Public Company Accounting and Finance

Second Edition

Steven M. Bragg

For more information about AccountingTools® products, visit our Web site at www.accountingtools.com.

ISBN-13: 978-1-938910-90-6

Printed in the United States of America

Table of Contents

Preface

The accounting requirements and financing opportunities for a publicly-held company are significantly different from those for a private company. There are a number of additional reporting requirements, complex filings with the Securities and Exchange Commission, and much more interaction with the company's auditors. There are also a number of avenues for raising money, which may require the filing of a registration statement, or its avoidance with several possible exemptions.

In *Public Company Accounting and Finance*, we address the additional burdens placed on the accounting staff in such areas as earnings per share calculations, segment reporting, and interim reporting. The book also covers many of the filing requirements of a public company, including the annual Form 10-K and the quarterly Form 10-Q. We then turn to possible financing options, including the initial public offering, Regulation A stock sales, and Regulation D stock sales. The book concludes with a number of accounting management topics that are of particular concern in a public company – closing the books and creating an adequate system of controls.

You can find the answers to many questions about public accounting and finance in the following chapters, including:

- How do I decide which parts of a business are to be treated as reporting segments?
- How do I account for the sale of stock?
- What are Staff Accounting Bulletins, and how do they impact the accounting for a public company?
- How do I pay the Securities and Exchange Commission a required fee for the filing of a registration statement?
- How can a business go public through a reverse merger?
- How can investors sell their shares without waiting to have them registered?
- How can employees sell their shares without being accused of insider trading?
- Which additional steps are needed by a public company to close its books?

Public Company Accounting and Finance is designed for the practicing accountant and finance person who is either involved in a public company or contemplating taking a company public. Given its broad coverage of the public company concept, *Public Company Accounting and Finance* may earn a permanent place on your book shelf.

Centennial, Colorado
July 2017

About the Author

Steven Bragg, CPA, has been the chief financial officer or controller of four companies, as well as a consulting manager at Ernst & Young. He received a master's degree in finance from Bentley College, an MBA from Babson College, and a Bachelor's degree in Economics from the University of Maine. He has been a two-time president of the Colorado Mountain Club, and is an avid alpine skier, mountain biker, and certified master diver. Mr. Bragg resides in Centennial, Colorado. He has written the following books and courses:

7 Habits of Effective CEOs	Cost Accounting (college textbook)
7 Habits of Effective CFOs	Cost Accounting Fundamentals
7 Habits of Effective Controllers	Cost Management Guidebook
Accountant Ethics [for multiple states]	Credit & Collection Guidebook
Accountants' Guidebook	Developing and Managing Teams
Accounting Changes and Error Corrections	Employee Onboarding
Accounting Controls Guidebook	Enterprise Risk Management
Accounting for Casinos and Gaming	Fair Value Accounting
Accounting for Derivatives and Hedges	Financial Analysis
Accounting for Earnings per Share	Financial Forecasting and Modeling
Accounting for Inventory	Fixed Asset Accounting
Accounting for Investments	Foreign Currency Accounting
Accounting for Intangible Assets	Fraud Examination
Accounting for Leases	Fraud Schemes
Accounting for Managers	GAAP Guidebook
Accounting for Stock-Based Compensation	Governmental Accounting
Accounting Procedures Guidebook	Health Care Accounting
Agricultural Accounting	Hospitality Accounting
Behavioral Ethics	How to Run a Meeting
Bookkeeping Guidebook	Human Resources Guidebook
Budgeting	IFRS Guidebook
Business Combinations and Consolidations	Interpretation of Financial Statements
Business Insurance Fundamentals	Inventory Management
Business Ratios	Investor Relations Guidebook
Business Valuation	Lean Accounting Guidebook
Capital Budgeting	Mergers & Acquisitions
CFO Guidebook	Negotiation
Change Management	New Controller Guidebook
Closing the Books	Nonprofit Accounting
Coaching and Mentoring	Partnership Accounting
Conflict Management	Payables Management
Constraint Management	Payroll Management
Construction Accounting	Project Accounting
Corporate Cash Management	Project Management
Corporate Finance	Public Company Accounting

(continued)

Purchasing Guidebook	The MBA Guidebook
Real Estate Accounting	The Soft Close
Records Management	The Statement of Cash Flows
Recruiting and Hiring	The Year-End Close
Revenue Recognition	Treasurer's Guidebook
Sales and Use Tax Accounting	Working Capital Management

On-Line Resources by Steven Bragg

Steven maintains the accountingtools.com web site, which contains continuing professional education courses, the Accounting Best Practices podcast, and thousands of articles on accounting subjects.

Public Company Accounting and Finance is also available as a continuing professional education (CPE) course. You can purchase the course (and many other courses) and take an on-line exam at:

www.accountingtools.com/cpe

Chapter 1
The Public Company Environment

Introduction

A company that wants to be a publicly-held entity will find that the accounting, reporting, and fund raising rules are substantially different than in the private sector. Additional accounting standards are applied to publicly-held businesses, while the Securities and Exchange Commission (SEC) requires that highly detailed reports be filed with it on a rigid schedule. If an organization wishes to sell securities to investors, there are a number of requirements that must first be met.

In this chapter, we provide a broad overview of the types of accounting and financing issues that a public company faces, and note which chapters later in this book contain more detailed information. In addition, we provide an overview of several topics that are prevalent throughout the book – the SEC, Generally Accepted Accounting Principles (GAAP), and several lesser but related topics.

Public Company Accounting

The accounting situation in a publicly-held company varies markedly from what is encountered in a private entity. The first issue is that a private company may have been using cash basis accounting, where revenues are recognized as cash is received, and expenses are recognized when cash is paid. This is not acceptable for a public company, which must use the accrual basis of accounting, where revenue is recognized as it is earned, and expenses are recognized when incurred. More specifically, a publicly-held company follows the accounting standards set forth under GAAP, which is described in the next section. These principles are highly detailed, and require that business transactions be recorded and reported in a very specific way. The financial statements of a publicly-held company must be audited, and the auditors will not issue a clean audit opinion unless the statements follow GAAP. Consequently, a public company must ensure that its accounting systems meet the requirements of GAAP.

In addition to GAAP, the SEC has created an additional set of accounting rules that only apply to public entities, which are its Staff Accounting Bulletins (SABs). Each SAB typically deals with a very specific situation, some of which are only applicable to a certain industry. Some companies may find that SABs do not apply to them at all, and so only have to follow the dictates of GAAP. Nonetheless, we have included a summary of the SAB mandates in the Staff Accounting Bulletins chapter.

The second issue for a public company is that it must incorporate into its financial statements additional information that is not required for a private company. The following topics are only required for a public company:

- *Earnings per share.* This is a calculation of earnings per share that can be complicated, depending on the equity structure of the business. This topic is covered in the Earnings per Share Reporting chapter.
- *Segment information.* This is the separate reporting of various types of information about the different business segments that comprise the company. This topic is covered in the Segment Reporting chapter.
- *Interim reporting.* This is a more loosely-defined set of concepts regarding how information is to be reported in the quarterly financial statements leading up to the full-year financial statements. This topic is addressed in the Interim reporting chapter.

In addition, there are two topics that a publicly-held company is likely to address more frequently than a private one. Since one of the main reasons for going public is to raise money, it can be reasonably presumed that a public business will actively sell shares, and may also issue bonds to investors. Given the greater likelihood of these activities, we have also covered the accounting for stock sales and debt issuances in the Stock Issuances Accounting and Debt Accounting chapters, respectively. The accounting for these activities is not different for public companies – it is just more frequently used.

A third issue for a public company is the amount of reporting that must be filed with the SEC. The quarterly results of the business must be filed every three months on the Form 10-Q, while annual reports are filed following the end of the fiscal year on the Form 10-K. In addition, any material events (covering a broad swathe of company activities) must be filed on the Form 8-K. A private company controller may be astounded at the excruciating level of detail required for these filings, especially the Form 10-K. To emphasize the draconian level of reporting required, we have provided extensive documentation and examples of the Form 10-K in the Annual and Quarterly Reporting chapter, which also addresses the Form 10-Q. The requirements of the Form 8-K are noted in the Form 8-K Reporting chapter.

The accountant may also be called upon to keep track of changes in the holdings of company securities by various corporate insiders and major stockholders. These individuals are personally responsible for reporting such changes to the SEC, but they frequently shift the reporting burden to the company. If so, the accountant needs to know about the Forms 3, 4, and 5, which are described in the Insider Securities Reporting chapter.

A fourth issue is one that primarily impacts the controller and CFO – that of accounting information released to the investment community. The individual responsible for this information release is the investor relations officer, who may push for the use of non-standard ratios and formulas in order to present the best possible picture of company performance to investors. This can be a major concern for the accounting manager, since the SEC has imposed strict rules on how non-GAAP information is to be presented and reconciled back to GAAP-compliant information. We address these SEC rules in the Non-GAAP Reporting chapter.

A fifth issue is payments to the SEC. Most periodic filings with the SEC are free. However, when a public company wants to raise money, it must file a registration statement with the SEC, for which a fee is charged. The accounting department is typically in charge of paying these fees, for which a special procedure must be followed. In the Fedwire Payments chapter, we describe exactly how to pay the SEC.

There are also procedural changes that a publicly-held company must make in order to create GAAP-compliant financial statements, have them approved by various individuals, reviewed or audited by the outside auditors, and filed with the SEC. Further, since the Forms 10-K and 10-Q are governed by tight filing deadlines, there is a need to close the books as rapidly as possible, while minimizing the number of accounting errors that reach the financial statements. Consequently, we note in the Closing the Books chapter the organizational steps needed to ensure that these filings are completed in a timely manner.

A final concern for a public company is a heightened level of control over the business. The Sarbanes-Oxley Act mandates a higher level of control by public companies, which calls for an additional controls examination by the outside auditors, which could reasonably be considered an oppressive amount of additional work. The outcome may be the imposition of a number of additional controls. We point out several controls in the Accounting and Finance Controls chapter that may be of use.

In short, there are a multitude of additional accounting issues that a public company must deal with that a private company may never have to consider. In the following chapters, we provide a considerable amount of detail about these accounting issues to show how company systems should be modified to raise them to the level of a public company, as well as which additional accounting standards are now applicable.

Generally Accepted Accounting Principles

The term GAAP is referenced throughout this book. GAAP is short for Generally Accepted Accounting Principles. GAAP is a large group of accounting standards and common industry usage that have been developed over many years. It is used by businesses to properly organize their financial information into accounting records and summarize it into financial statements, as well as disclose certain supporting information. One of the reasons for using GAAP is so that anyone reading the financial statements of multiple companies has a reasonable basis for comparison, since all companies using GAAP have created their financial statements using the same set of rules.

GAAP is derived from the pronouncements of a series of government-sponsored accounting entities of which the Financial Accounting Standards Board (FASB) is the latest. The SEC also issues accounting pronouncements through its Accounting Staff Bulletins and other announcements that are applicable only to publicly-held companies and which are considered to be part of GAAP. GAAP is codified into the Accounting Standards Codification, which is available on-line at asc.fasb.org in a rudimentary format and in a more easily searchable printed four-volume series.

For a detailed examination of GAAP, see the latest annual edition of the author's *GAAP Guidebook*.

Public Company Finance

One of the greatest temptations that a private company sees in going public is the opportunity to raise a large amount of money from investors. Doing so could jumpstart a moribund business by allowing it to invest heavily in product development, advertising, acquisitions, and so forth. However, going public is not so easy, and requires a large amount of cash. We describe the process of going public in the Initial Public Offering chapter. An alternative to the IPO is the reverse merger, where a private company buys a public shell company and takes itself public. Though initially much less expensive than an IPO, a reverse merger does not provide an initial surge of cash from the sale of securities, and also does not provide a ready market for the company's stock. Despite these shortcomings, reverse mergers continue to be popular for small businesses seeking to go public. We describe the reverse merger concept in the Reverse Merger chapter.

If a company wants to sell shares, it is much easier to gain investor acceptance if the shares are registered, which means that investors can re-sell the shares to third parties. However, the stock registration process is lengthy and expensive. In the Registration Statements chapter, we describe the contents of the Form S-1 registration statement, as well as the requirements for using the simpler Form S-3.

The stock registration process can be so difficult for some companies that they prefer to use other alternatives to raise capital. Two of the more common alternatives are found in the SEC's exemptions from the registration process, using either Regulation A or Regulation D. Regulation A allows for a reduced amount of fund raising in exchange for easier filing requirements, while Regulation D allows for an expanded amount of fund raising, but only to qualified investors, and only when the sales are restricted from resale. These options are discussed in the Regulation A Stock Sales chapter and the Sale of Unregistered Securities – Regulation D chapter.

There is also the option of raising money through crowdfunding, which is the concept of obtaining small individual amounts from a large number of investors. An initial set of guidelines for doing so were laid out in the Jumpstart Our Business Startups Act, which are stated in the chapter of the same name. The SEC is still defining how to regulate crowdfunding, but an initial view of the likely outcome is that the regulations will be too costly for businesses when compared to the limited amounts of funding that can be raised through this method.

A final financing concern for a publicly-held business is how to deal with company securities that are held by third parties – investors and employees. If shares are not registered, a company will find itself under continuing pressure from investors to file for registration. An alternative that can be presented to these investors is SEC Rule 144, which allows investors to sell restricted stock under certain limited circumstances. We discuss this option in the Sale of Unregistered

Securities – Rule 144 chapter. This option does not work especially well, since it may take many months (or years) for an investor to liquidate his holdings.

If investors are also company employees, they may be further restricted in their ability to sell securities, since they could be accused of trading on inside information. This legal conundrum can be avoided by engaging in a 10b5-1 stock plan, where an employee sets up a plan to buy or sell company securities in advance, and has a third party conduct the trades without further input from the employee. This topic is covered in the Rule 10b5-1 Stock Sales chapter.

In short, it is both time-consuming and expensive to raise money through the classic approach of selling registered company securities. A larger business can avoid some of this annoyance by shifting to the Form S-3 to register securities, while a smaller business should consider the Regulation A and Regulation D exemptions to achieve more cost-effective fundraising.

The Securities and Exchange Commission

A large part of this book refers to the requirements of and interactions with the Securities and Exchange Commission (SEC). We will briefly diverge from the accounting and finance topics of this chapter to give an overview of the SEC.

The mission of the SEC is to "protect investors, maintain fair, orderly, and efficient markets, and facilitate capital formation." To achieve this mission, the main focus of the SEC is in requiring that listed companies issue a comprehensive set of information about themselves and their securities to the investment community, so that all investors have access to the same investment information. The SEC also oversees the activities of the key participants in the investment community, including the securities exchanges, brokers and dealers, investment advisors, and mutual funds. Where the SEC finds that individuals or entities are engaged in fraudulent activities, it can bring civil enforcement actions against them for violation of the securities laws.

The SEC is managed by five commissioners, who have staggered five-year terms. One of the commissioners is designated by the President as the Chairman of the SEC, and is essentially the chief executive officer of the organization. The SEC is comprised of five divisions, which are as follows:

- *Division of Corporation Finance.* Oversees corporate disclosures of information to the investing public. This group routinely reviews the disclosure documents filed by companies, and may issue comment letters. This is the division that a publicly-held company is most likely to deal with.
- *Division of Trading and Markets.* Provides day-to-day oversight of the major securities market participants, such as the securities exchanges, the Financial Industry Regulatory Authority, clearing agencies, transfer agents, credit rating agencies, and so forth.
- *Division of Investment Management.* Oversees the investment management industry, such as mutual funds, professional fund managers, analysts, and investment advisors.

- *Division of Enforcement.* Recommends the commencement of investigations of securities law violations, and prosecutes these cases on behalf of the SEC. From the perspective of the public company, it is useful to understand which actions are most likely to trigger an SEC investigation. These actions are:
  - o The misrepresentation or omission of important information about securities
  - o Manipulating the market prices of securities
  - o Insider trading
  - o Selling unregistered securities
- *Division of Economic and Risk Analysis.* Conducts economic analysis and data analytics to support the activities of the other divisions of the SEC. This information is used by the SEC for policymaking, rulemaking, enforcement, and examinations. For example, this division may review the potential economic effects of proposed new rules, or help to focus on the early identification of illegal activities.

The accountant is more likely to run afoul of the SEC in certain reporting areas. The SEC has presumably found a higher incidence of reporting problems in these areas, and so has instructed its staff to be especially careful in perusing disclosures in these areas. The result may be a comment letter from the SEC, requesting clarification about statements made, and perhaps even advising that a filing be replaced with modified information. Consequently, be especially careful to present complete information, without hyperbole, in the following areas:

- *Goodwill impairment.* The amount of the goodwill asset on the books of a company can represent a disproportionate amount of its total assets. As such, the SEC expects a business to routinely examine this asset to see if it is impaired, and write down the asset as necessary. Consequently, the SEC may question insufficient documentation of the amount of goodwill impairment testing.
- *Judgment areas.* Management is expected to exercise judgment in prudently deciding upon reserves and fair values. The SEC may issue a comment letter if it feels that the management team is making overly optimistic assumptions in areas where judgment can alter the financial outcome.
- *Management discussion and analysis (MD&A).* The clear SEC favorite for criticizing a filing is the MD&A section of the annual Form 10-K and quarterly Form 10-Q. The SEC staff wants to see interpretive comments from a company regarding the results of operations, rather than the usual dry recitation of the percentages by which revenues and expenses changed in the past year, with boilerplate reasoning given for changes in performance.
- *Non-GAAP measurements.* Companies like to enhance their reported results by using measurements that are not used in Generally Accepted Accounting Principles. The SEC is distinctly not pleased with the use of these measures,

and will closely examine their use. When in doubt, do not use them at all. See the Non-GAAP Reporting chapter for more information.

- *Related-party transactions.* Despite being publicly held, many entities are controlled by a small number of individuals. If so, clearly state how the entity does business with them. The SEC will insist on a high degree of clarity in this area.
- *Revenue recognition.* The manner in which a business recognizes revenue is persistently subject to fraud, so expect the SEC to closely examine the methodology under which a company claims to be recognizing revenue.
- *Segment reporting.* Companies tend to recast their reportable business segments over time, resulting in inconsistency in how they report the types and results of segments. The SEC looks for these inconsistencies over multiple reporting periods, and will call out the company if it sees problems.

In short, the public company continually deals with the SEC; this is usually in regard to the clarification of information provided in filings, but can involve more detailed examinations if the SEC believes that the organization has engaged in activities that may be illegal.

Through the remainder of this book, we will refer to the Securities and Exchange Commission by its acronym, the SEC.

The Issuer and Registrant Concepts

The securities regulations use several terms when referring to a publicly-held entity. One common term is the *issuer*. An issuer is considered to be an entity that registers and sells securities in order to finance its operations. An issuer is most commonly a corporation, but it could also be a government (such as a state government that issues bonds) or an investment trust. An issuer is responsible for the obligations associated with each securities issuance, such as dividend payments for common stock or interest payments for bonds.

In its regulations, the SEC frequently refers to the *registrant*. This is the issuer of securities for which a registration statement (see the Registration Statements chapter) is filed. A registration statement is used to apply to the SEC to have shares registered, so that the holders of the shares can sell them to third parties.

The issuer and registrant concepts are not quite the same. An issuer may have issued securities, but has not necessarily registered them. Conversely, a registrant may not yet have issued securities – it may be waiting for registration approval from the SEC before doing so.

In this book, we do not differentiate between the two concepts. Instead, we tend to use the more generic "company," "entity," or "organization" terms to refer to any entity that is considered to be publicly-held.

The Decline in Public Companies

The number of companies listed on stock exchanges and in the over-the-counter market has clearly declined. There are a number of possible reasons for this change, including the following:

- *Reporting and control requirements.* The SEC has continually increased its reporting requirements over time, to the point where a smaller organization will find that a significant proportion of its profits are consumed by the additional overhead required to maintain an appropriate level of controls and issue the necessary reports.
- *Delisting.* The management of a company may want to continue to be listed on a public exchange, but its fundamentals (such as its stock price) have declined so far that it is delisted by the exchange. Being then thrust into the over-the-counter market, these firms find no further value in being publicly-held, and so take themselves private.
- *Private equity buyouts.* A small number of buyout firms have developed an effective business model for buying out low-performing public companies and spending several years fixing their fundamentals while outside of the public eye. Some of these firms are then taken public again, while others are sold off to other companies for a premium.
- *Economics for smaller firms.* One of the main reasons for the decline in public firms is that the economics of the stock markets make it increasingly difficult for a smaller firm to create any level of active trading in its stock. As trading commissions have declined over time, brokers find that they earn reduced fees for pushing the stock of smaller firms, since there are so few shares to trade. The result is that smaller firms go public, find that they cannot maintain an adequate float, and take themselves private again.
- *IPO cost.* The preceding points show why the overall number of existing public firms is declining. In addition, the number of initial public offerings (IPOs) is so low that they are not replenishing the number of firms departing the public markets. This is largely because the cost of an IPO continues to increase, to the point where it is uneconomical for a smaller firm to even consider going public. The minimum threshold at which to consider going public has now risen to the general vicinity of $100 million (which also depends on the profits being reported).

In short, the reasons noted here point toward a decline in the number of smaller publicly-held companies. This does not mean that the public ownership model is dead – the number of publicly-held entities is growing in other countries than the United States, partially due to less oppressive reporting and control requirements.

An ancillary result of the trend away from going public is that private companies tend to stay private longer. This delay has led to the appearance of *unicorns*, which are startup companies with a valuation of at least $1 billion. Private companies wait to go public in order to gain mass, so that going public at a later date is more economical. However, by delaying the date at which they go public, most of the growth years of a company tend to occur when it is private, which means that the gains in overall company valuation tend to accrue to private investors before the going-public stage. By the time a business finally goes public, it has already amassed significant market share and has settled into a reasonable market niche – which means that additional outsized gains in the value of the company are less likely to occur, yielding reduced profits for anyone investing *after* the company has gone public.

Summary

We cannot emphasize enough the extent of the additional accounting required for a publicly-held business. The accounting manager should consider a significant ramp-up in the number of accounting staff to handle the added workload. This increase should be completed well before the business has actually gone public, so that the new staff will have sufficient time to understand how the business works, and the functions of its accounting systems.

Fund raising is both expensive and time-consuming for a public company. Given the high cost and annoyance of maintaining public-company status with the SEC, it is no surprise that a large number of companies have concluded that there are easier ways to raise money than by going public. These entities have taken themselves private and pursued private stock and debt placements in order to achieve adequate funding levels. In short, fund raising in the public markets is not an easy goal to achieve, and so should be considered just one of many financing alternatives.

The managers of a public company may not deal all that frequently with the SEC, especially if the company has retained securities attorneys who address the bulk of all SEC inquiries. Nonetheless, it is useful to understand which SEC division is communicating with the company, and what their priorities are in contacting the company.

In the following chapters, we provide considerably greater detail regarding the general topics that were touched upon in this chapter, beginning with those elements of GAAP that were specifically designed for publicly-held companies – earnings per share, segment reporting, and interim reporting.

Chapter 2
Earnings per Share Reporting

Introduction

A publicly-held company is required to report either one or two types of earnings per share information within its financial statements, depending on the types of its outstanding equity. In this chapter, we describe how to calculate both basic and diluted earnings per share, as well as how to present this information within the financial statements.

Basic Earnings per Share

Basic earnings per share is the amount of a company's profit or loss for a reporting period that is available to the shares of its common stock that are outstanding during a reporting period. If a business only has common stock in its capital structure, it presents only its basic earnings per share for income from continuing operations and net income. This information is reported on its income statement.

The formula for basic earnings per share is:

$$\frac{\text{Profit or loss attributable to common equity holders of the parent business}}{\text{Weighted average number of common shares outstanding during the period}}$$

In addition, this calculation must be subdivided into:

- The profit or loss from continuing operations attributable to the parent company
- The total profit or loss attributable to the parent company

When calculating basic earnings per share, incorporate into the numerator an adjustment for dividends. Deduct from the profit or loss the after-tax amount of any dividends declared on non-cumulative preferred stock, as well as the after-tax amount of any preferred stock dividends, even if the dividends are not declared; this does not include any dividends paid or declared during the current period that relate to previous periods.

Also, incorporate the following adjustments into the denominator of the basic earnings per share calculation:

- *Contingent stock.* If there is contingently issuable stock, treat it as though it were outstanding as of the date when there are no circumstances under which the shares would *not* be issued.
- *Weighted-average shares.* Use the weighted-average number of shares during the period in the denominator. Do this by adjusting the number of

shares outstanding at the beginning of the reporting period for common shares repurchased or issued in the period. This adjustment is based on the proportion of the days in the reporting period that the shares are outstanding.

EXAMPLE

Lowry Locomotion earns a profit of $1,000,000 net of taxes in Year 1. In addition, Lowry owes $200,000 in dividends to the holders of its cumulative preferred stock. Lowry calculates the numerator of its basic earnings per share as follows:

$1,000,000 Profit - $200,000 Dividends = $800,000

Lowry had 4,000,000 common shares outstanding at the beginning of Year 1. In addition, it sold 200,000 shares on April 1 and 400,000 shares on October 1. It also issued 500,000 shares on July 1 to the owners of a newly-acquired subsidiary. Finally, it bought back 60,000 shares on December 1. Lowry calculates the weighted-average number of common shares outstanding as follows:

Date	Shares	Weighting (Months)	Weighted Average
January 1	4,000,000	12/12	4,000,000
April 1	200,000	9/12	150,000
July 1	500,000	6/12	250,000
October 1	400,000	3/12	100,000
December 1	-60,000	1/12	-5,000
			4,495,000

Lowry's basic earnings per share calculation is:

$800,000 adjusted profits ÷ 4,495,000 weighted-average shares = $0.18 per share

---

Diluted Earnings per Share

Diluted earnings per share is the profit for a reporting period per share of common stock outstanding during that period; it includes the number of shares that would have been outstanding during the period if the company had issued common shares for all potential dilutive common stock outstanding during the period.

If a company has more types of stock than common stock in its capital structure, it must present both basic earnings per share and diluted earnings per share information; this presentation must be for both income from continuing operations and net income. This information is reported on the company's income statement.

To calculate diluted earnings per share, include the effects of all dilutive potential common shares. This means it is necessary to increase the number of shares outstanding by the weighted average number of additional common shares that would have been outstanding if the company had converted all dilutive potential common stock to common stock. This dilution may affect the profit or loss in the numerator of the dilutive earnings per share calculation. The formula is:

$$\frac{\text{(Profit or loss attributable to common equity holders of parent company}}{\text{(Weighted average number of common shares outstanding during the period}}$$

(Profit or loss attributable to common equity holders of parent company
+ After-tax interest on convertible debt + Convertible preferred dividends)
(Weighted average number of common shares outstanding during the period
+ All dilutive potential common stock)

It may be necessary to make two adjustments to the *numerator* of this calculation. They are:

- *Interest expense*. Eliminate any interest expense associated with dilutive potential common stock, since the assumption is that these shares are converted to common stock. The conversion would eliminate the company's liability for the interest expense.
- *Dividends*. Adjust for the after-tax impact of dividends or other types of dilutive potential common shares.

Additional adjustments may be required for the *denominator* of this calculation. They are:

- *Anti-dilutive shares*. If there are any contingent stock issuances that would have an anti-dilutive impact on earnings per share, do not include them in the calculation. This situation arises when a business experiences a loss, because including the dilutive shares in the calculation would reduce the loss per share.
- *Dilutive shares*. If there is potentially dilutive common stock, add all of it to the denominator of the diluted earnings per share calculation. Unless there is more specific information available, assume that these shares are issued at the beginning of the reporting period.
- *Dilutive securities termination*. If a conversion option lapses during the reporting period for dilutive convertible securities, or if the related debt is extinguished during the reporting period, the effect of these securities should still be included in the denominator of the diluted earnings per share calculation for the period during which they were outstanding.

In addition to these adjustments to the denominator, also apply all of the adjustments to the denominator already noted for basic earnings per share.

Tip: The rules related to diluted earnings per share appear complex, but they are founded upon one principle – that the intent is to establish the absolute worst-case scenario to arrive at the smallest possible amount of earnings per share. If faced with an unusual situation involving the calculation of diluted earnings per share and there is uncertainty about what to do, that rule will likely apply.

In addition to the issues just noted, here are a number of additional situations that could impact the calculation of diluted earnings per share:

- *Most advantageous exercise price.* When calculating the number of potential shares that could be issued, do so using the most advantageous conversion rate from the perspective of the person or entity holding the security to be converted.
- *Settlement assumption.* If there is an open contract that could be settled in common stock or cash, assume that it will be settled in common stock, but only if the effect is dilutive. The presumption of settlement in stock can be overcome if there is a reasonable basis for expecting that settlement will be partially or entirely in cash.
- *Effects of convertible instruments.* If there are convertible instruments outstanding, include their dilutive effect if they dilute earnings per share. Consider convertible preferred stock to be anti-dilutive when the dividend on any converted shares is greater than basic earnings per share. Similarly, convertible debt is considered anti-dilutive when the interest expense on any converted shares exceeds basic earnings per share. The following example illustrates the concept.

EXAMPLE

Lowry Locomotion earns a net profit of $2 million, and it has 5 million common shares outstanding. In addition, there is a $1 million convertible loan that has an eight percent interest rate. The loan may potentially convert into 500,000 of Lowry's common shares. Lowry's incremental tax rate is 35 percent.

Lowry's basic earnings per share is $2,000,000 ÷ 5,000,000 shares, or $0.40/share. The following calculation shows the compilation of Lowry's diluted earnings per share:

Net profit	$2,000,000
+ Interest saved on $1,000,000 loan at 8%	80,000
- Reduced tax savings on foregone interest expense	-28,000
= Adjusted net earnings	$2,052,000
Common shares outstanding	5,000,000
+ Potential converted shares	500,000
= Adjusted shares outstanding	5,500,000
Diluted earnings per share ($2,052,000 ÷ 5,500,000)	**$0.37/share**

- *Option exercise.* If there are any dilutive options and warrants, assume that they are exercised at their exercise price. Then, convert the proceeds into the total number of shares that the holders would have purchased, using the average market price during the reporting period. Then use in the diluted earnings per share calculation the difference between the number of shares assumed to have been issued and the number of shares assumed to have been purchased. The following example illustrates the concept.

EXAMPLE

Lowry Locomotion earns a net profit of $200,000, and it has 5,000,000 common shares outstanding that sell on the open market for an average of $12 per share. In addition, there are 300,000 options outstanding that can be converted to Lowry's common stock at $10 each.

Lowry's basic earnings per share is $200,000 ÷ 5,000,000 common shares, or $0.04 per share.

Lowry's controller wants to calculate the amount of diluted earnings per share. To do so, he follows these steps:

1. *Calculate the number of shares that would have been issued at the market price.* Thus, he multiplies the 300,000 options by the average exercise price of $10 to arrive at a total of $3,000,000 paid to exercise the options by their holders.
2. *Divide the amount paid to exercise the options by the market price to determine the number of shares that could be purchased.* Thus, he divides the $3,000,000 paid to exercise the options by the $12 average market price to arrive at 250,000 shares that could have been purchased with the proceeds from the options.
3. *Subtract the number of shares that could have been purchased from the number of options exercised.* Thus, he subtracts the 250,000 shares potentially purchased from the 300,000 options to arrive at a difference of 50,000 shares.
4. *Add the incremental number of shares to the shares already outstanding.* Thus, he adds the 50,000 incremental shares to the existing 5,000,000 to arrive at 5,050,000 diluted shares.

Based on this information, the controller arrives at diluted earnings per share of $0.0396, for which the calculation is:

$200,000 Net profit ÷ 5,050,000 Common shares

- *Put options.* If there are purchased put options, only include them in the diluted earnings per share calculation if the exercise price is higher than the average market price during the reporting period.
- *Written put options.* If there is a written put option that requires a business to repurchase its own stock, include it in the computation of diluted earnings per share, but only if the effect is dilutive. If the exercise price of such a put option is above the average market price of the company's stock during the reporting period, this is considered to be "in the money," and the dilutive effect is to be calculated using the following method, which is called the *reverse treasury stock method*:

1. Assume that enough shares were issued by the company at the beginning of the period at the average market price to raise sufficient funds to satisfy the put option contract.
2. Assume that these proceeds are used to buy back the required number of shares.
3. Include in the denominator of the diluted earnings per share calculation the difference between the numbers of shares issued and purchased in steps 1 and 2.

EXAMPLE

A third party exercises a written put option that requires Armadillo Industries to repurchase 1,000 shares from the third party at an exercise price of $30. The current market price is $20. Armadillo uses the following steps to compute the impact of the written put option on its diluted earnings per share calculation:

1. Armadillo assumes that it has issued 1,500 shares at $20.
2. The company assumes that the "issuance" of 1,500 shares is used to meet the repurchase obligation of $30,000.
3. The difference between the 1,500 shares issued and the 1,000 shares repurchased is added to the denominator of Armadillo's diluted earnings per share calculation.

- *Call options.* If there are purchased call options, only include them in the diluted earnings per share calculation if the exercise price is lower than the market price.

> **Tip:** There is only a dilutive effect on the diluted earnings per share calculation when the average market price is greater than the exercise prices of any options or warrants.

- *Contingent shares in general.* Treat common stock that is contingently issuable as though it was outstanding as of the beginning of the reporting period, but only if the conditions have been met that would require the company to issue the shares. If the conditions were not met by the end of the period, then include in the calculation, as of the beginning of the period, any shares that would be issuable if the end of the reporting period were the end of the contingency period, and the result would be dilutive.
- *Contingent shares dependency.* If there is a contingent share issuance that is dependent upon the future market price of the company's common stock, include the shares in the diluted earnings per share calculation, based on the market price at the end of the reporting period; however, only include the issuance if the effect is dilutive. If the shares have a contingency feature, do not include them in the calculation until the contingency has been met.
- *Issuances based on future earnings and stock price.* There may be contingent stock issuances that are based on future earnings and the future price of

a company's stock. If so, the number of shares to include in diluted earnings per share should be based on the earnings to date and the current market price as of the end of each reporting period. If both earnings and share price targets must be reached in order to trigger a stock issuance and both targets are not met, then do not include any related contingently issuable shares in the diluted earnings per share calculation.

- *Compensation in shares*. If employees are awarded shares that have not vested or stock options as forms of compensation, then treat these grants as options when calculating diluted earnings per share. Consider these grants to be outstanding on the grant date, rather than any later vesting date.

Always calculate the number of potential dilutive common shares independently for each reporting period presented in the financial statements.

Disclosure of Earnings per Share

The basic and diluted earnings per share information is normally listed at the bottom of the income statement, and should be listed there for every period included in the income statement. Also, if diluted earnings per share information is reported in *any* of the periods included in a company's income statement, it must be reported for *all* of the periods included in the statement. The following sample illustrates the concept.

Sample Presentation of Earnings per Share

Earnings per Share	20x3	20x2	20x1
From continuing operations			
Basic earnings per share	$1.05	$0.95	$0.85
Diluted earnings per share	1.00	0.90	0.80
From discontinued operations			
Basic earnings per share	$0.20	$0.17	$0.14
Diluted earnings per share	0.15	0.08	0.07
From total operations			
Basic earnings per share	$1.25	$1.12	$0.99
Diluted earnings per share	1.15	0.98	0.87

Note that, if the company reports a discontinued operation, it must present the basic and diluted earnings per share amounts for this item. The information can be included either as part of the income statement or in the accompanying notes. The preceding sample presentation includes a disclosure for earnings per share from discontinued operations.

> **Tip:** If the amounts of basic and diluted earnings per share are the same, it is allowable to have a dual presentation of the information in a single line item on the income statement.

In addition to the earnings per share reporting format just noted, a company is also required to report the following information:

- *Reconciliation.* State the differences between the numerators and denominators of the basic and diluted earnings per share calculations for income from continuing operations.
- *Preferred dividends effect.* State the effect of preferred dividends on the computation of income available to common stockholders for basic earnings per share.
- *Potential effects.* Describe the terms and conditions of any securities not included in the computation of diluted earnings per share due to their antidilutive effects, but which could potentially dilute basic earnings per share in the future.
- *Subsequent events.* Describe any transactions occurring after the latest reporting period but before the issuance of financial statements that would have a material impact on the number of common or potential common shares if they had occurred prior to the end of the reporting period.

Summary

It will have been evident from the discussions of earnings per share that the computation of diluted earnings per share can be quite complex if there is a correspondingly complex equity structure. In such a situation, it is quite likely that diluted earnings per share will be incorrectly calculated. To improve the accuracy of the calculation, create an electronic spreadsheet that incorporates all of the necessary factors impacting diluted earnings per share. Further, save the calculation for each reporting period on a separate page of the spreadsheet; by doing so, there will be an excellent record of how these calculations were managed in the past.

Chapter 3
Segment Reporting

Introduction

If a company is publicly-held, it needs to report segment information, which is part of the disclosures attached to the financial statements. This information is supposedly needed to give the readers of the financial statements more insights into the operations and prospects of a business, as well as to allow them to make more informed judgments about a public entity as a whole. In this chapter, we describe how to determine which business segments to report separately, and how to report that information.

Overview of Segment Reporting

An operating segment is a component of a public entity, and which possesses the following characteristics:

- *Business activities.* It has business activities that can generate revenues and cause expenses to be incurred. This can include revenues and expenses generated by transactions with other operating segments of the same public entity. It can also include activities that do not yet include revenues, such as a start-up business.
- *Results reviewed.* The chief operating decision maker of the public entity regularly reviews its operating results, with the intent of assessing its performance and making decisions about allocating resources to it.
- *Financial results.* Financial results specific to it are available.

Generally, an operating segment has a manager who is accountable to the chief operating decision maker, and who maintains regular contact with that person, though it is also possible that the chief operating decision maker directly manages one or more operating segments.

If a company has a matrix form of organization, where some managers are responsible for geographic regions and others are responsible for products and services, the results of the products and services are considered to be operating segments.

Some parts of a business are not considered to be reportable business segments under the following circumstances:

- *Corporate overhead.* The corporate group does not usually earn outside revenues, and so is not considered a segment.
- *Post-retirement benefit plans.* A benefit plan can earn income from investments, but it has no operating activities, and so is not considered a segment.

- *One-time events*. If an otherwise-insignificant segment has a one-time event that boosts it into the ranks of reportable segments, do not report it, since there is no long-term expectation for it to remain a reportable segment.

The primary issue with segment reporting is determining which business segments to report. The rules for this selection process are quite specific. An organization should report segment information if a business segment passes any one of the following three tests:

1. *Revenue*. The revenue of the segment is at least 10% of the consolidated revenue of the entire business; or
2. *Profit or loss*. The absolute amount of the profit or loss of the segment is at least 10% of the greater of the combined profits of all the operating segments reporting a profit, or of the combined losses of all operating segments reporting a loss (see the following example for a demonstration of this concept); or
3. *Assets*. The assets of the segment are at least 10% of the combined assets of all the operating segments of the business.

If the preceding tests are run and the result is a group of reportable segments whose combined revenues are not at least 75% of the consolidated revenue of the entire business, then add more segments until the 75% threshold is surpassed.

If there is a business segment that used to qualify as a reportable segment and does not currently qualify, but for which there is an expectation that it will qualify in the future, continue to treat it as a reportable segment.

If there are operating segments that have similar economic characteristics, their results can be aggregated into a single operating segment, but only if they are similar in all of the following areas:

- The nature of their products and services
- The nature of their systems of production
- The nature of their regulatory environments (if applicable)
- Their types of customers
- Their distribution systems

The number of restrictions on this type of reporting makes it unlikely that an entity would be able to aggregate reportable segments.

After all of the segment testing has been completed, it is possible that there will be a few residual segments that do not qualify for separate reporting. If so, combine the information for these segments into an "other" category and include it in the segment report for the entity. Be sure to describe the sources of revenue included in this "other" category.

Finally, if an operating segment does not meet any of the preceding criteria, it can still be treated as a reportable segment if management decides that information about the segment may be of use to readers of the company's financial statements.

> **Tip:** The variety of methods available for segment testing makes it possible that there will be quite a large number of reportable segments. If so, it can be burdensome to create a report for so many segments, and it may be confusing for the readers of the company's financial statements. Consequently, consider limiting the number of reportable segments to ten; a business can aggregate the information for additional segments for reporting purposes.

EXAMPLE

Lowry Locomotion has six business segments whose results it reports internally. Lowry's controller needs to test the various segments to see which ones qualify as being reportable. He collects the following information:

Segment	(000s) Revenue	(000s) Profit	(000s) Loss	(000s) Assets
Diesel locomotives	$120,000	$10,000	$--	$320,000
Electric locomotives	85,000	8,000	--	180,000
Maglev cars	29,000	--	-21,000	90,000
Passenger cars	200,000	32,000		500,000
Toy trains	15,000	--	-4,000	4,000
Trolley cars	62,000	--	-11,000	55,000
	$511,000	$50,000	-$36,000	$1,149,000

In the table, the total profit exceeds the total loss, so the controller uses the total profit for the 10% profit test. The controller then lists the same table again, but now with the losses column removed and with test thresholds at the top of the table that are used to determine which segments are reported. An "X" mark below a test threshold indicates that a segment is reportable. In addition, the controller adds a new column on the right side of the table, which is used to calculate the total revenue for the reportable segments.

Segment	(000s) Revenue	(000s) Profit	(000s) Assets	75% Revenue Test
Reportable threshold (10%)	**$51,100**	**$5,000**	**$114,900**	
Diesel locomotives	X	X	X	$120,000
Electric locomotives	X	X	X	85,000
Maglev cars				
Passenger cars	X	X	X	200,000
Toy trains				
Trolley cars	X			62,000
			Total	$467,000

This analysis shows that the diesel locomotive, electric locomotive, passenger car, and trolley car segments are reportable, and that the combined revenue of these reportable segments easily exceeds the 75% reporting threshold. Consequently, the company does not need to separately report information for any additional segments.

Segment Disclosure

This section contains the disclosures for various aspects of segment reporting that are required under GAAP. At the end of each set of requirements is a sample disclosure containing the more common elements of the reporting requirements.

Segment Disclosure

The key requirement of segment reporting is that the revenue, profit or loss, and assets of each segment be separately reported for any period for which an income statement is presented. In addition, reconcile this segment information back to the company's consolidated results, which requires the inclusion of any adjusting items. Also disclose the methods by which the entity determined which segments to report. The essential information to include in a segment report includes:

- The types of products and services sold by each segment
- The basis of organization (such as by geographic region or product line)
- Revenues from external customers
- Revenues from inter-company transactions
- Interest income
- Interest expense
- Depreciation, depletion, and amortization expense
- Material expense items
- Income tax expense or income
- Other material non-cash items
- Profit or loss

If an operating segment only has minimal financial operations, it is not necessary to report any information about interest income or interest expense.

The following two items must also be reported if they are included in the determination of segment assets, or are routinely provided to the chief operating decision maker:

- Equity method interests in other entities.
- The total expenditure for additions to fixed assets. Expenditures for most other long-term assets are excluded from this requirement.

The preceding disclosures should be presented along with the following reconciliations, which should be separately identified and described:

Category	Reconciliation
Revenues	Total company revenues to reportable segment revenues
Profit or loss	Total consolidated income before income taxes and discontinued operations to reportable segment profit or loss
Assets	Consolidated assets to reportable segment assets
Other items	Consolidated amounts to reportable segment amounts for every other significant item of disclosed segment information

If an operating segment qualifies for the first time as being reportable, also report the usual segment information for it in any prior period segment data that may be presented for comparison purposes, even if the segment was not reportable in the prior period. An exemption is allowed for this prior period reporting if the required information is not available, or if it would be excessively expensive to collect the information.

The operating segment information reported should be the same information reported to the chief operating decision maker for purposes of assessing segment performance and allocating resources. This may result in a difference between the information reported at the segment level and in the public entity's consolidated financial results. If so, disclose the differences between the two figures. This may include a discussion of any policies for the allocation of costs that have been centrally incurred, or the allocation of jointly-used assets.

The following additional items should also be included in the disclosure of operating segment information:

- The basis of accounting for any inter-segment transactions.
- Any changes in the methods used to measure segment profit or loss from the prior period, and the effect of those changes on the reported amount of segment profit or loss.
- A discussion of any asymmetrical allocations, such as the allocation of depreciation expense to a segment without a corresponding allocation of assets.

If a business is reporting condensed financial statements for interim periods, it must disclose the following information for each reportable segment:

- Revenues from external customers for the current quarter and year-to-date, with comparable information for the preceding year
- Revenues from inter-company transactions for the current quarter and year-to-date, with comparable information for the preceding year
- Profit or loss for the current quarter and year-to-date, with comparable information for the preceding year
- Total assets for which there has been a material change from the last annual disclosure
- A description of any differences in the basis of segmentation from the last annual disclosure, or in the method of measuring segment profit or loss

- A reconciliation of the aggregate segment profit or loss to the consolidated income before income taxes, and discontinued operations for the public company

If a public entity alters its internal structure to such an extent that the composition of its operating segments is changed, restate its reported results for earlier periods, as well as interim periods, to match the results and financial position of the new internal structure. This requirement is waived if it is impracticable to obtain the required information. The result may be the restatement of some information, but not all of the segment information. If an entity does alter its internal structure, it should disclose whether there has also been a restatement of its segment information for earlier periods. If the entity does not change its prior period information, it must report segment information in the current period under both the old basis and new basis of segmentation, unless it is impracticable to do so.

EXAMPLE

The controller of Lowry Locomotion produces the following segment report for the segments identified in the preceding example:

(000s)	Diesel	Electric	Passenger	Trolley	Other	Consolidated
Revenues	$120,000	$85,000	$200,000	$62,000	$44,000	$511,000
Interest income	11,000	8,000	28,000	8,000	2,000	57,000
Interest expense	--	--	--	11,000	39,000	50,000
Depreciation	32,000	18,000	50,000	6,000	10,000	116,000
Income taxes	4,000	3,000	10,000	-3,000	-7,000	7,000
Profit	10,000	8,000	32,000	-11,000	-25,000	14,000
Assets	320,000	180,000	500,000	55,000	94,000	1,149,000

Products, Services, and Customer Disclosure

A publicly-held entity must report the sales garnered from external customers for each product and service or group thereof, unless it is impracticable to compile this information.

The entity must also describe the extent of its reliance on its major customers. In particular, if revenues from a single customer exceed 10% of the entity's revenues, this fact must be disclosed, along with the total revenues garnered from each of these customers and the names of the segments in which these revenues were earned.

It is not necessary to disclose the name of a major customer.

If there is a group of customers under common control (such as different departments of the federal government), the revenues from this group should be reported in aggregate as though the revenues were generated from a single customer.

EXAMPLE

Armadillo Industries reports the following information about its major customers:

Revenues from one customer of Armadillo's home security segment represented approximately 12% of the company's consolidated revenues in 20X2, and 11% of consolidated revenues in 20X1.

Geographic Area Disclosure

A publicly-held entity must disclose the following geographic information, unless it is impracticable to compile:

- *Revenues*. All revenues generated from external customers and attributable to the entity's home country, and all revenues attributable to foreign countries. Foreign-country revenues by individual country shall be stated if these country-level sales are material. There must also be disclosure of the basis under which revenues are attributed to individual countries.
- *Assets*. All long-lived assets (for which the definition essentially restricts reporting to fixed assets) that are attributable to the entity's home country, and all such assets attributable to foreign countries. Foreign-country assets by individual country shall be stated if these assets are material.

It is also acceptable to include in this reporting subtotals of geographic information by groups of countries.

Geographic area reporting is waived if providing it is impracticable. If so, the entity must disclose the fact.

EXAMPLE

Armadillo Industries reports the following geographic information about its operations:

	Revenues	Long-Lived Assets
United States	$27,000,000	$13,000,000
Mexico	23,000,000	11,000,000
Chile	14,000,000	7,000,000
Other foreign countries	8,000,000	2,000,000
Total	$72,000,000	$33,000,000

Summary

The determination of whether a business has segments is, to a considerable extent, based upon whether a business tracks information internally at the segment level.

Thus, if a company's accounting systems are sufficiently primitive, or if management is sufficiently disinterested to not review information about business segments, it is entirely possible that even a publicly-held company will have no reportable business segments.

If there are a number of reportable segments, consider using the report writing software in the accounting system to create a standard report that automatically generates the entire segment report for the financial statement disclosures. By using this approach, the accounting staff will not waste time manually compiling the information, and will avoid running the risk of making a mistake while doing so. However, if reportable segments change over time, it will be necessary to modify the report structure to match the new group of segments.

Chapter 4
Interim Reporting

Introduction

The SEC requires that a publicly-held entity file a variety of quarterly information on the Form 10-Q. This information is a reduced set of the requirements for the more comprehensive annual Form 10-K. The requirement to issue these additional financial statements may appear to be simple enough, but the accountant must consider whether to report information assuming that quarterly results are stand-alone documents, or part of the full-year results of the business. This chapter discusses the disparities that these different viewpoints can cause in the financial statements, as well as how to report changes in accounting principle and estimate.

Overview of Interim Reporting

A business will periodically create financial statements for shorter periods than the fiscal year, which are known as *interim periods*. The most common examples of interim periods are monthly or quarterly financial statements, though any period of less than a full fiscal year can be considered an interim period. The concepts related to interim periods are most commonly applicable to the financial statements of publicly-held companies, since they are required to issue quarterly financial statements that must be reviewed by their outside auditors; these financials must account for certain activities in a consistent manner, as well as prevent readers from being misled about the results of the business on an ongoing basis.

General Interim Reporting Rule

The general rule for interim period reporting is that the same accounting principles and practices be applied to interim reports that are used for the preparation of annual financial statements. The following bullet points illustrate revenues and expenses that follow the general rule, and therefore do not change for interim reporting:

- *Revenue*. Revenue is recognized in the same manner that is used for annual reporting, with no exceptions.
- *Costs associated with revenue*. If a cost is typically assigned to a specific sale (such as cost of goods sold items), expense recognition is the same as is used for annual reporting.
- *Direct expenditures*. If an expense is incurred in a period and relates to that period, it is recorded as an expense in that period. An example is salaries expense.

- *Accruals for estimated expenditures.* If there is an estimated expenditure to be made at a later date but which relates to the current period, it is recorded as an expense in the current period. An example is accrued wages.
- *Depreciation and amortization.* If there is a fixed asset, depreciation (for tangible assets) or amortization (for intangible assets) is ratably charged to all periods in its useful life.

In addition, there are cases where a company is accustomed to only making a year-end adjustment, such as to its reserves for doubtful accounts, obsolete inventory, and/or warranty claims, as well as for year-end bonuses. Where possible, these adjustments should be made in the interim periods, thereby reducing the amount of any residual adjustments still required in the year-end financial statements.

Variations from the Interim Reporting Rule

There are other cases in which the treatment of certain transactions will vary for interim periods. The following rules should be applied in these cases:

- *Expense allocation.* Non-product expenses are allocated among interim periods based on time expired, usage, or benefits received. In most cases, this means that expenditures will simply be charged to expense in the current period, with no allocation to other interim periods. However, it could result in spreading expense recognition over several quarters.
- *Arbitrary assignments.* It is not allowable to make arbitrary assignments of costs to certain interim periods.
- *Gains and losses.* Gains and losses that arise in an interim period shall be recognized at once, and not be deferred to any later interim periods.

EXAMPLE

Armadillo Industries incurs an annual property tax charge of $60,000. Also, Armadillo has historically earned an annual volume discount of $30,000 per year, based on its full-year purchases from a major supplier.

Since the property tax charge is applicable to all months in the year, the controller accrues a $5,000 monthly charge for this expense. Similarly, the volume discount relates back to volume purchases throughout the year, not just the last month of the year, in which the discount is retroactively awarded. Accordingly, the controller creates a monthly credit of $2,500 to reflect the expected year-end volume discount of $30,000.

The concepts of recognizing expenses are more thoroughly discussed in the next two sections, which address the integral view and the discrete view of how to handle interim expense recognition.

There are several specific areas in which the accounting for interim reporting can differ from what is used for annual reporting. In particular:

- *Estimated inventory*. It is acceptable to use the gross profit method or other methods to estimate the cost of goods sold during interim periods. This is allowed in order to reduce the amount of time required to derive the cost of goods sold using a formal count of the ending inventory. The gross profit method is described in a later sub-section.
- *LIFO layers*. If a company uses the last in, first out (LIFO) method of calculating inventory, existing inventory cost layers may be liquidated during an interim period. If such a cost layer is expected to be replaced by the end of the fiscal year, the cost of sales for the interim period can include the expected replacement cost of that LIFO cost layer.
- *Lower of cost or market*. If there is a reduction in the market value of inventory, the difference between the market value and its cost should be charged to expense in an interim period. However, it is allowable to offset the full amount of these losses with any market value gains in subsequent periods within the same fiscal year on the same inventory items. Alternatively, it is acceptable to avoid recognizing these losses in an interim period if there are seasonal price fluctuations that are expected to result in an offsetting increase in market prices by the end of the year.
- *Purchase price and volume variances*. If a company uses a standard costing system to assign costs to its inventory items, it is acceptable to defer the recognition of any variances from standard cost in interim periods, if it has already been planned that these variances will have been absorbed by the end of the fiscal year. However, if there are unexpected purchase price or volume variances, recognize them in the interim period in which they occur.

EXAMPLE

Pianoforte International writes down the value of its mahogany wood holdings, due to a crash in world mahogany prices. The amount of the first-quarter write down is $100,000. By year-end, the market price has stabilized at a higher level, allowing Pianoforte to reverse $62,000 of the original write down and report the change in its fiscal year-end results.

Changes in Accounting Principle in Interim Periods

An accounting principle is an acceptable method for recording and reporting an accounting transaction. There is a change in accounting principle when:

- There are several accounting principles that apply to a situation, and the entity switches to a principle that it has not used in the past; or
- When the accounting principle that formerly applied to the situation is no longer generally accepted; or
- The company changes the method of applying the principle.

Only change an accounting principle when doing so is required by GAAP, or there is a justifiable reason for using the new principle. If management elects to proceed with a change in accounting principle, apply it retrospectively to all prior periods, including all interim reporting, unless it is impractical to do so. To complete a retrospective application of a change in accounting principle, do the following:

1. Include the cumulative effect of the change on periods prior to those presented in the carrying amount of assets and liabilities as of the beginning of the first period in which the entity is presenting financial statements; and
2. Enter an offsetting amount in the beginning retained earnings balance of the first period in which financial statements are presented; and
3. Adjust all presented financial statements to reflect the change to the new accounting principle.

From a reporting perspective, a change in accounting principle requires disclosure of the change in principle from those applied in the comparable interim period of the prior annual period, as well as the preceding interim periods in the current fiscal year, and in the annual report for the prior fiscal year.

Changes in Accounting Estimate in Interim Periods

There is a change in accounting estimate when there is a change that affects the carrying amount of an existing asset or liability, or that alters the subsequent accounting for existing or future assets or liabilities. A change in estimate arises from the appearance of new information that alters the existing situation.

Changes in estimate are a normal part of accounting, and an expected part of the ongoing process of reviewing the current status and future benefits and obligations related to assets and liabilities. All of the following are situations where there is likely to be a change in accounting estimate:

- Allowance for doubtful accounts
- Reserve for obsolete inventory
- Changes in the useful life of depreciable assets
- Changes in the salvage values of depreciable assets
- Changes in the amount of expected warranty obligations
- Changes in the estimated effective annual tax rate

When there is a change in estimate, account for it in the period of change. There is no need to restate earlier financial statements; thus, there is no need to restate any prior-period interim reporting. There should be disclosure in the current and subsequent interim periods of the effect on earnings of the change in estimate, if material in relation to any of the reporting periods presented. This disclosure should continue to be made for as long as necessary, to avoid any misleading comparisons between periods.

> **Tip:** Where possible, adopt accounting changes during the first interim period of a fiscal year. Doing so eliminates any comparability problems between the interim periods for the remainder of the fiscal year.

Error Correction in Interim Periods

When determining the materiality of an error, relate the amount to the estimated profit for the entire fiscal year and the effect on the earnings trend, rather than for the current interim period. Otherwise, a disproportionate number of error corrections will be separately reported within the financial statements.

If an error correction is considered material at the interim period level but not for the full fiscal year, disclose the error in the interim report.

EXAMPLE

Armadillo Industries has profits of $1,000,000 in its first quarter, and expects to generate $4,000,000 of profits for the entire fiscal year. The company has historically considered materiality to be 5% of its profits. In the first quarter, the accounting department uncovers a $100,000 error. Though this amount is 10% of first-quarter profits, it is only 2.5% of full-year expected profits. Given the minimal impact on full-year profits, Armadillo does not have to segregate this information for reporting purposes in its first quarter interim reporting, though it must still disclose the information.

Adjustments to Prior Interim Periods

If an item impacting a company's profits occurs during an interim period other than the first interim period of the fiscal year, and some portion or all of it is an adjustment relating to a prior interim period of the current fiscal year, report the item as follows:

- Include that portion of the item that relates to the current interim period in the results of the current interim period
- Restate the results of prior interim periods to include that portion of the item relating to each interim period
- If there are any portions of the item relating to activities in prior fiscal years, include the change in a restatement of the first interim period of the current fiscal year

Gross Profit Method

As noted earlier, the gross profit method is an acceptable approach to estimate the amount of ending inventory in an interim period. Follow these steps to calculate ending inventory using the gross profit method:

1. Add together the cost of beginning inventory and the cost of purchases during the period to arrive at the cost of goods available for sale.

2. Multiply (1 - expected gross profit percentage) by sales during the period to arrive at the estimated cost of goods sold.
3. Subtract the estimated cost of goods sold (step 2) from the cost of goods available for sale (step 1) to arrive at the ending inventory.

EXAMPLE

Mulligan Imports is calculating its month-end golf club inventory for March. Its beginning inventory was $175,000 and its purchases during the month were $225,000. Thus, its cost of goods available for sale is:

$$\$175,000 \text{ beginning inventory} + \$225,000 \text{ purchases}$$

$$= \$400,000 \text{ cost of goods available for sale}$$

Mulligan's gross margin percentage for all of the past 12 months was 35%, which is considered a reliable long-term margin. Its sales during March were $500,000. Thus, its estimated cost of goods sold is:

$$(1 - 35\%) \times \$500,000 = \$325,000 \text{ cost of goods sold}$$

By subtracting the estimated cost of goods sold from the cost of goods available for sale, Mulligan arrives at an estimated ending inventory balance of $75,000.

There are several issues with the gross profit method that make it unreliable as a long-term method for determining the value of inventory, which are:

- *Applicability.* The calculation is most useful in retail situations where a company is simply buying and reselling merchandise. If a company is instead manufacturing goods, the components of inventory must also include labor and overhead, which make the gross profit method too simplistic to yield reliable results.
- *Historical basis.* The gross profit percentage is a key component of the calculation, but the percentage is based on a company's historical experience. If the current situation yields a different percentage (as may be caused by a special sale at reduced prices), the gross profit percentage used in the calculation will be incorrect.
- *Inventory losses.* The calculation assumes that the long-term rate of losses due to theft, obsolescence, and other causes is included in the historical gross profit percentage. If not, or if these losses have not previously been recognized, the calculation will likely result in an inaccurate estimated ending inventory (and probably one that is too high).

In short, this method is most useful for a small number of consecutive accounting periods, after which the estimated ending balance should be updated with a physical inventory count.

The Integral View

Under the integral view of producing interim reports, there is an assumption that the results reported in interim financial statements are an integral part of the full-year financial results (hence the name of this concept). This viewpoint produces the following accounting issues:

- *Accrue expenses not arising in the period.* If an expense will be paid later in the year that is incurred at least partially in the reporting period, accrue some portion of the expense in the reporting period. Here are several examples:

  - *Advertising.* If the company pays in advance for advertising that is scheduled to occur over multiple time periods, recognize the expense over the entire range of time periods. Also, if there are clear benefits from an initial advertising expenditure that extend beyond the interim period in which the expenditure was made, expense recognition can be deferred to later periods (this concept may be difficult to prove to the auditors).
  - *Bonuses.* If there are bonus plans that may result in bonus payments later in the year, accrue the expense in all accounting periods. Only accrue this expense if one can reasonably estimate the amount of the bonus, which may not always be possible during the earlier months covered by a performance contract.
  - *Contingencies.* If there are contingent liabilities that will be resolved later in the year, and which are both probable and reasonably estimated, then accrue the related expense.
  - *Profit sharing.* If employees are paid a percentage of company profits at year-end, and the amount can be reasonably estimated, then accrue the expense throughout the year as a proportion of the profits recognized in each period.
  - *Property taxes.* A local government entity issues an invoice to the company at some point during the year for property taxes. These taxes are intended to cover the entire year, so accrue a portion of the expense in each reporting period.

- *Tax rate.* A company is usually subject to a graduated income tax rate that incrementally escalates through the year as the business generates more profit. Under the integral view, use the expected tax rate for the entire year in every reporting period, rather than the incremental tax rate that applies only to the profits earned for the year to date.

EXAMPLE

The board of directors of Lowry Locomotion approves a senior management bonus plan for the upcoming year that could potentially pay the senior management team a maximum of $240,000. It initially seems probable that the full amount will be paid, but by the third quarter it appears more likely that the maximum amount to be paid will be $180,000. In addition, the company pays $60,000 in advance for a full year of advertising in *Locomotive Times* magazine. Lowry recognizes these expenses as follows:

	Quarter 1	Quarter 2	Quarter 3	Quarter 4	Full Year
Bonus expense	$60,000	$60,000	$30,000	$30,000	$180,000
Advertising	15,000	15,000	15,000	15,000	60,000

The accounting staff spreads the recognition of the full amount of the projected bonus over the year, but then reduces its recognition of the remaining expense starting in the third quarter, to adjust for the lowered bonus payout expectation.

The accounting staff initially records the $60,000 advertising expense as a prepaid expense, and recognizes it ratably over all four quarters of the year, which matches the time period over which the related advertisements are run by *Locomotive Times*.

One problem with the integral view is that it tends to result in a significant number of expense accruals. Since these accruals are usually based on estimates, it is entirely possible that adjustments should be made to the accruals later in the year, as the company obtains more precise information about the expenses that are being accrued. Some of these adjustments could be substantial, and may materially affect the reported results in later periods.

The Discrete View

Under the discrete view of producing interim reports, the assumption is that the results reported for a specific interim period are *not* associated with the revenues and expenses arising during other reporting periods. Under this view, record the entire impact of a transaction within the reporting period, rather than ratably over the entire year. The following are examples of the situations that can arise under the discrete method:

- *Reduced accruals.* A substantially smaller number of accruals are likely under the discrete method, since the assumption is that one should not anticipate the recordation of transactions that have not yet arisen.
- *Gains and losses.* Do not spread the recognition of a gain or loss across multiple periods. If the accounting department were to do so, it would allow a company to spread a loss over multiple periods, thereby making the loss look smaller on a per-period basis than it really is.

Comparison of the Integral and Discrete Views

The integral view is clearly the better method from a theoretical perspective, since the causes of some transactions can span an entire year. For example, a manager may be awarded a bonus at the end of December, but he probably had to achieve specific results throughout the year to earn it. Otherwise, if one were to adopt the discrete view, interim reporting would yield exceedingly varied results, with some periods revealing inordinately high or low profitability.

However, a business should adopt the integral view from the perspective of accounting efficiency; that is, it is very time-consuming to maintain a mass of revenue and expense accruals, their ongoing adjustments, and documentation of the reasons for them throughout a year. Instead, use the integral view only for the more material transactions that are anticipated, and use the discrete view for smaller transactions. Thus, an organization could accrue the expense for property taxes throughout the year if the amount is significant, or simply record it in the month when the invoice is received, if the amount is small.

Disclosures for Interim Reporting

The level of financial reporting contained within the interim reports of publicly-held companies is lower than the requirements for annual financial statements, which is necessary in order to release interim reports on an accelerated schedule. To prevent an excessive reduction in the level of reporting, GAAP requires the following minimum content in the financial statements:

- *Financial statement items*. Includes sales, provision for income taxes, net income, and comprehensive income.
- *Earnings per share*. Includes both basic and diluted earnings per share.

The following additional disclosures are specific to interim reports:

- *Cost of goods sold derivation*. If a different method is used during an interim period than at year-end to derive the cost of goods sold, this different method must be disclosed, as well as any significant adjustments resulting from a reconciliation with the annual physical inventory count.
- *Expenses charged wholly within current period*. If there are costs wholly charged to expense within an interim period, and for which there are no comparable expenses in the corresponding interim period of the preceding year, the nature and amount of the expense should be disclosed.
- *Prior period adjustment*. If there is a material retroactive prior period adjustment made during any interim period, disclosure must be made of the effect on net income and earnings per share of any prior period included in the report, as well as on retained earnings.
- *Seasonality*. When there are seasonal variations in a business, disclose the seasonal nature of its activities, thereby avoiding confusion about unusually high or low results in an interim period. It may also be necessary to supplement interim reports with financial results for the 12-month periods ended at the interim date for the current and preceding years.

In addition, GAAP requires that the following standard disclosures found in annual reports also be addressed in interim reports:

- Asset and liability fair value information
- Business combinations (involves pro forma disclosure of the financial statements for the current and preceding year to reflect the combined results of the businesses)
- Changes in accounting estimate
- Changes in accounting principle
- Contingent items (the significance of which is judged in relation to the annual financial statements)
- Defined benefit pension plan disclosures
- Derivative instrument information
- Disposals of a material component of the business, or material items considered unusual or infrequent
- Financial instrument fair value information
- Investments in debt and equity securities
- Other-than-temporary impairments
- Segment information
- Significant changes in financial position
- Significant changes in the provision for income taxes

Tip: The SEC allows line items in the balance sheet to be aggregated if a line item is less than 10% of total assets and the amount has not changed by more than 25% since the end of the preceding fiscal year. The same concept applies to the income statement, except that the thresholds are 15% of average net income for the last three fiscal years (not including loss years) and the change limit is 20% from the corresponding interim period of the preceding fiscal year. For the statement of cash flows, the threshold is 10% of the average of net cash flows from operating activities for the last three years.

The SEC requires that the disclosures in interim reports not be misleading. This means that a material change from any disclosure in the most recent annual report should be noted in the next interim report. However, even if there is no significant change in a material contingency, the matter must continue to be disclosed until resolved.

Finally, the SEC requires that quarterly filings with it must include the following financial statements:

- A balance sheet as of the end of the most recent fiscal quarter
- A balance sheet as of the end of the preceding fiscal year
- An income statement for the most recent fiscal quarter and for the corresponding prior-year period
- An income statement for the fiscal year-to-date and for the corresponding prior-year period

- A statement of cash flows for the fiscal year-to-date
- A statement of cash flows for the corresponding prior-year periods

Summary

When creating interim financial reports, one should judiciously apply the integral and discrete views to the statements – that is, the integral method is more accurate, but the discrete view is more efficient; and a key factor in closing the books for an interim period is that there is less time than usual in which to complete all closing activities. Thus, it will be necessary to restrict the integral view to material transactions, and apply the discrete view to all other transactions.

Chapter 5
Stock Issuances Accounting

Introduction

One of the main reasons why a company goes public is to raise funds by selling its stock to the investment community. In addition, a publicly-held entity is much more likely to take full advantage of the situation by issuing stock options and warrants, which have real value to the recipients. There may be a number of related actions, such as issuing cash dividends or stock dividends, or engaging in stock splits, or setting up employee share purchase plans.

In this chapter, we describe the accounting and related disclosures associated with all of these activities. We do not describe other equity topics that are less specific to the activities of a public company, such as the repurchase of company stock or the use of spinoffs. For a more complete analysis of these additional topics, see the author's latest annual edition of the *GAAP Guidebook*.

The Sale of Stock

A common fund raising activity for a publicly-held entity is to sell stock – usually its common stock. The structure of the journal entry to record the sale of stock depends upon the existence and size of any par value associated with the stock. Par value is the legal capital per share, and the amount is printed on the face of each stock certificate. A portion of the price at which each share is sold is recorded in either the common stock or preferred stock account (depending on the type of share sold) in the amount of the par value, with the remainder being recorded in the additional paid-in capital account. Both entries are credits. The offsetting debit is to the cash account.

EXAMPLE

Arlington Motors sells 10,000 shares of its common stock for $8 per share. The stock has a par value of $0.01. Arlington records the share issuance with the following entry:

	Debit	Credit
Cash	80,000	
Common stock ($0.01 par value)		100
Additional paid-in capital		79,900

If Arlington were to only sell the stock for an amount equal to the par value, the entire credit would be to the common stock account; there would be no entry to the additional paid-in capital account. If the company were to sell preferred stock instead of common stock, the entry would be the same, except that the accounts in which the entries are made would be identified as preferred stock accounts, not common stock accounts.

Dividend Payments

The cash dividend is by far the most common of the dividend types used. On the date of declaration, the board of directors resolves to pay a certain dividend amount in cash to those investors holding the company's stock on a specific date. The date of record is the date on which dividends are assigned to the holders of the company's stock. On the date of payment, the company issues dividend payments.

EXAMPLE

On February 1, Milagro Corporation's board of directors declares a cash dividend of $0.50 per share on the company's 2,000,000 outstanding shares, to be paid on June 1 to all shareholders of record on April 1. On February 1, the company records this entry:

	Debit	Credit
Retained earnings	1,000,000	
Dividends payable		1,000,000

On June 1, Milagro pays the dividends and records the transaction with this entry:

	Debit	Credit
Dividends payable	1,000,000	
Cash		1,000,000

Stock Dividends and Stock Splits

A company may issue additional shares to its shareholders, which is called a stock dividend. This type of dividend does not involve the reduction of any company assets, nor does it increase the cash inflow to the recipient, so it can be considered a neutral event that has no impact on either party. However, the sheer volume of shares issued can have an effect on the value of the shareholdings of the recipient, which calls for different types of accounting. The two volume-based accounting treatments are:

- *Low-volume stock issuance.* If a stock issuance is for less than 20% to 25% of the number of shares outstanding prior to the issuance, account for the transaction as a stock dividend.
- *High-volume stock issuance.* If a stock issuance is for more than 20% to 25% of the number of shares outstanding prior to the issuance, account for the transaction as a stock split.

The dividing line between these two treatments is an estimate provided in GAAP, based on the assumption that a relatively small stock issuance will not appreciably alter the price of a share, which therefore creates value for the recipient of these shares. A larger share issuance is presumed to reduce the market price of shares outstanding, so that share recipients do not experience a net increase in the value of their shares.

If there are an ongoing series of stock issuances that would individually be accounted for as stock dividends, consider aggregating these issuances to see if the result would instead trigger treatment as a stock split.

Stock Dividend

When there is a stock dividend, transfer from retained earnings to the capital stock and additional paid-in capital accounts an amount equal to the fair value of the additional shares issued. The fair value of the additional shares issued is based on their market value after the dividend is declared. A stock dividend is never treated as a liability, since it does not reduce assets.

EXAMPLE

Davidson Motors declares a stock dividend to its shareholders of 10,000 shares. The fair value of the stock is $5.00, and its par value is $1.00. Davidson's controller records the following entry:

	Debit	Credit
Retained earnings	50,000	
Common stock, $1 par value		10,000
Additional paid-in capital		40,000

Stock Split

When a stock issuance is sufficiently large to be classified as a stock split, the only accounting is to ensure that the legally-required amount of par value has been properly designated as such in the accounting records. If a company's stock has no par value, then no reallocation of funds into the par value account is required.

EXAMPLE

Davidson Motors declares a stock dividend to its shareholders of 1,000,000 shares, which represents a doubling of the prior number of shares outstanding. Davidson's stock has a par value of $1, so the controller records the following entry to ensure that the correct amount of capital is apportioned to the par value account:

	Debit	Credit
Additional paid-in capital	1,000,000	
Common stock, $1 par value		1,000,000

Equity-Based Payments to Non-Employees

An equity-based payment is one in which a business pays a provider of goods or services with its equity, such as shares or warrants. The accounting for equity-based payments depends upon the definition of the recipient, since the accounting for a payment to an employee differs from the accounting when payment is made to anyone else. In this section, we deal with the accounting for equity-based payments to non-employees. See the Overview of Stock Compensation section for the accounting treatment of equity-based payments to employees.

The two main rules for equity-based payments are to:

- Recognize the fair value of the equity instruments issued or the fair value of the consideration received, whichever can be more reliably measured; and
- Recognize the asset or expense related to the provided goods or services at the same time.

The following additional conditions apply to more specific circumstances:

- *Fully vested equity issued.* If fully vested, nonforfeitable equity instruments are issued, the grantor should recognize the equity on the date of issuance. The offset to this recognition may be a prepaid asset, if the grantee has not yet delivered on its obligations.
- *Option expiration.* If the grantor recognizes an asset or expense based on its issuance of stock options to a grantee, and the grantee does not exercise the options, do not reverse the asset or expense.
- *Sales incentives.* If sales incentives are paid with equity instruments, measure them at the fair value of the equity instruments or the sales incentive, whichever can be more reliably measured.

The grantor usually recognizes an equity-based payment as of a measurement date. The measurement date is the earlier of:

- The date when the grantee's performance is complete; or
- The date when the grantee's commitment to complete is probable, given the presence of large disincentives related to nonperformance. Note that forfeiture of the equity instrument is not considered a sufficient disincentive to trigger this clause.

It is also possible to reach the measurement date when the grantor issues fully vested, nonforfeitable equity instruments to the grantee, since the grantee does not have an obligation to perform in order to receive payment.

If the grantor issues a fully vested, nonforfeitable equity instrument that can be exercised early if a performance target is reached, the grantor measures the fair value of the instrument at the date of grant. If early exercise is granted, then measure and record the incremental change in fair value as of the date of revision to the terms of the instrument. Also, recognize the cost of the transaction in the same period as if the company had paid cash, instead of using the equity instrument as payment.

EXAMPLE

Armadillo Industries issues fully vested warrants to a grantee. The option agreement contains a provision that the exercise price will be reduced if a project on which the grantee is working is completed to the satisfaction of Armadillo management by a certain date.

In another arrangement, Armadillo issues warrants that vest in five years. The option agreement contains a provision that the vesting period will be reduced to six months if a project on which the grantee is working is accepted by an Armadillo client by a certain date.

In both cases, the company should record the fair value of the instruments when granted, and then adjust the recorded fair values when the remaining provisions of the agreements have been settled.

In rare cases, it may be necessary for the grantor to recognize the cost of an equity payment before the measurement date. If so, measure the fair value of the equity instrument at each successive interim period until the measurement date is reached. If some terms of the equity instrument have not yet been settled during these interim periods (as is the case when the amount of equity paid will vary based on market conditions or counterparty performance), measure the instrument at its lowest aggregate fair value during each interim period, until all terms have been settled.

The grantee must also record payments made to it with equity instruments. The grantee should recognize the fair value of the equity instruments paid using the same rules applied to the grantor. If there is a performance condition, the grantee may have to alter the amount of revenue recognized, once the condition has been settled.

EXAMPLE

Gatekeeper Corporation operates a private toll road. It contracts with International Bridge Development (IBD) to build a bridge along the toll way. Gatekeeper agrees to pay IBD $10,000,000 for the work, as well as an additional 1,000,000 warrants if the bridge is completed by a certain date. IBD agrees to forfeit $2,000,000 of its fee if the bridge has not been completed by that date. The forfeiture clause is sufficiently large to classify the arrangement as a performance commitment.

Gatekeeper should measure the 1,000,000 warrants at the performance commitment date, which have a fair value of $500,000. Gatekeeper should then charge the $500,000 to expense over the normal course of the bridge construction project, based on milestone and completion payments.

EXAMPLE

Archaic Corporation hires a writer to create a series of books about ancient Greece. The terms of the deal are that Archaic will pay the writer $20,000 and 10,000 warrants per book completed. There is no penalty associated with the writer declining to continue writing books for the series. The writer completes work on the first book in the series on October 31, and then refuses to continue writing books for Archaic.

Archaic should recognize the fair value of the 10,000 warrants associated with the writer's completion of the first book when the writer completes the manuscript on October 31. On that date, the warrants have a fair value of $5,000, so Archaic should recognize a total expense of $25,000, which is comprised of the cash and warrant portions of the payment.

Overview of Stock Compensation

A company may issue payments to its employees in the form of shares in the business. When these payments are made, the essential accounting is to recognize the cost of the related services as they are received by the company, at their fair value. The offset to this expense recognition is either an increase in an equity or liability account, depending on the nature of the transaction. In rare cases, the cost of the services received by the company may be capitalized into a fixed asset, if the services are related to the acquisition or construction of the asset.

The following issues relate to the measurement and recognition of stock-based compensation:

- *Employee designation.* The accounting for stock compensation noted in this chapter only applies to employees. It also applies to the board of directors, as long as they were elected by company shareholders. However, the accounting only applies to stock grants issued in compensation for their services as directors, not for other services provided.
- *Employee payments.* If an employee pays the issuer an amount in connection with an award, the fair value attributable to employee service is net of the amount paid. For example, if a stock option has a fair value on the grant date of $100, and the recipient pays $20 for the option, the award amount attributable to employee service is $80.

EXAMPLE

Armadillo Industries issues 1,000 shares of common stock to Mr. Jones, the vice president of sales, at a large discount from the market price. On the grant date, the fair value of these shares is $20,000. Mr. Jones pays $1,000 to the company for these shares. Thus, the amount that can be attributed to Mr. Jones' services to the company is $19,000 (calculated as $20,000 fair value - $1,000 payment).

- *Expense accrual.* When the service component related to a stock issuance spans several reporting periods, accrue the related service expense based on the probable outcome of the performance condition. Thus, always accrue the expense when it is probable that the condition will be achieved. Also, accrue the expense over the initial best estimate of the employee service period, which is usually the service period required in the arrangement related to the stock issuance.

EXAMPLE

The board of directors of Armadillo Industries grants stock options to its president that have a fair value of $80,000, which will vest in the earlier of four years or when the company achieves a 20% market share in a new market that the company wants to enter. Since there is not sufficient historical information about the company's ability to succeed in the new market, the controller elects to set the service period at four years, and accordingly accrues $20,000 of compensation in each of the next four years.

If both performance conditions had been required before the stock options would be awarded, and there was no way of determining the probability of achieving the 20% market share condition, the controller would only begin to accrue any compensation expense after it became probable that the market share condition could be achieved. In this latter case, compensation expense would be recognized at once for all of the earlier periods during which no compensation expense had been accrued.

- *Expired stock options.* If stock option grants expire unused, do not reverse the related amount of compensation expense.
- *Fair value determination.* Stock-based compensation is measured at the fair value of the instruments issued as of the grant date, even though the stock may not be issued until a much later date. Fair value is based on the share price at the grant date. The fair value of a stock option is estimated with a valuation method, such as an option-pricing model.
- *Fair value of nonvested shares.* The fair value of a nonvested share is based on its value as though it were vested on the grant date.
- *Fair value of restricted shares.* The fair value of a restricted share is based on its value as a *restricted* share, which is likely to be less than the fair value of an *unrestricted* share.
- *Fair value restrictions.* If a restriction is imposed on awarded equity instruments that continue after the required service period, such as being unable to sell shares for a period of time, this restriction is considered in determining the fair value of the stock award.
- *Grant date.* The date on which a stock-based award is granted is assumed to be the date when the award is approved under the corporate governance requirements. The grant date can also be considered the date on which an employee initially begins to benefit from or be affected by subsequent

changes in the price of a company's stock, as long as subsequent approval of the grant is considered perfunctory.

- *Non-compete agreement*. If a share-based award contains a non-compete agreement, the facts and circumstances of the situation may indicate that the non-compete is a significant service condition. If so, accrue the related amount of compensation expense over the period covered by the non-compete agreement.

EXAMPLE

Armadillo Industries grants 200,000 restricted stock units (RSUs) to its chief high-pressure module design engineer, which are vested on the grant date. The fair value of the grant is $500,000, which is triple his compensation for the past year. Under the terms of the arrangement, the RSUs will only be transferred to the engineer ratably over the next five years if he complies with the terms of the non-compete agreement.

Since the RSUs are essentially linked to the non-compete agreement, and the amount of the future payouts are quite large, it is evident that the arrangement is really intended to be compensation for future services yet to be rendered to the company. Consequently, the appropriate accounting treatment is not to recognize the expense at once, but rather to recognize it ratably over the remaining term of the non-compete agreement.

- *Payroll taxes*. Accrue an expense for the payroll taxes associated with stock-based compensation at the same time as the related compensation expense.
- *Reload valuation*. A compensation instrument may have a reload feature, which automatically grants additional options to an employee once that person exercises existing options that use company shares to pay the exercise price. Do not include the value of the reload feature in the fair value of an award. Instead, measure reload options as separate awards when they are granted.
- *Service not rendered*. If an employee does not render the service required for an award, the company may then reverse any related amount of compensation expense that had previously been recognized.

EXAMPLE

Uncanny Corporation grants 5,000 restricted stock units (RSUs) to its vice president of sales, with a three-year cliff vesting provision. The fair value of the RSUs on the grant date is $60,000, so the company accrues $20,000 of compensation expense per year for three years.

One week prior to the cliff vesting date, the vice president of sales unexpectedly resigns. Since the award has not yet vested, the company reverses all of the accrued compensation expense.

- *Service period.* The service period associated with a stock-based award is considered to be the vesting period, but the facts and circumstances of the arrangement can result in a different service period for the purpose of determining the number of periods over which to accrue compensation expense. This is called the *implicit service period.*

EXPENSE

Mrs. Smith is granted 10,000 stock options by the board of directors of Uncanny Corporation, which vest over 24 months. There is no service specified under the arrangement, so the service period is assumed to be the 24-month vesting period. Thus, the fair value of the award should be recognized ratably over the vesting period.

- *Service rendered prior to grant date.* If some or all of the requisite service associated with stock-based compensation occurs prior to the grant date, accrue the compensation expense during these earlier reporting periods, based on the fair value of the award at each reporting date. When the grant date is reached, adjust the compensation accrued to date based on the per-unit fair value assigned on the grant date. Thus, the initial recordation is a best guess of what the eventual fair value will be.
- *Subsequent changes.* If the circumstances later indicate that the number of instruments to be granted has changed, recognize the change in compensation cost in the period in which the change in estimate occurs. Also, if the initial estimate of the service period turns out to be incorrect, adjust the expense accrual to match the updated estimate.

EXAMPLE

The board of directors of Armadillo Industries initially grants 5,000 stock options to the engineering manager, with a vesting period of four years. The shares are worth $100,000 at the grant date, so the controller plans to recognize $25,000 of compensation expense in each of the next four years. After two years, the board is so pleased with the performance of the engineering manager that they accelerate the vesting schedule to the current date. The controller must therefore accelerate the remaining $50,000 of compensation expense that had not yet been recognized to the current date.

If the offsetting increase to stock-based compensation is equity, it should be to the paid-in capital account, as noted in the following example.

EXAMPLE

Armadillo Industries issues stock options with 10-year terms to its employees. All of these options vest at the end of four years (known as *cliff vesting*). The company uses a lattice-based valuation model to arrive at an option fair value of $15.00. The company grants

100,000 stock options. On the grant date, it assumes that 10% of the options will be forfeited. The exercise price of the options is $25.

Given this information, Armadillo charges $28,125 to expense in each month. The calculation of this compensation expense accrual is:

($15 Option fair value × 100,000 Options × 90% Exercise probability) ÷ 48 Months

= $28,125

The monthly journal entry to recognize the compensation expense is:

	Debit	Credit
Compensation expense	28,125	
Additional paid-in capital		28,125

Armadillo is subject to a 35% income tax rate, and expects to have sufficient future taxable income to offset the deferred tax benefits of the share-based compensation arrangements. Accordingly, the company records the following monthly entry to recognize the deferred tax benefit:

	Debit	Credit
Deferred tax asset	9,844	
Deferred tax benefit		9,844

Thus, the net after-tax effect of the monthly compensation expense recognition is $18,281 (calculated as $28,125 compensation expense - $9,844 deferred tax benefit).

At the end of the vesting period, the actual number of forfeitures matches the originally estimated amount, leaving 90,000 options. All of the 90,000 options are exercised once they have vested, which results in the following entry to record the conversion of options to shares:

	Debit	Credit
Cash (90,000 shares × $25/share)	2,250,000	
Additional paid-in capital	1,350,000	
Common stock		3,600,000

The Volatility Concept

A key component of the value of a company's stock is its volatility, which is the range over which the price varies over time, or is expected to vary. Since an employee holding a stock option can wait for the highest possible stock price before exercising the option, that person will presumably wait for the stock price to peak before exercising the option. Therefore, a stock that has a history or expectation of high volatility is worth more from the perspective of an option holder than one that has little volatility. The result is that a company with high stock price volatility will likely charge more employee compensation to expense for a given number of shares than a company whose stock experiences low volatility.

Stock price volatility is partially driven by the amount of leverage that a company employs in its financing. Thus, if a business uses a large amount of debt to fund its operations, its profit will fluctuate in a wider range than a business that uses less debt, since the extra debt can be used to generate more sales, but the associated interest expense will reduce net profits if revenues decline.

Fair Value Calculation Alternatives

When a publicly-held company issues stock compensation, it can derive fair value from the current market price of its stock, which is readily available. When it is not possible to estimate the fair value of an equity instrument, it is permissible to use an alternative valuation technique, as long as it is applied consistently, reflects the key characteristics of the instrument, and is based on accepted standards of financial economic theory. Models that are commonly used to derive fair value are the Black-Scholes-Merton formula and the lattice model. Key characteristics of these models are:

- *Black-Scholes-Merton formula.* Assumes that options are exercised at the end of the arrangement period, and that price volatility, dividends, and interest rates are constant through the term of the option being measured.
- *Lattice model.* Can incorporate ongoing changes in price volatility and dividends over successive time periods in the term of an option. The model assumes that at least two price movements are possible in each measured time period.

EXAMPLE

Armadillo Industries grants an option on $25 stock that will expire in 12 months. The exercise price of the option matches the $25 stock price. Management believes there is a 40% chance that the stock price will increase by 25% during the upcoming year, a 40% chance that the price will decline by 10%, and a 20% chance that the price will decline by 50%. The risk-free interest rate is 5%. The steps required to develop a fair value for the stock option using the lattice model are:

1. Chart the estimated stock price variations.
2. Convert the price variations into the future value of options.
3. Discount the options to their present values.

Stock Issuances Accounting

The following lattice model shows the range and probability of stock prices for the upcoming year:

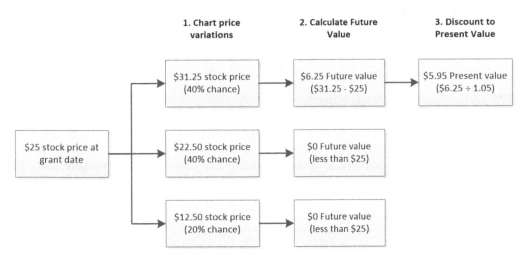

In short, the option will expire unexercised unless the stock price increases. Since there is only a 40% chance of the stock price increasing, the present value of the stock option associated with that scenario can be assigned the following expected present value for purposes of assigning a fair value to the option at the grant date:

$5.95 Option present value × 40% Probability = $2.38 Option value at grant date

---

It is acceptable to employ a different valuation model to develop the fair value of different equity instruments. It is also permissible to switch valuation methods if the replacement method can yield a better estimate of fair value.

Whatever valuation method is used, it must take into account the exercise price and expected term of the option being measured, the risk-free interest rate over the expected term of the option, and the expected dividends and volatility of the underlying shares. Accounting notes related to these inclusions are:

- *Interest-free rate.* Use the implied yield on U.S. Treasury zero-coupon issuances over the term of the option.
- *Expected term.* The expected term of an option is generally shorter than its contractual term, and can be based on historical experience. Another choice is to estimate the term based upon expected future price points of the underlying stock.
- *Volatility.* A reasonable way to estimate volatility is the historical pattern of changes in the price of a company's stock, adjusted for anticipated future issues that may impact volatility.
- *Dividends.* Include the historical pattern of changes in dividend payments in the estimation of future dividends.

When developing estimates for these inputs to the valuation model, select the amount that is the most likely; if no value appears to be the most likely, use an average of the range of possible outcomes.

> **Tip:** From an accounting efficiency perspective, it is useful to aggregate individual awards into homogeneous groups for valuation purposes.

Awards Classified as Equity

In this section, we address a number of variations on how to account for awards that are classified as equity arrangements (that is, the offset to compensation expense is an increase in equity). The bulk of these issues relate to subsequent modifications of existing stock-based awards.

Award Measurement Problems

When it is not possible to reasonably estimate the fair value of a stock-based award at its grant date, continue to remeasure the award at each successive reporting date until the award has been settled. Once the award has been settled, adjust the compensation-to-date associated with the award to the intrinsic value of the award. Intrinsic value is the excess amount of the fair value of a share over the exercise price of an underlying stock option.

Contingent Features

If there is a contingent feature in a stock-based award that allows the recipient to return equity instruments earned or to pay for equity instruments at less than their fair value when sold, account for the feature only if it is actually used.

Award Modifications

If a stock-based award is modified, treat the modification as an exchange of the original award for an entirely new award. Thus, the company is assumed to buy back the original award and exchange it for an award of equal or greater value. The accounting for a modified award includes the following points:

- *Fair value basis.* If there is an incremental change in value between the "old" and "new" awards, this is treated as additional compensation expense. The amount of expense is calculated by determining the fair value of the "old" award immediately prior to the terms modification, and subtracting it from the fair value of the modified award.
- *Intrinsic value basis.* If intrinsic value is being used instead of fair value to calculate the associated cost of compensation, measure the incremental change in value by comparing the intrinsic value of the award just prior to modification with the intrinsic value of the modified award.
- *Short-term inducements.* If the company offers short-term inducements to convince employees to accept an alteration of their stock-based compensa-

tion plans, only treat these inducements as modifications if they are accepted by employees.

- *Equity restructuring.* If there is an equity restructuring and awards are replaced with new ones that have the same fair values, do not alter the existing accounting. However, if the fair values have changed, treat the effects of the equity restructuring as a modification.
- *Repurchase of award.* If the company repurchases an award, it should charge the amount of the payment to equity, up to the amount of the fair value of the instruments repurchased. If the amount paid exceeds the fair value of the instruments repurchased, charge the difference to compensation expense.
- *Cancellation and replacement.* If the company cancels a stock-based award and concurrently grants a replacement award or other form of payment, treat these two events as the modification of terms of the original award.
- *Award cancellation.* If the company cancels an award outright, without any offer to replace the award, accelerate the recognition of any remaining unrecognized compensation expense to the cancellation date.

EXAMPLE

Armadillo Industries issues 10,000 stock options to various employees in 20X1. The designated exercise price of the options is $25, and the vesting period is four years. The total fair value of these options is $20,000, which the company charges to expense ratably over four years, which is $5,000 per year.

One year later, the market price of the stock has declined to $15, so the board of directors decides to modify the options to have an exercise price of $15.

Armadillo incurs additional compensation expense of $30,000 for the amount by which the fair value of the modified options exceeds the fair value of the original options as of the date of the modification. The accounting department adds this additional expense to the remaining $15,000 of compensation expense associated with the original stock options, which is a total unrecognized compensation expense of $45,000. The company recognizes this amount ratably over the remaining three years of vesting, which is $15,000 per year.

Awards Classified as Liabilities

A key element of stock-based compensation arrangements is whether these arrangements result in an offsetting increase in equity or liabilities. The following situations indicate the presence of a liability:

- *Cash settlement.* An employee can require the issuing company to settle an option by paying in cash or other assets, rather than stock.
- *Indexing.* An award is indexed to some additional factor, such as the market price of a commodity.

- *Puttable shares.* An employee has the right to require the issuing company to repurchase shares at their fair value, where the put feature essentially allows the employee to avoid the risks associated with owning stock.
- *Share classification.* Certain types of share-based payments, such as mandatorily-redeemable shares, are themselves classified as liabilities.

If an award is classified as a liability, the offsetting expense should be remeasured at its fair value as of the end of each reporting period, until the related service has been completed. Any change in value is to be recognized in the measurement period, adjusted for the percentage of required service rendered through the reporting period. Thus, the measurement date for a liability is the settlement date, not the grant date.

If an award is modified, treat it as the exchange of the "old" award for a "new" award. However, since the accounting for awards classified as liabilities already provides for the ongoing remeasurement of a liability, there is no need for any additional accounting for a modified award.

EXAMPLE

Uncanny Corporation grants 20,000 stock appreciation rights (SARs) to its chief executive officer (CEO). Each SAR entitles the CEO to receive a cash payment that equates to the increase in value of one share of company stock above a baseline value of $25. The award cliff vests after two years. The fair value of each SAR is calculated to be $11.50 as of the grant date. The entry to record the associated amount of compensation expense for the first year, along with the company's deferred tax asset at its 35% income tax rate, is:

	Debit	Credit
Compensation expense	115,000	
Share-based compensation liability		115,000

	Debit	Credit
Deferred tax asset	40,250	
Deferred tax benefit		40,250

At the end of the first year of vesting, the fair value of each SAR has increased to $12.75, so an additional entry is needed to adjust the vested amount of compensation expense and deferred tax asset for the $12,500 incremental increase in the value of the award over the first year (calculated as $1.25 increase in SAR fair value × 20,000 SARs × 0.5 service period).

At end of the vesting period, the fair value of each SAR has increased again, to $13.00, which increases the total two-year vested compensation expense for the CEO to $260,000. Since $127,500 of compensation expense has already been recognized at the end of the first year, the company must recognize an additional $132,500 of compensation expense, along with the related amount of deferred tax asset. When the cash payment is made to the CEO, the entry is:

	Debit	Credit
Share-based compensation liability	260,000	
Cash		260,000

Employee Share Purchase Plans

A company may offer its employees the opportunity to directly purchase shares in the business through an employee share purchase plan (ESPP). These plans frequently offer sales without any brokerage charge, and possibly also at a price somewhat below the market rate.

From an accounting perspective, the main issue with an ESPP is whether it represents a form of compensation to employees. An ESPP is not considered compensatory if it meets all of the following criteria:

- *Employee qualification.* Essentially all employees meeting a limited set of employment qualifications can participate in the plan.
- *Favorable terms.* The terms offered under the plan are no more favorable than those available to investors at large, or does not offer a purchase discount of greater than five percent (which is considered the per-share cost that would otherwise be required to raise funds through a public offering). It is possible to justify a percentage greater than five percent, but the justification must be reassessed on an annual basis.
- *Option features.* The plan only allows a maximum 31-day notice period to enroll in the plan after the share price has been fixed, the share price is based only on the market price on the purchase date, and employees can cancel their participation before the purchase date.

Under the following circumstances, an ESPP is considered to be compensatory, which means that the company must record the difference between the market price of the stock and the lower price at which employees purchase the shares as compensation expense:

- The purchase discount offered under the plan is greater than five percent.
- The purchase price is the lesser of the market price on the grant date or the market price on the purchase date.

EXAMPLE

Armadillo Industries has an employee stock purchase plan, under which employees can purchase shares for a 10% discount from the market price of the company's stock. In the most recent quarter, employees authorized the deduction of $90,000 from their pay, which was used to purchase $100,000 of company stock. Since the discount exceeds the 5% threshold, Armadillo must record the $10,000 discount as compensation expense.

Equity Disclosures

There are a large number of disclosures related to the equity topic, so the disclosures related to each topic are addressed separately within the following sub-sections.

Rights and Privileges

Disclose a summary of the rights and privileges accorded to the holders of the various securities outstanding during the presented accounting periods. This may include the following items, or other rights and privileges:

- Conversion rights to other securities (and the associated prices and dates)
- Dividends
- Liquidation rights
- Participation rights
- Special voting rights

Preferred Stock

If there is preferred stock outstanding and those shares have a liquidation preference that significantly exceeds their par value, disclose the aggregate liquidation preference on the balance sheet. Also disclose the following information anywhere in the financial statements:

- *Arrearages*. The amount by which there are cumulative preferred dividends in arrears, both in aggregate and on a per-share basis.
- *Redemption*. The amounts of preferred stock subject to redemption, both in aggregate and on a per-share basis.

Contingently Convertible Securities

Disclose the significant conversion terms associated with contingently convertible securities. There must be sufficient information for readers to understand the contingent conversion option and what the impact of the conversion would be. The following disclosures would be helpful for gaining this understanding:

- Events that would alter the terms of the contingency
- Events that would trigger the contingency
- The conversion price

- The number of shares into which a security can be converted
- The timing of conversion rights
- The type of settlement (such as in cash or shares)

EXAMPLE

Armadillo Industries includes the following disclosure in the notes that accompany its financial statements, regarding the issuance of shares related to a recent acquisition:

> The company issued 2,000,000 shares of its common stock to the shareholders of Susquehanna Plating when it acquired that entity. If the market price of Armadillo's stock declines below $10 per share before December 31, 20X4, the company will be obligated to issue an additional 500,000 shares of its common stock to those shareholders.

Also disclose the excess amount by which the aggregate fair value of the securities to be issued at conversion exceeds the proceeds received, as well as the time period over which the discount would be amortized.

Redeemable Securities

If a business issues redeemable securities, disclose the redemption requirements in each of the five years following the date of the last balance sheet presented. The disclosure can be in aggregate or separately for each issuance of these securities.

Changes in Shareholders' Equity

If both the income statement and balance sheet are presented, disclose the changes in the shareholders' equity accounts, as well as any changes in shares outstanding during at least the most recent fiscal year and subsequent interim periods. A sample statement, not including changes in shares outstanding, is shown in the following exhibit.

Statement of Retained Earnings

	Common Stock, $1 Par	Additional Paid-In Capital	Retained Earnings	Total Shareholders' Equity
Retained earnings at December 31, 20X2	$10,000	$40,000	$100,000	$150,000
Net income for the year ended 12/31/X3			40,000	40,000
Dividends paid to shareholders			-25,000	-25,000
Retained earnings at December 31, 20X3	$10,000	$40,000	$115,000	$165,000

The SEC also requires disclosure of adjustments to the beginning balance in this reconciliation for items that were retroactively applied to prior periods.

Equity-Based Payments to Non-Employees

There may be situations where a company issues fully vested, non-forfeitable equity instruments in exchange for goods or services. A likely outcome of this arrangement is that the goods or services have not yet been provided or performed, and so are recorded as a prepaid asset. This prepaid asset should be included within the assets section of the balance sheet, not as a deduction from equity.

Stock-Based Compensation Disclosures

A company that issues stock-based compensation should disclose sufficient information to ensure that users of its financial statements are aware of the nature of these arrangements, the effect of the resulting compensation cost on the income statement, how the fair value of the services received or instruments granted is derived, and the cash flow effects of these arrangements. Disclosure at this level of detail is not required for interim financial statements.

The following disclosures are considered to be the minimum level of information required to meet the preceding disclosure requirements:

- *General description.* The general terms of the arrangements, including service periods, the maximum term of stock options, and the number of shares authorized for awards.
- *Cash payments.* The cash paid by the company to settle equity instruments that were granted under share-based compensation arrangements.
- *Cash receipts.* The cash paid to the company for the exercise of stock options, and the tax benefit realized from the exercised stock options.
- *Compensation cost not recognized.* As of the latest balance sheet date, the total cost of compensation related to unvested awards not yet recognized, and the weighted-average period over which this cost will be recognized.
- *Compensation cost.* For each year in which an income statement is presented, the aggregate compensation cost recognized that was related to share-based payment arrangements, net of taxes, as well as any amount capitalized. Also, the terms of any modifications and the related change in cost, and the number of employees affected by the modifications.
- *Fair value assumptions.* For each year for which an income statement is presented, the method used to estimate fair value, and the assumptions incorporated into these estimations, including expected option terms (which includes expected employee behavior), expected volatility and how it is estimated, expected dividends, the risk-free rate, and the discount for post-vesting restrictions.
- *Fair values.* For the most recent year, the number and weighted-average grant-date fair values of those stock options nonvested at the beginning and end of the year, and for those granted, vested, and forfeited during the year.

- *Measurement*. The method used to measure compensation cost from these stock-based payment arrangements.
- *Multi-year information*. For each year for which an income statement is presented, the weighted-average grant date fair values of stock options granted, the intrinsic value of options exercised, share-based liabilities paid, and the aggregate fair value of shares vested.
- *Option information*. For the most recent year, the number and weighted-average exercise prices of those stock options at the beginning and end of the year, as well as for those exercisable at year-end, and for those granted, exercised, forfeited, and expired during the year.
- *Policy*. The company policy for issuing shares related to exercised stock options, including the source of the shares (such as treasury stock). If this policy will result in the repurchase of shares in a later period, state the range or estimated amount of shares that will be repurchased.
- *Vested information*. For stock options that have vested or are expected to vest by the balance sheet date, the number of options outstanding, as well as their weighted-average exercise price, aggregate intrinsic value, and weighted-average remaining option term, stated both for options outstanding and options currently exercisable.

EXAMPLE

Armadillo Industries discloses the following information about its stock options as part of its year-end financial statements:

The company's 20X2 employee stock option plan permits the granting of stock options to its employees for up to 2,000,000 shares of common stock. All option awards are granted with an exercise price equal to the market price of Armadillo's stock on the grant date. Option awards vest after four years of service and have 10-year terms. All awards issued thus far vest on an accelerated basis if there is a change in control of the company.

The fair values of all option awards are estimated using a lattice-based model that uses as inputs the assumptions noted in the following table:

	20X2	20X1
Expected dividends	2%	0%
Expected term (years)	4.8 – 7.7	4.3 – 7.2
Expected volatility	30% - 55%	35% - 60%
Weighted-average volatility	45%	47%
Risk-free rate	2.3% - 3.0%	2.5% - 3.2%

The expected term of options granted is based on historical experience; expected volatility ranges are based on the implied volatilities of an industry index of stocks; the risk-free rate is based on the U.S. Treasury yield curve on the grant dates.

Option activity under the Armadillo stock option plan as of December 31, 20X2, and changes during that year are noted in the following table:

Options	Shares (000s)	Weighted-Average Exercise Price	Weighted-Average Remaining Contractual Term	Aggregate Intrinsic Value ($000s)
Outstanding at 1/1/X2	985	$18		
Granted	420	25		
Exercised	-570	17		
Expired or forfeited	-120	23		
Outstanding at 12/31/X2	715	20	5.3	$2,860
Exercisable at 12/31/X2	405	18	4.9	$1,620

The weighted-average grant-date fair value of stock options granted during the years 20X2 and 20X1 were $10.15 and $9.68, respectively. The total intrinsic value of options exercised during the years ended 20X2 and 20X1 were $953,000 and $802,000, respectively.

Nonvested share activity as of December 31, 20X2 and changes during that year are noted in the following table:

Nonvested Shares	Shares (000s)	Weighted-Average Grant-Date Fair Value
Nonvested at 1/1/X1	500	$19.80
Granted	75	24.17
Vested	-120	18.25
Forfeited	-20	23.50
Nonvested at 12/31/X2	435	20.52

As of December 31, 20X2, $8,900,000 of compensation cost related to nonvested share-based compensation arrangements had not yet been recognized. We estimate that this cost will be recognized over a weighted-average period of 4.2 years. The total fair value of shares vested in 20X2 and 20X1 was $2,190,000 and $1,990,000, respectively.

Summary

It is relatively common for a publicly-held entity to pay for goods and services with equity instruments, so the accountant should be familiar with the concepts related to how these instruments are recognized. The level of judgment and accounting complexity increases when a business enters into arrangements where the issuance of equity instruments is subject to several variables. Consequently, it is best to provide advice on these arrangements before the business is contractually committed to them, in order to have commitments that require the least accounting effort and measurement uncertainty.

The measurement of stock-based compensation can be complex, but is not inordinately so, as long as the accounting staff develops a standard procedure for dealing with these arrangements and follows it consistently. It is also useful to gain the cooperation of the human resources department in formulating compensation arrangements that consistently include the same terms, so that the pre-existing accounting procedures can be readily applied to them. The worst-case scenario is when stock-based compensation plans are issued with substantially different terms, which forces the accounting department to adopt unique and detailed accounting plans to deal with each one. In short, a consistently-applied pay system greatly reduces the effort of accounting for stock-based compensation.

Chapter 6
Debt Accounting

Introduction

A publicly-held entity is likely to obtain financing through the sale of stock – but it can also do so by obtaining debt from investors. If so, the debt may contain features that allow investors to convert the debt into company stock, or to exercise attached warrants. In this chapter, we describe the accounting for a number of variations on the concept of debt with conversion features. We also describe how to account for the interest on a debt that does not match the market interest rate.

Debt with Conversion and Other Options

Debt that converts into the equity of the issuing entity presents a number of challenges from an accounting perspective, based on the variety of ways in which the conversion can take place. Each of the following sub-sections addresses a different variation on the convertible debt concept.

Debt Instruments with Detachable Warrants

A debt instrument may be issued with warrants that allow an investor to acquire shares in the issuing company. Typically, the warrants exist independently from the debt, which may allow investors to sell the warrants to third parties. Investors have the right to use the warrants to buy company stock, or to let the warrants expire unused.

When a company issues a combination of debt and warrants, investors are willing to accept a lower interest rate, since they are also obtaining a valuable right to buy company stock at a fixed price at some future date.

When a company sells a debt instrument with attached warrants, it should account for the transaction by allocating funds received to the two elements of the instrument based on their relative fair values as of the issuance date. The allocated funds are then accounted for as follows:

- *Warrants*. Record the funds assigned to the warrants in the paid-in capital account.
- *Debt*. Record the remaining funds as debt. This will probably also result in a discount on the debt, which is the difference between the value assigned to the debt instrument and its face amount.

EXAMPLE

Armadillo Industries issues $500,000 of convertible debt that has 50,000 detachable warrants associated with it. The convertible debt is convertible at $18, which is also the fair value of the company's stock. The ratio of the fair values of the convertible debt and the warrants is 90:10. The company records the transaction by allocating 90% of the proceeds, or $450,000, to the convertible debt liability and 10% of the proceeds, or $50,000, to the detached warrants (which is recorded in the paid-in capital account).

Convertible Securities

A convertible security is a debt instrument that gives the holder the right to convert it into a certain number of shares of the stock of the issuing entity. This type of security has value to the investor, who can either receive interest payments on the debt or elect to acquire stock that may have increased in value. Because of this added value, the issuing company can achieve a lower interest rate on its debt than would normally be the case.

The accounting for a debt instrument that is converted into a company's equity under an inducement offer is to recognize an expense in the amount of:

(Fair value of all securities and other consideration transferred) – (Fair value of securities issued)

The fair value in this calculation is based on the fair values of the securities when a conversion inducement offer is accepted.

If there is no inducement offer, and instead the conversion of a debt instrument into a company's equity is based on the original conversion privileges stated in the debt instrument, do not recognize a gain or loss on the transaction.

EXAMPLE

Armadillo Industries issues a $1,000 face amount convertible bond that sells for $1,000. The bond is convertible into Armadillo stock at a conversion price of $20. To induce holders of the bonds to convert them into company stock, Armadillo issues an offer to reduce the conversion price to $10, if the conversion takes place within the next 30 days.

A number of investors accept the new conversion terms and convert their bonds into company stock. The market price of Armadillo's stock on the conversion date is $30. Based on this information, the calculation of the incremental consideration paid by Armadillo to effect the conversion is:

Value of securities issued to debt holders (using inducement):		
Face amount	$1,000	
÷ New conversion price	÷ $10	Per share
= Number of shares issued upon conversion	= 100	Shares
× Market price per common share	× $30	Per share
= Value of securities issued	$3,000	

Value of securities issued to debt holders (prior to inducement):		
Face amount	$1,000	
÷ Old conversion price	÷ $20	Per share
= Number of shares issued upon conversion	= 50	Shares
× Market price per common share	× $30	Per share
= Value of securities issued	$1,500	

By subtracting the value of the equity securities prior to the inducement price from the value of the securities including the inducement price, we arrive at the following fair value of the incremental consideration:

$3,000 Value of securities with inducement - $1,500 Value of securities prior to inducement

= $1,500 Fair value of incremental consideration

Based on this information, Armadillo records the following entry to document the conversion of a bond to company stock:

	Debit	Credit
Convertible debt	1,000	
Debt conversion expense	1,500	
Common stock		2,500

Beneficial Conversion Features

When a business issues a convertible security, it can include a beneficial conversion feature in the agreement. This feature allows for conversion into the common stock of the issuer at the lower of a fixed conversion rate or a fixed discount to the market price of the stock on the conversion date. This conversion feature may even be adjustable, depending on such future events as a change in control of the business or an initial public offering at a lower share price.

To account for an embedded beneficial conversion feature, record it separately from the convertible security at the issuance date. The amount to assign to the feature is its intrinsic value. Record the amount in the additional paid-in capital account. Do not recognize this feature in earnings until the contingent feature of the instrument has been resolved.

Use the following steps to determine the intrinsic value of a beneficial conversion feature:

1. Allocate the proceeds to the debt instrument and any detachable instruments based on their relative fair values.
2. Calculate an effective conversion price and use it to measure the intrinsic value of the conversion option. The *intrinsic value* is the difference between the conversion price and the fair value of the securities into which the instrument is convertible, multiplied by the number of shares into which the instrument converts.

EXAMPLE

Luminescence Corporation is a privately-held company. It issues a $5,000,000 convertible debt instrument that can be converted to the company's common stock in two years at a conversion price of $12 (which is also the current fair value of the stock). There is an additional provision in the debt agreement that the conversion price drops to $8 in 18 months if Luminescence does not complete an initial public offering by that date.

The intrinsic value of the conversion option is calculated as follows:

(Funding obtained ÷ Final conversion price) × Difference in conversion prices)

= ($5,000,000 ÷ $8) × ($12 - $8) = $2,500,000

Luminescence should recognize the intrinsic value of the conversion option when it issues the convertible instrument.

Additional issues related to the assignment of value to beneficial conversion features are as follows:

- *Not beneficial.* If an embedded feature is not beneficial to the debt holder, do not assign any of the proceeds to that feature.
- *Multi-step discount.* If there is a multi-step discount feature in the debt instrument, compute its intrinsic value based on those terms most beneficial to the instrument holder.

EXAMPLE

Armadillo Industries issues a convertible debt instrument that includes a multi-step discount that begins with a 20% discount from the market price of the company's stock if conversion is within the next year, to a 28% discount if conversion is between three and four years in the future. Since the computation of intrinsic value is based on the most beneficial terms to the investor, the 28% discount rate should be used.

- *Instrument paid in kind (mandatory).* If dividend or interest payments made to investors are with more of the convertible instrument on a mandatory basis, use the original commitment date for the instrument to determine the number of additional convertible instruments to issue, and value the intrinsic value of the conversion option at the fair value of the issuer's stock at the commitment date for the original issuance of the instrument.
- *Instrument paid in kind (not mandatory).* If an instrument is paid in kind, but the issuance of additional debt instruments in payment of dividends or interest is not mandatory, the commitment date moves forward to the date when the dividends or interest are accrued (see the preceding bullet for additional valuation information).
- *Instrument swapped for nonconvertible instrument.* If a convertible instrument is issued in exchange for a nonconvertible instrument, use the fair value of the new issuance as the redemption amount, if the original instrument has matured and this is not a troubled debt restructuring.
- *Discount accretion and amortization.* If a debt discount is recognized because a portion of the funds received are allocated to a beneficial conversion feature, the following accounting variations may apply:
  - If the instrument has a stated redemption date, discount amortization occurs between the dates of issuance and stated redemption, irrespective of when conversions actually occur.
  - If the instrument has a multiple-step discount and there is no stated redemption date, cumulative amortization should be the greater of the results of the effective yield method that is based on the conversion terms most beneficial to the investor, or the discount amount that the investor can realize at each interim date.
  - For all other convertible preferred securities, amortize from the date of issuance the discount using the effective yield method.
  - For all other convertible debt securities, use the effective yield method to recognize the discount as interest expense.
  - If the beneficial conversion feature terminates after a certain period of time and the instrument results in an equity share that must be redeemed when the conversion feature expires, treat the feature as a liability when the feature expires, measured at its fair value as of the expiration date. This will require an offsetting reduction in equity.

o If the beneficial conversion feature terminates after a certain period of time and must then be redeemed at a premium, amortize the resulting discount to the mandatory redemption amount.

In general, when a company issues a convertible instrument at a substantial premium, it is reasonable to assume that some portion of the funds received relate to a conversion feature, and so should be recorded within the paid-in capital account.

One or more accounting actions may be triggered when the holder of a convertible instrument exercises the related call option to convert the instrument into the equity of the issuer. The following options are possible outcomes:

- *Unamortized discount.* If a convertible instrument contains a beneficial conversion feature, and the holder of the instrument converts it, recognize the unamortized discount as of the conversion date. The amount recognized may be either interest expense or a dividend, depending upon the nature of the underlying instrument.
- *Substantive conversion feature.* If there is a substantive conversion feature, do not recognize a gain or loss on the issuance of equity securities.
- *No substantive conversion feature.* If there is no substantive conversion feature, account for the issuance of equity securities as a debt retirement. Thus, use the fair value of the equity securities to determine the cost of debt reacquisition.

Since the accounting for a conversion varies so much depending on whether there is a substantive conversion feature, it is of some importance to determine the nature of this feature. The key issue indicating a substantive conversion is when it is reasonably possible that the feature will be exercised. A high conversion price would make exercise less possible.

Interest Forfeiture

When a convertible debt instrument is converted into the equity of the issuer, the terms of the agreement may state that any accrued but unpaid interest as of the conversion date is retained by the issuer. This situation most commonly occurs when conversion happens between scheduled interest payment dates, but can also occur when zero-interest debt is converted. To account for interest forfeiture, charge the amount forfeited between the date of the last interest payment and the conversion date, net of any income tax effects to interest expense, with the offset to a capital account.

Induced Conversions

The issuer of a convertible debt instrument may have the right to alter the terms of the arrangement, such as by paying additional consideration to debt holders to convert their holdings to company stock.

Conversion by Exercise of Call Option

The issuer of a convertible debt instrument can exercise a call option that requires debt holders to convert their debt instruments into the company's equity.

Convertible Instruments Issued to Nonemployees as Payment

A company may issue a convertible instrument to a person or entity who is not an employee in exchange for the provision of goods or services by the third party. The accounting for this situation is to recognize a related expense for the cost of the goods or services received.

To measure the intrinsic value of the conversion option, compare the proceeds received to the fair value of the shares the counterparty would receive by exercising the conversion option. Use the following guidance to determine the fair value of the convertible instrument:

1. Use the fair value of the goods or services received, if this amount can be determined reliably and the company has not issued similar convertible instruments recently; or
2. Use the fair value of similar convertible instruments for cash to independent third parties that have been issued recently; or
3. Use as a minimum value the fair value of the equity shares into which the instrument can be converted, if the first two alternatives are not viable.

Contingent Conversion Option

The conversion terms associated with a convertible debt instrument may be altered in the future, based on future events that are not controlled by the issuing company. If so, do not recognize the intrinsic value of these conversion changes until a triggering event occurs, and then make the following computation:

1. Calculate the number of shares that would be issued to the recipient, based on the revised conversion price.
2. Compare the number of shares issued to the number that the counterparty would have received prior to the contingent event.
3. Multiply the excess number of shares by the stock price on the commitment date to arrive at the incremental intrinsic value resulting from resolution of the contingency.
4. Recognize this incremental amount when the triggering event occurs.

If there is recognition, the accounting entry is an increase in equity, with an offset to the discount for the convertible instrument.

Own-Share Lending Arrangements

A company may enter into a share lending arrangement with its investment bank that is connected to an offering of convertible debt. In this situation, the share lending arrangement is designed to enhance the ability of investors to hedge their option to convert the company's debt into its equity. The typical terms of such an arrangement require the company to loan shares to the investment bank in exchange for a small loan processing fee that equals the par value of the stock. Once the convertible instrument matures or is converted, the investment bank returns the loaned shares to the company. During the period when the investment bank is holding the company's shares, it is not allowed to vote the shares, and must return any dividends associated with the shares.

The accounting for an own-share lending arrangement is to be measured at its fair value and recognized as a cost of issuing the associated debt. The offset to this cost is the additional paid-in capital account.

If it is probable that the counterparty in such an arrangement will default, recognize an expense that equals the fair value of all shares not yet returned by the counterparty, less the amount of any probable recoveries. The offset to this expense is the additional paid-in capital account. Continue to remeasure the fair value of all shares that have not yet been returned until the amount of the eventual repayment (if any) has been settled. All of these subsequent remeasurements of the missing shares should be recognized in earnings.

Own-Share Lending Arrangements (EPS Calculations)

If a company lends its shares to an investment bank as part of an own-share lending arrangement, exclude these shares from the calculation of basic and diluted earnings per share. However, if the investment bank defaults on the arrangement and retains the shares, include the shares in these earnings per share calculations.

If the dividends on loaned shares are not returned to the issuing company, include the dividend amounts in the calculation of income available to common shareholders in the earnings per share calculations.

Overview of Imputed Interest

When two parties enter into a business transaction that involves payment with a note, the default assumption is that the interest rate associated with the note will be close to the market rate of interest. However, there are times when no interest rate is stated, or when the stated rate departs significantly from the market rate.

If the stated and market interest rates are substantially different, it is necessary to record the transaction using an interest rate that more closely accords with the market rate. The rate that should be used is one that approximates the rate that would have been used if an independent borrower and lender had entered into a similar arrangement under comparable terms and conditions. This guidance does not apply to the following situations:

- Receivables and payables using customary trade terms that do not exceed one year
- Advances, deposits, and security deposits
- Customer cash lending activities of a financial institution

- When interest rates are affected by a governmental agency (such as a tax-exempt bond)
- Transactions between commonly-owned entities (such as between subsidiaries)

If available, the preferred option for deriving imputed interest is to locate the established exchange price of the goods or services involved in the transaction, and use that as the basis for calculating the interest rate. The exchange price is presumed to be the price paid in a cash purchase. In essence, this means that goods or services shall be recorded at their fair value. Any difference between the present value of the note and the fair value of the goods or services shall then be accounted for as a change in interest expense (i.e., as a note discount or premium) over the life of the note.

If it is not possible to determine the established exchange price, an applicable interest rate must be derived at the time the note is issued. The rate selected should be the prevailing rate for similar borrowers with similar credit ratings, which may be further adjusted for the following factors:

- The credit standing of the borrower
- Restrictive covenants on the note
- Collateral on the note
- Tax consequences to the buyer and seller
- The rate at which the borrower can obtain similar financing from other sources

Any subsequent changes in the market interest rate shall be ignored for the purposes of this transaction.

> **Tip:** Selecting a justifiable imputed interest rate is a matter of some importance, since an incorrect interest rate that is applied to a sufficiently large and long-term debt can result in the inaccurate acceleration or deferral of earnings.

Once the correct interest rate has been selected, use it to amortize the difference between the imputed interest rate and the rate on the note over the life of the note, with the difference being charged to the interest expense account. This is called the *interest method*. The following example illustrates the concept.

EXAMPLE

Armadillo Industries issues a $5,000,000 bond at a stated rate of 5% interest, where similar issuances are being purchased by investors at 8% interest. The bonds pay interest annually, and are to be redeemed in six years.

In order to earn the market rate of 8% interest, investors purchase the Armadillo bonds at a discount. The following calculation is used to derive the discount on the bond, which is comprised of the present values of a stream of interest payments and the present value of $5,000,000 payable in six years, with both calculations based on the 8% interest rate:

Present value of 6 payments of $250,000	= $250,000 × 4.62288	$1,155,720
Present value of $5,000,000	= $5,000,000 × 0.63017	3,150,850
	Total of present values	$4,306,570
	Less: Stated bond price	$5,000,000
	Bond discount	$693,430

The initial entry to record the sale of bonds is:

	Debit	Credit
Cash	4,306,570	
Discount on bonds payable	693,430	
Bonds payable		5,000,000

The controller of Armadillo creates the following table, which shows the derivation of how much of the discount should be charged to interest expense in each of the following years. In essence, the annual amortization of the discount is added back to the present value of the bond, so that the bond's present value matches its $5,000,000 stated value by the date when the bonds are scheduled for redemption from the bond holders.

Year	Beginning Present Value of Bond	Unamortized Discount	Interest Expense*	Cash Payment**	Discount Reduction***
1	$4,306,570	$693,430	$344,526	$250,000	$94,526
2	4,401,096	598,904	352,088	250,000	102,088
3	4,503,184	496,816	360,255	250,000	110,255
4	4,613,439	386,561	369,075	250,000	119,075
5	4,732,514	267,486	378,601	250,000	128,601
6	4,861,115	138,885	388,885	250,000	138,885
7	$5,000,000	$0			

* Bond present value at the beginning of the period, multiplied by the 8% market rate
** Scheduled annual interest payment for the bond
*** Interest expense, less the cash payment

As an example of the entries that the controller would derive from this table, the entry for the first annual interest payment would be:

	Debit	Credit
Interest expense	344,526	
Discount on bonds payable		94,526
Cash		250,000

The reasoning behind the entry is that Armadillo is only obligated to make a cash payment of $250,000 per year, despite the higher 8% implicit interest rate that its investors are earning on the issued bonds. The difference between the actual interest of $344,526 and the cash payment represents an increase in the amount of the bond that the company must eventually pay back to its investors. Thus, by the end of the first year, the present value of Armadillo's obligation to pay back the bond has increased from $4,306,570 to $4,401,096. By the end of the six-year period, the present value of the amount to be paid back will have increased to $5,000,000.

Tip: GAAP requires that the interest method be used to amortize any discount or premium associated with a note. However, other methods can be used if the results do not differ materially from those of the interest method. Accordingly, we suggest using the simpler straight-line method if the results do not differ materially from those of the interest method.

Debt Disclosures

The following sub-sections address several financial statement disclosure issues related to debt.

Long-Term Obligations

If a company has long-term debt obligations, disclose the aggregate amount of the maturities and sinking fund requirements for these borrowings for each of the five years after the balance sheet date. If there is a debt violation for a long-term debt agreement, and the borrower has continued to classify the debt on the grounds that it is probable that the violation can be cured in a timely manner, disclose the circumstances.

EXAMPLE

Armadillo Industries discloses the following information about its long-term debt obligations, which are divided into bonds and preferred stock. One bond has a sinking fund requirement that calls for continuing debt reductions in each year, while another bond is to be paid off in its entirety in five years. There is also preferred stock outstanding that is subject to a 10% annual buyback. The disclosure of this information follows:

The maturities and ongoing sinking fund requirements for the company's long-term debt obligations and outstanding preferred stock for the next five years are as follows:

(000s)	Long-Term Debt	Preferred Stock
20X2	$15,000	$3,275
20X3	15,000	3,275
20X4	15,000	3,275
20X5	15,000	3,275
20X6	175,000	--

Short-Term Obligations to be Refinanced

If a short-term obligation is classified as a long-term obligation due to its refinancing after the balance sheet date, disclose the general terms of the refinancing agreement, as well as the terms of the replacement debt or equity.

EXAMPLE

Armadillo Industries enters into a long-term financing arrangement that allows it to entirely refinance an obligation that is coming due within the current year. Its disclosure of the refinancing arrangement follows:

> The company has entered into a five-year financing arrangement with an industrial bank that allows the company to borrow up to $20,000,000 at the prime lending rate of the bank, plus 1%. Under the arrangement, the company must pay a ¼% commitment fee per year on any unused portion of the commitment, and also agrees to not issue dividends during the term of the agreement. The lender can terminate the agreement if the company's reported current ratio falls below 1.5 to 1. In July 20X3, the company borrowed $4,000,000 at a 6.5% interest rate and used the funds to liquidate a 5.25% current obligation.

Summary

A publicly-held firm may find that it is much easier to sell debt when that debt has warrants attached. The circumstances may never allow investors to exercise the warrants, depending on the subsequent prices at which the company's stock sells. Consequently, there may be no subsequent need to account for an actual warrant conversion. However, there will always be a need to account for the initial debt and equity components of these multi-part securities. This means that the accountant should pay particular attention to the valuations assigned to the debt and equity portions of a debt-and-warrant package.

It is also possible that debt will be sold at an interest rate that diverges significantly from the market rate. If so, be particularly careful in determining and documenting the market interest rate used to impute interest, as well as the calculation of any discounts or premiums, since the company's auditors are likely to reconstruct the imputed interest calculations as part of their annual audit activities.

Chapter 7
Staff Accounting Bulletins

Introduction

A *Staff Accounting Bulletin* (SAB) is a summarization of the views of the SEC's staff regarding how GAAP is to be applied. A common result is that the requirements of an SAB are more conservative and/or restrictive than the GAAP from which they are derived.

The views stated in an SAB are followed by the staffs of the Office of the Chief Accountant and the Division of Corporate Finance when reviewing the filings of publicly-held companies. For this reason, SABs are closely adhered to by entities registering their securities within the United States. If a publicly-held company does not incorporate the concepts in these bulletins into their financial statements and disclosures, it may receive a comment letter from the SEC.

In this chapter, we summarize the key points made in the various SABs; rather than itemizing accounting issues by individual SAB, they are stated by topic; this makes it easier to locate information on specific topics. The question-and-answer format used here is a close approximation of the fact-question-interpretation format used by the SEC in its Codification of Staff Accounting Bulletins. This presentation is a compressed version of the actual text in the SABs, which does not include any industry-specific information. Instead, the focus is on SAB content that applies to general situations.

Financial Statement Topics

Of all the topics covered by the SABs, the issue that a public company accountant should pay the most attention to is the proper recognition and treatment of material misstatements in the financial statements, which is covered in one of the following sub-sections. This is a topic that the accountant will likely deal with on a regular basis, especially if the accounting systems are somewhat rudimentary, and so yield inconsistent results.

Overhead Allocations

Situation: A company operates as a subsidiary of another company (the parent). Certain expenses incurred by the parent on behalf of the subsidiary have not been charged to the subsidiary in the past. The subsidiary files a registration statement in connection with an initial public offering.

Should the subsidiary's historical income statements reflect all of the expenses that the parent incurred on its behalf? In general, the historical income statements of a company should reflect all of its costs of doing business. Therefore, in specific situations, the SEC has required the subsidiary to revise its financial statements to include certain expenses incurred by the parent on its behalf. Examples of such expenses may include, but are not necessarily limited to, the following:

- Officer and employee salaries
- Rent or depreciation
- Advertising
- Accounting and legal services
- Other selling, general and administrative expenses

How should the amount of expenses incurred on the subsidiary's behalf by its parent be determined, and what disclosure is required in the financial statements? Any expenses clearly applicable to the subsidiary are to be reflected in its income statements. However, in some situations a reasonable method of allocating common expenses to the subsidiary (e.g., incremental or proportional cost allocation) must be chosen because specific identification of expenses is not practicable. In these situations, include an explanation of the allocation method used in the notes to the financial statements along with management's assertion that the method used is reasonable. In addition, since agreements with related parties are by definition not at arm's length and may be changed at any time, make a footnote disclosure of management's estimate of what the expenses would have been on a stand-alone basis, that is, the cost that would have been incurred if the subsidiary had operated as an unaffiliated entity.

What are the staff's views with respect to the accounting for and disclosure of the subsidiary's income tax expense? A parent company may sell an interest in a subsidiary, but retains a sufficient ownership interest to permit continued inclusion of the subsidiary in its consolidated tax return. It is material to investors to know what the effect on income would have been if the company had not been eligible to be included in a consolidated income tax return with its parent. Some of these subsidiaries have calculated their tax provision on the separate return basis, which is the preferable method. When the historical income statements in the filing do not reflect the tax provision on the separate return basis, the SEC has required a pro forma income statement for the most recent year and interim period reflecting a tax provision calculated on the separate return basis.

Should the historical income statements reflect a charge for interest on intercompany debt if no such charge had been previously provided? The financial statements are more useful to investors if they reflect all costs of doing business, including interest costs. Because of the inherent difficulty in distinguishing the elements of a subsidiary's capital structure, the SEC has not insisted that the historical income statements include an interest charge on intercompany debt if such a charge was not provided in the past, except when debt specifically related to the operations of the subsidiary and previously carried on the parent's books will henceforth be recorded in the subsidiary's books. In any case, financing arrangements with the parent must be discussed in a note to the financial statements. In this connection, where an interest charge on intercompany debt has not been provided, appropriate disclosure would include an analysis of the intercompany accounts as well as the average balance due to or from related parties for each period for which an income statement is required.

Pro Forma Financial Statements

What disclosure should be made if the company's historical financial statements are not indicative of the ongoing entity? The registration statement should include pro forma financial information that reflects the impact of terminated or revised cost sharing agreements and other significant changes.

What is the staff's position with respect to dividends declared by the subsidiary subsequent to the balance sheet date? Such dividends should either be given retroactive effect in the balance sheet with appropriate footnote disclosure, or reflected in a pro forma balance sheet. In addition, when the dividends are to be paid from the proceeds of the offering, it is appropriate to include pro forma per share data (for the latest year and interim period only) giving effect to the number of shares whose proceeds were to be used to pay the dividend. A similar presentation is appropriate when dividends exceed earnings in the current year, even though the stated use of proceeds is other than for the payment of dividends. In these situations, pro forma per share data should give effect to the increase in the number of shares which, when multiplied by the offering price, would be sufficient to replace the capital in excess of earnings being withdrawn.

Materiality

Situation: During the course of preparing or auditing year-end financial statements, financial management or the company's independent auditor becomes aware of misstatements in the company's financial statements. When combined, the misstatements result in a 4% overstatement of net income and a \$.02 (4%) overstatement of earnings per share. Because no item in the company's consolidated financial statements is misstated by more than 5%, management and the independent auditor conclude that the deviation from GAAP is immaterial and that the accounting is permissible.

In the staff's view, may a company or the auditor of its financial statements assume the immateriality of items that fall below a percentage threshold set by management or the auditor to determine whether amounts and items are material to the financial statements? No. The SEC is aware that certain companies, over time, have developed quantitative thresholds as "rules of thumb" to assist in the preparation of their financial statements, and that auditors also have used these thresholds in their evaluation of whether items might be considered material to users of a company's financial statements. One rule of thumb in particular suggests that the misstatement or omission of an item that falls under a 5% threshold is not material in the absence of particularly egregious circumstances, such as self-dealing or misappropriation by senior management. The SEC reminds companies and the auditors of their financial statements that exclusive reliance on this or any percentage or numerical threshold has no basis in the accounting literature or the law.

The use of a percentage as a numerical threshold, such as 5%, may provide the basis for a preliminary assumption that a deviation of less than the specified percentage with respect to a particular item on the company's financial statements is unlikely to be material. The SEC has no objection to such a "rule of thumb" as an initial step in assessing materiality. But quantifying, in percentage terms, the magnitude of a misstatement is only the beginning of an analysis of materiality; it cannot appropriately be used as a substitute for a full analysis of all relevant considerations. Materiality concerns the significance of an item to users of a company's financial statements. A matter is "material" if there is a substantial likelihood that a reasonable person would consider it important.

As a result of the interaction of quantitative and qualitative considerations in materiality judgments, misstatements of relatively small amounts that come to the auditor's attention could have a material effect on the financial statements. Among the considerations that may well render material a quantitatively small misstatement of a financial statement item are the following:

- Whether the misstatement arises from an item capable of precise measurement or whether it arises from an estimate and, if so, the degree of imprecision inherent in the estimate
- Whether the misstatement masks a change in earnings or other trends
- Whether the misstatement hides a failure to meet analysts' consensus expectations for the enterprise
- Whether the misstatement changes a loss into income or vice versa
- Whether the misstatement concerns a segment or other portion of the company's business that has been identified as playing a significant role in the company's operations or profitability
- Whether the misstatement affects the company's compliance with regulatory requirements
- Whether the misstatement affects the company's compliance with loan covenants or other contractual requirements
- Whether the misstatement has the effect of increasing management's compensation; for example, by satisfying requirements for the award of bonuses or other forms of incentive compensation
- Whether the misstatement involves concealment of an unlawful transaction

For the reasons noted above, a company and the auditors of its financial statements should not assume that even small intentional misstatements in financial statements, for example those pursuant to actions to "manage" earnings, are immaterial.

The materiality of a misstatement may turn on where it appears in the financial statements. For example, a misstatement may involve a segment of the company's operations. In that instance, in assessing materiality of a misstatement to the financial statements taken as a whole, companies and their auditors should consider not only the size of the misstatement but also the significance of the segment information to the financial statements taken as a whole.

In determining whether multiple misstatements cause the financial statements to be materially misstated, companies and the auditors of their financial statements should consider each misstatement separately and the aggregate effect of all misstatements. If the misstatement of an individual amount causes the financial statements as a whole to be materially misstated, that effect cannot be eliminated by other misstatements whose effect may be to diminish the impact of the misstatement on other financial statement items. To take an obvious example, if a company's revenues are a material financial statement item and if they are materially overstated, the financial statements taken as a whole will be materially misleading even if the effect on earnings is completely offset by an equivalent overstatement of expenses.

Even though a misstatement of an individual amount may not cause the financial statements taken as a whole to be materially misstated, it may nonetheless, when aggregated with other misstatements, render the financial statements taken as a whole to be materially misleading. Companies and the auditors of their financial statements accordingly should consider the effect of the misstatement on subtotals or totals. The auditor should aggregate all misstatements that affect each subtotal or total and consider whether the misstatements in the aggregate affect the subtotal or total in a way that causes the company's financial statements taken as a whole to be materially misleading.

Companies and auditors also should consider the effect of misstatements from prior periods on the current financial statements. This may be particularly the case where immaterial misstatements recur in several years and the cumulative effect becomes material in the current year.

Situation: During the course of preparing annual financial statements, a company is evaluating the materiality of an improper expense accrual (e.g., overstated liability) in the amount of $100, which has built up over 5 years, at $20 per year. The company previously evaluated the misstatement as being immaterial to each of the prior year financial statements (i.e., years 1-4). For the purpose of evaluating materiality in the current year (i.e., year 5), the company quantifies the error as a $20 overstatement of expenses.

Has the company appropriately quantified the amount of this error for the purpose of evaluating materiality for the current year? No. In this example, the company has only quantified the effects of the identified unadjusted error that arose in the current year income statement. Prior year misstatements should be considered in quantifying misstatements in current year financial statements.

The techniques most commonly used in practice to accumulate and quantify misstatements are generally referred to as the "rollover" and "iron curtain" approaches. The rollover approach, which is the approach used in the example, quantifies a misstatement based on the amount of the error originating in the current year income statement. This approach ignores the effects of correcting the portion of the current year balance sheet misstatement that originated in prior years (i.e., it ignores the "carryover effects" of prior year misstatements). The iron curtain approach quantifies a misstatement based on the effects of correcting the misstatement existing in the balance sheet at the end of the current year, irrespective of the misstatement's year(s) of origination. Had the company in this fact pattern applied the iron curtain approach, the misstatement would have been quantified as a $100 misstatement based on the end of year balance sheet misstatement. Thus, the adjustment needed to correct the financial statements for the end of year error would be to reduce the liability by $100 with a corresponding decrease in current year expense.

As demonstrated in this example, the primary weakness of the rollover approach is that it can result in the accumulation of significant misstatements on the balance sheet that are deemed immaterial in part because the amount that originates in each year is quantitatively small.

In contrast, the primary weakness of the iron curtain approach is that it does not consider the correction of prior year misstatements in the current year (i.e., the reversal of the carryover effects) to be errors. Therefore, in this example, if the misstatement was corrected during the current year such that no error existed in the balance sheet at the end of the current year, the reversal of the $80 prior year misstatement would not be considered an error in the current year financial statements under the iron curtain approach. Implicitly, the iron curtain approach assumes that because the prior year financial statements were not materially misstated, correcting any immaterial errors that existed in those statements in the current year is the "correct" accounting, and is therefore not considered an error in the current year. Thus, utilization of the iron curtain approach can result in a misstatement in the current year income statement not being evaluated as an error at all.

Companies must quantify the impact of correcting all misstatements, including both the carryover and reversing effects of prior year misstatements, on the current year financial statements. This can be accomplished by quantifying an error under both the rollover and iron curtain approaches and by evaluating the error measured under each approach. Thus, a company's financial statements would require adjustment when either approach results in quantifying a misstatement that is material, after considering all relevant quantitative and qualitative factors.

It is possible that correcting an error in the current year could materially misstate the current year's income statement. For example, correcting the $100 misstatement in the current year will:

- Correct the $20 error originating in the current year;
- Correct the $80 balance sheet carryover error that originated in Years 1 through 4; but also
- Misstate the current year income statement by $80.

If the $80 understatement of current year expense is material to the current year, after all of the relevant quantitative and qualitative factors are considered, the prior year financial statements should be corrected, even though such revision previously was and continues to be immaterial to the prior year financial statements. Correcting prior year financial statements for immaterial errors would not require previously filed reports to be amended. Such correction may be made the next time the company files the prior year financial statements.

Debt Issuance Costs

Situation: Company A is to acquire the net assets of Company B in a transaction to be accounted for as a business combination. In connection with the transaction, Company A has retained an investment banker to provide advisory services in structuring the acquisition and to provide the necessary financing. It is expected that the acquisition will be financed on an interim basis using "bridge financing" provided by the investment banker. Permanent financing will be arranged at a later date through a debt offering, which will be underwritten by the investment banker. Fees will be paid to the investment banker for the advisory services, the bridge financing, and the underwriting of the permanent financing. These services may be billed separately or as a single amount.

Should total fees paid to the investment banker for acquisition-related services and the issuance of debt securities be allocated between the services received? Yes. Fees paid to an investment banker in connection with a business combination or asset acquisition, when the investment banker is also providing interim financing or underwriting services, must be allocated between acquisition related services and debt issue costs.

When an investment banker provides services in connection with a business combination or asset acquisition and also provides underwriting services associated with the issuance of debt or equity securities, the total fees incurred by an entity should be allocated between the services received on a relative fair value basis. The objective of the allocation is to ascribe the total fees incurred to the actual services provided by the investment banker.

Redeemable Preferred Stock

Situation: Regulation S-X states that redeemable preferred stock is not to be included in amounts reported as stockholders' equity, and that their redemption amounts are to be shown on the face of the balance sheet. However, the SEC's rules and regulations do not address the carrying amount at which redeemable preferred stock should be reported, or how changes in its carrying amount should be treated in calculations of earnings per share and the ratio of earnings to combined fixed charges and preferred stock dividends.

How should the carrying amount of redeemable preferred stock be determined? The initial carrying amount of redeemable preferred stock should be its fair value at date of issue. Where fair value at date of issue is less than the mandatory redemption amount, the carrying amount shall be increased by periodic accretions, using the interest method, so that the carrying amount will equal the mandatory redemption amount at the mandatory redemption date. The carrying amount shall be further periodically increased by amounts representing dividends not currently declared or paid, but which will be payable under the mandatory redemption features, or for which ultimate payment is not solely within the control of the company (e.g., dividends that will be payable out of future earnings). Each type of increase in carrying amount shall be effected by charges against retained earnings or, in the absence of retained earnings, by charges against paid-in capital. This accounting would apply irrespective of whether the redeemable preferred stock may be voluntarily redeemed by the issuer prior to the mandatory redemption date, or whether it may be converted into another class of securities by the holder.

Equity Accounting Topics

The investment community appears to question the SEC more closely about the treatment of equity issues than most other topics, resulting in a larger-than-usual number of SEC opinions in this area. The topics appearing in this section were selected based on their applicability to the broadest possible range of public companies.

Subordinated Debt

Situation: Company E proposes to include in its registration statement a balance sheet showing its subordinated debt as a portion of stockholders' equity.

Is this presentation appropriate? Subordinated debt may not be included in the stockholders' equity section of the balance sheet. Any presentation describing such debt as a component of stockholders' equity must be eliminated. Furthermore, any caption representing the combination of stockholders' equity and only subordinated debts must be deleted.

S Corporations

Situation: An S corporation has undistributed earnings on the date its S election is terminated.

How should such earnings be reflected in the financial statements? Such earnings must be included in the financial statements as additional paid-in capital. This assumes a constructive distribution to the owners followed by a contribution to the capital of the corporation.

Change in Capital Structure

Situation: A capital structure change to a stock dividend, stock split or reverse split occurs after the date of the latest reported balance sheet but before the release of the financial statements or the effective date of the registration statement, whichever is later.

What effect must be given to such a change? Such changes in the capital structure must be given retroactive effect in the balance sheet. An appropriately cross-referenced note should disclose the retroactive treatment, explain the change made and state the date the change became effective.

Receivables from the Sale of Stock

Situation: Capital stock is sometimes issued to officers or other employees before the cash payment is received.

How should the receivables from the officers or other employees be presented in the balance sheet? The amount recorded as a receivable should be presented in the balance sheet as a deduction from stockholders' equity. It should be noted generally that all amounts receivable from officers and directors resulting from sales of stock or from other transactions (other than expense advances or sales on normal trade terms) should be separately stated in the balance sheet irrespective of whether such amounts may be shown as assets or are required to be reported as deductions from stockholders' equity.

Limited Partnerships

Situation: There exist a number of publicly held partnerships having one or more corporate or individual general partners and a relatively larger number of limited partners. There are no specific requirements or guidelines relating to the presentation of the partnership equity accounts in the financial statements. In addition, there are many approaches to the parallel problem of relating the results of operations to the two classes of partnership equity interests.

How should the financial statements of limited partnerships be presented so that the two ownership classes can readily determine their relative participations in both the net assets of the partnership and in the results of its operations? The equity section of a partnership balance sheet should distinguish between amounts ascribed to each ownership class. The equity attributed to the general partners should be stated separately from the equity of the limited partners, and changes in the number of equity units authorized and outstanding should be shown for each ownership class. A statement of changes in partnership equity for each ownership class should be furnished for each period for which an income statement is included.

The income statements of partnerships should be presented in a manner which clearly shows the aggregate amount of net income (loss) allocated to the general partners and the aggregate amount allocated to the limited partners. The statement of income should also state the results of operations on a per unit basis.

Notes and Other Receivables from Affiliates

<u>Situation</u>: The balance sheet of a corporate general partner is often presented in a registration statement. Frequently, the balance sheet of the general partner discloses that it holds notes or other receivables from a parent or another affiliate. Often the notes or other receivables were created in order to meet the "substantial assets" test which the Internal Revenue Service utilizes in applying its "Safe Harbor" doctrine in the classification of organizations for income tax purposes.

How should such notes and other receivables be reported in the balance sheet of the general partner? While these notes and other receivables evidencing a promise to contribute capital are often legally enforceable, they seldom are actually paid. In substance, these receivables are equivalent to unpaid subscriptions receivable for capital shares, which are to be deducted from the dollar amount of capital shares subscribed.

The balance sheet display of these or similar items is not determined by the quality or actual value of the receivable or other asset "contributed" to the capital of the affiliated general partner, but rather by the relationship of the parties and the control inherent in that relationship. Accordingly, in these situations, the receivable must be treated as a deduction from stockholders' equity in the balance sheet of the corporate general partner.

Miscellaneous Accounting Topics

This section contains a selection of SEC opinions regarding miscellaneous accounting topics, ranging from the expenses associated with securities offerings to the consistency of cash flow analysis when determining whether an asset has been impaired.

Expenses of Offering

<u>Situation</u>: Prior to the effective date of an offering of equity securities, Company Y incurs certain expenses related to the offering.

Should such costs be deferred? Specific incremental costs directly attributable to a proposed or actual offering of securities may properly be deferred and charged against the gross proceeds of the offering. However, management salaries or other general and administrative expenses may not be allocated as costs of the offering and deferred costs of an aborted offering may not be deferred and charged against proceeds of a subsequent offering. A short postponement (up to 90 days) does not represent an aborted offering.

Gain or Loss from Disposition of Equipment

<u>Situation</u>: Company A has adopted the policy of treating gains and losses from disposition of revenue-producing equipment as adjustments to the current year's

provision for depreciation. Company B reflects such gains and losses as a separate item in the statement of income.

Does the SEC have any views as to which method is preferable? Gains and losses resulting from the disposition of revenue producing equipment should not be treated as adjustments to the provision for depreciation in the year of disposition, but should be shown as a separate item in the statement of income.

If such equipment is depreciated on the basis of group of composite accounts for fleets of like vehicles, gains (or losses) may be charged (or credited) to accumulated depreciation with the result that depreciation is adjusted over a period of years on an average basis. It should be noted that the latter treatment would not be appropriate for (1) an enterprise (such as an airline) which replaces its fleet on an episodic rather than a continuing basis or (2) an enterprise (such as a car leasing company) where equipment is sold after limited use so that the equipment on hand is both fairly new and carried at amounts closely related to current acquisition cost.

Accounting Changes Not Retroactively Applied Due to Immateriality

Situation: A company is required to adopt an accounting principle by means of retrospective adjustment of prior periods' financial statements. However, the company determines that the accounting change does not have a material effect on prior periods' financial statements and, accordingly, decides not to retrospectively adjust such financial statements.

In these circumstances, is it acceptable to adjust the beginning balance of retained earnings of the period in which the change is made for the cumulative effect of the change on the financial statements of prior periods? No. If prior periods are not retrospectively adjusted, the cumulative effect of the change should be included in the statement of income for the period in which the change is made. Even in cases where the total cumulative effect is not significant, the amount should be reflected in the results of operations for the period in which the change is made. However, if the cumulative effect is material to current operations or to the trend of the reported results of operations, then the individual income statements of the earlier years should be retrospectively adjusted.

New Basis of Accounting Required in Certain Circumstances

Situation: Company A acquired substantially all of the common stock of Company B in a series of purchase transactions.

Must Company B's financial statements presented in either its own or Company A's subsequent filings with the SEC reflect the new basis of accounting arising from Company A's acquisition of Company B when Company B's separate corporate entity is retained? Yes. Purchase transactions that result in an entity becoming substantially wholly owned establish a new basis of accounting for the purchased assets and liabilities.

When the form of ownership is within the control of the parent, the basis of accounting for purchased assets and liabilities should be the same regardless of whether the entity continues to exist or is merged into the parent's operations. Therefore, Company B's separate financial statements should reflect the new basis of accounting recorded by Company A upon acquisition (i.e., "pushed down" basis).

What is the staff's position if Company A acquired less than substantially all of the common stock of Company B or Company B had publicly-held debt or preferred stock at the time Company B became wholly owned? The existence of outstanding public debt, preferred stock or a significant noncontrolling interest in a subsidiary might impact the parent's ability to control the form of ownership. Although encouraging its use, the SEC generally does not insist on the application of push down accounting in these circumstances.

Restructuring Charges

Situation: Restructuring charges often do not relate to a separate component of the entity, and, as such, they would not qualify for presentation as losses on the disposal of a discontinued operation.

May such restructuring charges be presented in the income statement as a separate caption after income from continuing operations before income taxes (i.e., preceding income taxes and/or discontinued operations)? No. Furthermore, a separately presented restructuring charge should not be preceded by a sub-total representing "income from continuing operations before restructuring charge."

Impairments

Has the SEC expressed any views with respect to company-determined estimates of cash flows used for assessing and measuring the impairment of assets? In providing guidance on the development of cash flows for purposes of determining asset impairment indicates that "estimates of future cash flows used to test the recoverability of a long-lived asset (asset group) shall incorporate the entity's own assumptions about its use of the asset (asset group) and shall consider all available evidence. The assumptions used in developing those estimates shall be reasonable in relation to the assumptions used in developing other information used by the entity for comparable periods, such as internal budgets and projections, accruals related to incentive compensation plans, or information communicated to others."

The SEC recognizes that various factors, including management's judgments and assumptions about the business plans and strategies, affect the development of future cash flow projections for purposes of applying impairment testing. The SEC, however, cautions companies that the judgments and assumptions made for purposes of applying impairment testing must be consistent with other financial statement calculations and disclosures in the Management's Discussion and Analysis (MD&A) section [presented in the Forms 10-K and 10-Q]. The SEC also expects that forecasts made for purposes of applying impairment testing be consistent with other forward-looking information prepared by the company, such as that used for internal budgets, incentive compensation plans, discussions with lenders or third parties, and/or reporting to management or the board of directors.

For example, the SEC has reviewed a fact pattern where a company developed cash flow projections for purposes of asset impairment testing using one set of assumptions and utilized a second, more conservative set of assumptions for purposes of determining whether deferred tax valuation allowances were necessary. In this case, the SEC objected to the use of inconsistent assumptions.

In addition to the disclosure of key assumptions used in the development of cash flow projections, the SEC also has required discussion in MD&A of the implications of assumptions. For example, do the projections indicate that a company is likely to violate debt covenants in the future? What are the ramifications to the cash flow projections used in the impairment analysis? If growth rates used in the impairment analysis are lower than those used by outside analysts, has the company had discussions with the analysts regarding their overly optimistic projections? Has the company appropriately informed the market and its shareholders of its reduced expectations for the future that are sufficient to cause an impairment charge? Cash flow projections used in the impairment analysis must be both internally consistent with the company's other projections and externally consistent with financial statement and other public disclosures.

Revenue Recognition Topics

There is extensive commentary on revenue recognition issues in the SABs. However, a new revenue recognition standard, *Revenue from Contracts with Customers*, has just been released that replaces a large part of the existing GAAP on this topic, so we will wait until a later edition to see if the SEC alters its SAB subject matter in the area of revenue recognition. Consult the author's *Revenue Recognition* course for more information about revenue recognition issues.

Summary

The bulk of the SAB content was not included in this chapter, since so many SAB topics address highly-specific situations that the typical public company will never see. Instead, we have focused on the most broad-based content that will be of the most use to the typical public company.

The information in an SAB does not apply to privately-held organizations, though they could consider using it if they intend to eventually go public, and would prefer to meet public company reporting standards as early as possible.

Staff Accounting Bulletins are issued by the SEC at relatively long intervals. The complete text of all current SABs is listed on the website of the Securities and Exchange Commission.

Chapter 8
Annual and Quarterly Reporting

Introduction

Accountants typically have a great deal of interest in the exact contents of the Forms 10-K and 10-Q, so the level of discussion in this chapter is quite detailed. We summarize the SEC's reporting requirements for all major reporting areas within the Form 10-K and also provide examples that are modified from actual filings with the SEC. The same level of detail is not used for the Form 10-Q, since the information supplied in that report is essentially a subset of the information reported in the Form 10-K.

The Form 10-K

A publicly-held company is required to issue the Form 10-K to report the results of its fiscal year. The Form 10-K includes not just the financial statements, but also a number of additional disclosures. The following table itemizes the more common disclosures. Examples of these disclosures are noted in the following sub-sections.

Selection of Form 10-K Disclosures

Item Header	Description
Item 1. Business	Provide a description of the company's purpose, history, operating segments, customers, suppliers, sales and marketing operations, customer support, intellectual property, competition, and employees. It should tell readers what the company does and describe its business environment.
Item 1A. Risk factors	A thorough listing of all risks that the company may experience. It warns investors of what could reduce the value of their investments in the company.
Item 1B. Unresolved staff comments	Disclose all unresolved comments received from the SEC if they are material. (only applies to written comments from the SEC received at least 180 days before the fiscal year-end by an accelerated or large accelerated filer)
Item 2. Properties	Describe the leased or owned facilities of the business, including square footage, lease termination dates, and lease amounts paid per month.

Item Header	Description
Item 3. Legal proceedings	Describe any legal proceedings currently involving the company, and its estimate of the likely outcome of those proceedings.
Item 4. Mine safety disclosures	If applicable, discuss mine safety laws, and the types of warnings and penalties that occurred during the reporting period.
Item 5. Market for company stock	Describe where the company's stock trades and the number of holders of record, as well as the high and low closing prices per share, by quarter.
Item 6. Selected financial data	For the last five years, state selected information from the company's income statement and balance sheet (should be in tabular comparative format).
Item 7. Management's discussion and analysis (MD&A)	Describe opportunities, challenges, risks, trends, future plans, and key performance indicators, as well as changes in revenues, the cost of goods sold, other expenses, assets, and liabilities.
Item 7A. Quantitative and qualitative disclosures about market risk	Quantify the market risk at the end of the last fiscal year for the company's market risk-sensitive instruments.
Item 8. Financial statements and supplementary data	Make all disclosures required by GAAP, including descriptions of: • Accrued liabilities • Acquisitions • Discontinued operations • Fixed assets • Income taxes • Related party transactions • Segment information • Stock options
Item 9. Changes in and disagreements with accountants on accounting and financial disclosure	Describe any disagreements with the auditors when management elects to account for or disclose transactions in a manner different from what the auditors want.
Item 9A. Controls and procedures	Generally describe the system of internal controls, testing of controls, changes in controls, and management's conclusions regarding the effectiveness of those controls.

Item Header	Description
Item 10. Directors, executive officers and corporate governance	Identify the executive officers, directors, promoters, and individuals classified as control persons.
Item 11. Executive compensation	Itemize the types of compensation paid to company executives.
Item 12. Security ownership of certain beneficial owners and management and related stockholder matters	State the number of shares of all types owned or controlled by certain individuals classified as beneficial owners and/or members of management.
Item 13. Certain relationships and related transactions, and director independence	If there were transactions with related parties during the past fiscal year, and the amounts involved exceeded $120,000, describe the transactions.
Item 14. Principal accountant fees and services	State the aggregate amount of any fees billed in each of the last two fiscal years for professional services rendered by the company's auditors for: • Reviews and audits; • Audit-related activities; • Taxation work; and • All other fees.
Item 15. Exhibits and financial statement schedules	Item 601 of Regulation S-K requires that a business attach a number of exhibits to the Form 10-K, including (but not limited to): • Code of ethics • Material contracts • Articles of incorporation • Bylaws • Acquisition purchase agreements

The Form 10-K must be filed within 60 days of the end of the fiscal year if the company is a large accelerated filer or an accelerated filer, or within 75 days of the end of the fiscal year if the company is an accelerated filer. If the company does not have either designation, then the 10-K must be filed within 90 days of the end of the fiscal year.

The following sub-sections contain examples of the items just noted for the Form 10-K.

Item 1. Business

The description of the business that is required by the SEC can be quite extensive. A summarized version of the SEC's requirements in this area is as follows:

- Describe the general development of the business during the past five years. Note the year of organization, and the form of organization, the nature and results of any bankruptcy proceedings, and the nature and results of any material mergers or consolidations.
- Report revenues, profit or loss, and assets for each business segment for each of the last three fiscal years. This presentation may be cross-referenced to the financial statements.
- Describe the business done by the company, and what it intends to do, focusing on the dominant segment or each reportable segment. This includes the company's principal products and services, and methods by which they are distributed. Also note the following:
  - For each of the last three years, the amount or percentage of total revenue contributed by each class of products or services which account for 10 percent or more of revenues.
  - The status of new products or services, without revealing information that would interfere with the competitive stance of the business.
  - The sources and availability of raw materials.
  - The duration and effect on the business of the patents, trademarks, licenses, concessions, and so forth that the organization holds.
  - The extent to which the business is seasonal.
  - The need for working capital within the industry, and by the company, such as to offer long credit terms to customers.
  - The dependence of the business on one or a few customers. Disclose the names of these customers if the amount sold to each one equals or exceeds 10 percent of the company's revenues.
  - The dollar amount of firm customer orders on backlog, as compared to a similar period in the preceding year. Also note any seasonal or other material aspects of the backlog.
  - Any material portion of the business that may be subject to renegotiation of profits, or in which contracts can be terminated by the government.
  - The competitive conditions in the industry, including an estimate of the number of competitors and the competitive position of the company within the industry. Dominant competitors should be identified. Note the principal methods of competition, such as by price, service level, or product performance.

- o The amount spent in each of the past three years on research and development activities.
- o The material effects that compliance with government regulations concerning the discharge of materials into the environment has had upon capital expenditures, earnings, and the company's competitive position.
- o The number of persons employed by the company.

- Describe the following financial information about the geographic areas in which the company did business for each of the last three fiscal years:

  - o Revenues from customers attributed to the company's home country, all foreign countries in total, and any individual foreign country, if material.
  - o Long-lived assets located in the company's home country, all foreign countries in total, and any individual foreign country, if material.

- Describe any risks related to the foreign operations and any dependence of the company's segments on its foreign operations.

This section of the Form 10-K can be massive. A much abbreviated example of Item 1 follows:

The mission of Ninja Cutlery is to be the premier provider of knives to commercial chefs, worldwide. The company was incorporated in New York in 19X5 by four partners, all professional chefs and amateur knife makers. All four partners remain with the company today in various senior management roles. Ninja began offering knife products in 19X5, and has continued to expand its product line since then.

Ninja has two operating segments. One follows the original mission of the company, manufacturing and distributing cutlery to commercial chefs. Distribution is through independent retailers and mailed catalogs. Only high-end knife products are sold, including carbon-steel blades and ceramic self-sharpening knives. The other segment serves the backwoods survival market with low-cost plastic-and-steel multi-purpose blades that are intended for abbreviated use. This segment sells direct to consumers through an on-line store, as well as through Army-Navy stores.

Ninja has a diverse customer base that includes many of the largest restaurant chains in the ten countries where Ninja products are sold. In 20X3, our largest customer was Lethal Sushi, which generated 8% of total sales for the commercial knife division. The Sharper Edge retail chain is the largest retail purchaser of the division's products, comprising 11% of the segment's sales in 20X3.

Ninja obtains the metal for its knife blades from Artisanal Metal Products, and its ceramic blades from Ferro-Cast Corporation. Knife handles are cast in-house, using commodity-grade rubber and plastic beads obtained from several suppliers.

Sales and marketing operations are conducted by an in-house direct sales staff for all sales in the United States. A locally-based sales staff is used to solicit sales in all other countries where Ninja sells its products. The survival market is serviced through an on-line store, as well as a separate in-house sales staff that maintains relations with Army-Navy stores. Marketing efforts include a well-maintained web site, a quarterly e-newsletter to selected retailers and restaurant chains, attendance at trade shows, participation in selected trade associations and an assortment of collateral materials.

Sales cycles are quite short. Customers place orders for standard products, and orders typically ship within two business days. We do not provide custom products, so there is no need for a produce-to-order system. Instead, goods are produced to stock and then shipped as needed.

We maintain a customer service department in our New York location, which is open during regular business hours to assist customers. All customer contacts handled through the customer service desk are tracked using a customer relationship database. We have posted training manuals on the company website that discuss the proper use and maintenance of all of our knife products.

The carbon blade knives used by the commercial chef segment rely heavily on intellectual property, since the blades use a patented technology developed by the company. Ferro-Cast Corporation is the only licensed user of this technology, and Ferro-Cast is only allowed to produce blades for Ninja. We regard our intellectual property as a valuable asset and use intellectual property laws, as well as confidentiality agreements with our employees and others to protect our rights. In addition, we exercise reasonable measures to protect our intellectual property rights and enforce these rights when we become aware of any potential or actual violation or misuse.

The dominant player in the knife marketplace is Universal Blades, which primarily sells knives for use in the residential kitchen. There is little direct competition with Universal, since the price points at which we sell our products are much too high for the typical home cook. Other competitors include The Point Brothers, Scissor Results, Carvers, Inc., and Chop Knives. These other companies occupy competitive positions with lower price points and product quality levels than Ninja's and so tend to compete more directly with Universal than with Ninja.

As of December 31, 20X3, we employed 240 employees, of which 10 were part time employees, and all of whom are located within the United States. The sales staff that sells in other countries is also based in the United States. None of the employees are represented by a collective bargaining agreement, and employee relations are considered to be good.

Item 1A. Risk Factors

The SEC insists on comprehensive statements regarding every possible risk factor to which a business may be subjected. More specifically, the SEC offers the following advice regarding the disclosure of risks:

- State the most significant risk factors that make the company's shares speculative or risky.
- Do not present risks that could apply to any company.
- Explain how the risk affects the company.
- The risk factors may include:
  - The lack of an operating history
  - The lack of profitable operations in recent periods
  - The financial position of the business
  - The business or proposed business

Corporate counsel also wants to include all possible risks, on the grounds that doing so gives investors reduced grounds for initiating lawsuits if they were already warned of risks. This typically results in long lists of risks, of which the following sample provides an overview:

> You should carefully consider the following risks and all of the other information set forth in this report. If any of the events or developments described below actually occurs, our business, financial condition, and results of operations may suffer. In that case, the trading price of our common stock may decline and you could lose all or part of your investment.

Some of the risks related to the business include:

- *Affiliate control.* Members of Ninja's Board of Directors and its executive officers, together with their affiliates, own a significant number of shares of Ninja outstanding common stock. Accordingly, these stockholders, if they act together, can have significant control over matters requiring approval of company stockholders, including the election of directors and approval of significant corporate transactions. The concentration of ownership, which could result in a continued concentration of representation on the Board of Directors, may delay, prevent or deter a change in control and could deprive stockholders of an opportunity to receive a premium for their common stock as part of a sale of our assets. Ninja's directors, executive officers and other affiliates will continue to exert significant control over the company's future direction, which could reduce its future sale value.

- *Customer concentrations.* In the commercial chef market, sales to large restaurant chains comprise a significant proportion of total company sales. The termination of sales to Ninja's five largest restaurant chain customers would eliminate 35% of that segment's total sales. The company cannot be certain that current customers will continue to purchase from it.

- *Dividends.* The company has never declared or paid any cash dividends or distributions on its common stock and intends to retain future earnings, if any, to support operations and to finance expansion. Therefore, the company does not anticipate paying any cash dividends on the common stock in the foreseeable future.

- *Funding availability.* Given the state of the current credit markets, it may be difficult to obtain funds for either operational needs or prospective acquisitions. Ninja currently has $3 million of debt funding available through a previously authorized loan through Fourth National Bank. The company's next-year budget projects sufficient cash requirements to use all but $500,000 of the available debt funding.

- *Growth strategy.* Ninja's growth strategy involves expanding into additional foreign markets. The company's ability to do so may be negatively impacted by the need to work with foreign partners, as well as to sell into markets where there may be currency restrictions. There may also be cases in which vigorous local competition from existing businesses could impede Ninja's ability to gain any significant market share.

- *Industry trends.* The company derives a large part of its revenue from customers in the commercial restaurant business. As a result, Ninja's business, financial condition, and results of operations depend upon the conditions and trends affecting this industry. For example, a decline in consumer spending could lead restaurant chains to reduce their spending on kitchen supplies, which would reduce Ninja's sales.

- *Patent protection.* The patent protecting the company's use of carbon blade knives will expire in 20X9. At that time, competitors may use the same technology to create their own knife blades, which could result in extensive price competition. If so, the company's margins on the sale of this product will likely decline.

- *Personnel loss.* The future success of the company depends in part on the continued service of the executive officers and other key management, sales, and operations personnel, and on the company's ability to continue to attract, motivate, and retain additional highly qualified employees. The loss of the services of one or more of these people, or the company's inability to recruit replacements for them or to otherwise attract, motivate, or retain qualified personnel could have an adverse effect on the business, its operating results, and financial condition.

- *Stock sales.* Sales of substantial amounts of Ninja common stock in the public market, or the perception that such sales could occur, could adversely affect the market price of its shares. Any sales of common stock by Ninja or its principal stockholders, or the perception that such sales might occur, could have a material adverse effect on the price of Ninja shares.

- *Stock price volatility.* The company's share price is likely to fluctuate in the future because of the volatility of the stock market in general and a variety of factors, many of which are beyond the control of the company, including:

- o Quarterly variations in actual or anticipated results of operations;
- o Changes in financial estimates by securities analysts;
- o Actions or announcements by the company or its competitors;
- o Regulatory actions;
- o Litigation;
- o Loss or gain of major customers;
- o Additions or departures of key personnel; and
- o Future sales of the company's common stock.

These fluctuations may result in an immediate and significant decline in the trading price of Ninja's common stock, which could cause a decline in the value of an investor's investment.

Item 1B. Unresolved Staff Comments

Certain types of companies are required to make note of any unresolved SEC staff comments regarding their reports. In these situations, disclose the substance of the unresolved comments that the company considers to be material. The company may also note its position regarding these comments. The following is a sample disclosure related to unresolved staff comments:

The company received a comment letter from the SEC dated November 10, 20X3 regarding its quarterly report on Form 10-Q for the quarter ended September 30, 20X3. These comments are unresolved as of March 2, 20X4. We have filed with the SEC a response to the comment letter. Additionally, we have incorporated into our subsequent periodic filings with the SEC additional disclosures that we believe are responsive to the SEC's comments.

In general, the unresolved staff comments relate to the methodologies used to determine a reserve for obsolete inventory, and how evenly those methodologies are applied across our various product lines. We believe that the ultimate resolution of these comments will not have a material impact on our consolidated financial statements and/or related footnotes.

Item 2. Properties

This section should contain descriptions of the leased or owned facilities of the business, as enumerated by the SEC:

- State the location and character of the principal plants, mines and other materially important physical properties of the company. In addition, identify the business segments that use the properties described. If any property is not held in fee or is held subject to a major encumbrance, describe the situation.
- In the case of an extractive business that does not involve oil and gas producing activities, describe production, reserves, locations, development, and the nature of the company's interest. If individual properties are of major significance to an industry segment, supply more detailed information and disclose the locations of these properties.

- In the case of extractive reserves other than oil and gas reserves, do not disclose estimates other than proven or probable reserves.

If there are a number of facilities, consider providing the information in a tabular format. Consider the following example text:

The company's principal locations, their purposes and the expiration dates for the leases on facilities at those locations as of June 30, 20X3 are shown in the table below. Ninja has renewal options on several of its leases.

Location	Purpose	Approximate Square Feet	Principal Lease Expiration Dates
Corning, New York	Corporate headquarters	30,000	Owned
Little Falls, New York	Main assembly facility	45,000	20X9
Port Jervis, New York	Knife handle production facility	52,000	20X8

Ninja owns its headquarters building, comprising approximately 30,000 square feet, as noted in the preceding table. The table excludes approximately 12,000 square feet for a storage facility that the company has classified as a discontinued operation. Ninja also leases facilities for its sales staff in each country where it conducts sales activities, including the United Kingdom, Italy, and France. The company believes its facilities are suitable and adequate for its current and near-term needs, and that it will be able to locate additional facilities as needed.

Item 3. Legal Proceedings

The legal proceedings of a business should be extensively described in the Form 10-K. The SEC gives the following instructions:

- Describe any material pending legal proceedings, other than ordinary routine litigation incidental to the business, to which the company is a party. Include the name of the court or agency in which the proceedings are pending, the date instituted, the principal parties, the factual basis alleged to underlie the proceeding and the relief sought.
- Do not include information about lawsuits that involve a claim for damages if the amount involved does not exceed 10 percent of the current assets of the company.
- Describe any material bankruptcy, receivership, or similar proceeding.
- Describe any material proceedings to which any director, officer or affiliate of the company, any owner of record or beneficially of more than five percent of any class of voting securities of the company, or security holder is a party adverse to the company.
- Describe any administrative or judicial proceeding arising under any government provisions regulating the discharge of materials into the envi-

ronment or for the purpose of protecting the environment, if material to the business.

For example:

> In August 20X2, Outdoor Devices (OD) brought suit against Ninja, seeking monetary damages and injunctive relief based on Ninja's alleged infringement of certain patents held by OD. Specifically, OD identified the company's FlipBlade product as infringing the patents OD is asserting. On the company's motion, the case was transferred to the United States District Court for New York. In October 20X2, OD voluntarily dismissed its claims asserted against the FlipBlade. In November 20X2, the court entered a final judgment in this case, dismissing OD's claim. The time for filing an appeal of the decision has now passed, and neither party filed an appeal.
>
> From time to time, the company has received notices from third parties alleging infringement of such parties' patent or other intellectual property rights by the company's products. In such cases it is the company's policy to defend the claims, or if considered appropriate, negotiate licenses on commercially reasonable terms. However, no assurance can be given that the company will be able to negotiate necessary licenses on commercially reasonable terms, or at all, or that any litigation resulting from such claims would not have a material adverse effect on the company's consolidated financial position, liquidity, operating results, or consolidated financial statements taken as a whole.

Item 4. Mine Safety Disclosures

The discussion of mine safety issues only applies to a minority of situations, and in all other cases can be tagged as not applicable. Where such disclosures *do* apply, make note of the following information:

- For each coal or other mine of which the company is an operator, identify the mine and disclose:
    - The total number of violations of mandatory health or safety standards that could significantly contribute to the cause and effect of a coal or other mine safety or health hazard for which the operator received a citation from the Mine Safety and Health Administration (MSHA)
    - The total number of orders issued by MSHA
    - The total number of citations and orders for unwarranted failure of the mine operator to comply with mandatory health or safety standards by MSHA
    - The total number of flagrant violations
    - The total number of imminent danger orders issued
    - The total dollar value of proposed assessments from MSHA
    - The total number of mining-related fatalities

- A list of the coal or other mines, of which the company is an operator, that receive written notice from MSHA of:
  - A pattern of violations of mandatory health or safety standards that are of such nature as could have significantly contributed to the cause and effect of coal or other mine health or safety hazards
  - The potential to have such a pattern
- Any pending legal action before the Federal Mine Safety and Health Review Commission involving such coal or other mine.

For example:

The following disclosures are provided pursuant to the Dodd-Frank Wall Street Reform and Consumer Protection Act and Item 104 of Regulation S-K, which requires certain disclosures by companies required to file periodic reports under the Exchange Act that operate mines regulated under the Federal Mine Safety and Health Act of 1988. Whenever the Federal Mine Safety and Health Administration MSHA) believes a violation of the Mine Act, any health or safety standard or any regulation has occurred, it may issue a citation which describes the alleged violation and fixes a time within which the operator must abate the alleged violation. In some situations, such as when MSHA believes that conditions pose a hazard to miners, MSHA may issue an order removing miners from the area of the mine affected by the condition until the alleged hazards are corrected.

When the MSHA issues a citation or order, it generally proposes a civil penalty, or fine, as a result of the alleged violation, that the operator is ordered to pay. Citations and orders can be contested and appealed, and as part of that process, are often reduced in severity and amount, and are sometimes dismissed. The following table reflects citations and orders issued to the company by MSHA during the year ended December 31, 20X3.

	Total Number of Significant and Substantial Violations	Total Number of Citations and Orders Issued	Total Number of Imminent Danger Orders	Total Amount of Proposed Assessments from MSHA
Meager Mine	4	1	1	$29,540

Item 5. Market for Company Stock

The SEC wants investors to understand the markets in which a company's stock is sold, the prices at which its shares have traded recently, who holds the stock, the amount of dividends paid out, and similar information. More specifically, the SEC mandates that the following information be disclosed:

- The principal United States market in which each class of the company's common stock is traded, or note if there is no established market for the stock. Also state the high and low sales prices for the stock for each full quarterly period within the two most recent fiscal years and any subsequent interim period.

- The approximate number of holders of each class of common stock of the company as of the latest practicable date.
- The frequency and amount of any cash dividends declared on each class of the company's common stock for the two most recent fiscal years and any subsequent interim period. Describe any restrictions on the ability of the company to pay dividends. If there is no intent to pay cash dividends in the foreseeable future, state that point. If an entity has a history of paying cash dividends, indicate whether there is an expectation to continue doing so in the future; if not, state the nature of the change in the amount or rate of cash dividend payments.
- For any equity compensation plans approved or not approved by shareholders, state the number of securities to be issued upon the exercise of outstanding options and similar instruments, the weighted-average price of these instruments, and the number of securities remaining available for future issuance under the plans. Also describe the material features of these plans.
- A line graph that compares the yearly percentage change in the company's cumulative total shareholder return on each class of registered common stock, alongside both of the following for comparison purposes:
  - The cumulative total return of the broad equity market index that includes companies whose equity securities are traded on the same exchange or are of comparable market capitalization
  - The cumulative total return of a published industry index, or a peer entity, or issuers with similar market capitalizations

For example:

Since February 15, 19X8, the company's stock has traded on the NASDAQ Capital Market under the trading symbol "NINJ". The following table sets forth the quarterly high and low selling prices for the company's stock as reported on the NASDAQ since January 1, 20X2.

	Common Stock	
	High	Low
Fiscal Year Ended December 31, 20X2	$15.50	$14.00
Fiscal quarter ended March 31, 20X2	$15.53	$13.91
Fiscal quarter ended June 30, 20X2	$15.10	$13.01
Fiscal quarter ended September 30, 20X2	$13.49	$12.81
Fiscal quarter ended December 31, 20X2		

	Common Stock	
	High	Low
Fiscal Year Ended December 31, 20X3		
Fiscal quarter ended March 31, 20X3	$13.58	$12.77
Fiscal quarter ended June 30, 20X3	$13.08	$12.20
Fiscal quarter ended September 30, 20X3	$12.34	$11.68
Fiscal quarter ended December 31, 20X3	$10.19	$10.00

As of February 4, 20X4, there were 1,512 holders of record of Ninja's common stock, and the closing stock price was $10.15.

The annual changes for the five-year period shown in the following graph are based on the assumption that $100 had been invested in Ninja stock, the Standard & Poor's 500 Stock Index (S&P 500) and the Dow Jones Industrial Average (DJIA) on December 31, 20X8, and that all quarterly dividends were reinvested. The total cumulative dollar returns shown on the graph represent the value that such investments would have had on December 31, 20X3.

Five-Year Financial Performance Graph

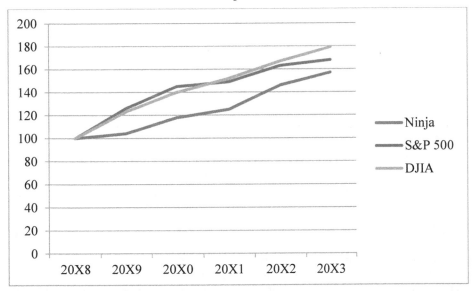

	20X8	20X9	20X0	20X1	20X2	20X3
Ninja	100	104	118	125	146	157
S&P 500	100	126	145	149	163	168
DJIA	100	123	140	152	167	179

Following is a summary of dividends declared per common share during the fiscal year 20X3 (in thousands, except per share amounts):

Date of Declaration	Dividend per Common Share	Date of Record	Date of Payment	Total Amount
December 8, 20X2	$0.15	January 10, 20X3	January 20, 20X3	$450
February 27, 20X3	0.15	April 12, 20X3	April 22, 20X3	525
June 7, 20X3	0.15	June 24, 20X3	July 5, 20X3	570
September 8, 20X3	0.20	September 19, 20X3	September 29, 20X3	590

The company will pay future dividends at the discretion of the board of directors. The continuation of these payments, the amount of such dividends, and the form in which the dividends are paid (cash or stock) depend on many factors, including the results of operations and the financial condition of the company. Subject to these qualifications, the company currently expects to pay dividends on a quarterly basis.

Item 6. Selected Financial Data

The SEC mandates that financial data be provided by the company that gives readers a view of performance levels over time. This information is to be provided in columnar format, and should include the following items for each of the last five years:

- Net sales or operating revenues
- Income or loss from continuing operations
- Income or loss from continuing operations per common share
- Total assets
- Long-term obligations and redeemable preferred stock
- Cash dividends declared per common share

Additional items may be included if doing so would enhance the understanding of the reader. Also note factors such as accounting changes, or business combinations or dispositions that materially affect the comparability of the information appearing in the selected financial data. Finally, discuss any material uncertainties where these issues might cause the data stated in this section to not be indicative of the company's future financial condition or its results of operations. A sample disclosure that follows these instructions is:

> The following selected data are derived from the company's consolidated financial statements and should be read in conjunction with "Item 7. Management's Discussion and Analysis of Financial Condition and Results of Operations" and "Item 8. Financial Statements and Supplementary Data". All financial information presented in the following table is in thousands, except per share amounts.

	December 31, 20X3	December 31, 20X2	December 31, 20X1	December 31, 20X0	December 31, 20X9
Sales	$61,700	$43,000	$38,200	$33,500	$29,000
Cost of goods sold	24,700	17,200	15,300	13,400	11,600
Gross profit	37,000	25,800	22,900	20,100	17,400
Administrative expenses	26,400	20,900	18,300	16,600	15,000
Operating income	10,600	$4,900	$4,600	$3,500	$2,400
Interest expense	3,600	300	--	--	--
Provision for income taxes	2,400	1,600	1,600	1,200	800
Net income	$4,600	$3,000	$3,000	$2,300	$1,600
Operating income per share	$5.30	$2.45	$2.30	$1.75	$1.20
Dividends declared per share	$1.37	$1.20	--	--	--
Total assets	$17,020	$11,860	$10,540	$9,250	$8,000
Long-term debt	$32,000	$5,000	--	--	--

Item 7. Management's Discussion and Analysis of Financial Condition and Results of Operation (MD&A)

This section of the Form 10-K traditionally receives the most attention from the accountant, since it is used to explain the information appearing in the financial statements. It is an area that also receives a detailed perusal from the SEC, and which may trigger occasional comment letters. Consequently, be especially careful to provide complete commentary on the following SEC disclosure requirements:

- Discuss the company's financial condition, changes in financial condition and results of operations for the years presented, which shall include the following items:
    - Identify trends, demands, commitments, events, or uncertainties that can reasonably result in material changes in the liquidity of the entity; if there is a material deficiency, note the course of action that has been or will be taken. Also describe the company's internal and external sources of liquidity, and discuss any material unused sources of liquid assets.
    - Describe the company's material commitments for capital expenditures; indicate their purpose, and the source of funds to fulfill these commitments. Also note any material trends in the company's capital resources. Further, describe any expected material changes in the mix and relative cost of these resources.
    - Describe any infrequent or unusual events or transactions or significant economic changes that materially affected the amount of reported income, and the extent to which income was affected.

- o Discuss other significant components of revenues and expenses that should be addressed in order to understand the company's results of operations.
- o Describe any trends or uncertainties that have had or that the company reasonably expects will have a material impact on net sales or income from operations.
- o Discuss the reasons for material increases in net sales, such as the impact of price or unit volume increases, or the introduction of new products.
- o Address the concept of inflation and changing prices on the company's net sales and income from operations.
- o Discuss any off-balance sheet arrangements that have had or will have a material effect on the company's financial statements. Also note the nature and purpose of these arrangements, and their importance to the company. Further, state the amounts of revenues, expenses and cash flows of the company arising from these arrangements, the nature and amounts of any interests retained, securities issued and other indebtedness incurred by the company in connection with these arrangements. In addition, note any other obligations of the company arising from these arrangements that could become material, as well as the triggering events that could cause them to arise.
- o Describe any known event, demand, commitment, trend or uncertainty that will likely result in the termination or material reduction in availability to the company of those off-balance sheet arrangements that provide material benefits to it, and the course of action the company has taken or can take in response to these circumstances.
- o Provide a summary of the company's contractual obligations in tabular format, showing payments due in total, in less than one year, in 1-3 years, in 3-5 years, and in more than 5 years, for the major classes of obligations. These classes may include long-term debt obligations, capital lease obligations, operating lease obligations, and so forth.

- If interim period financial statements are included, this section shall give sufficient information for the reader to assess material changes in financial condition and the results of operations. It is not necessary to discuss the impact of inflation and changing prices on operations for interim periods. Note any seasonal aspects of the business which have had a material effect on the financial condition or results of operation of the entity.

The MD&A sections of company filings can be extensive; the following example presents a compressed and non-inclusive set of statements taken from the MD&A language of an assortment of public companies:

The following discussion of our consolidated results of operations and financial condition should be read together with the other financial information and consolidated financial statements included in this Form 10-K. This discussion contains forward-looking statements that involve risks and uncertainties. Our actual results could differ materially from the results anticipated in the forward-looking statements as a result of a variety of factors, including those discussed in "Item 1A. Risk Factors" and elsewhere in this report.

The company's revenue has increased substantially over the past three years, primarily due to our ability to expand the existing product line into new foreign markets, and also the introduction of our new line of ceramic chef knives. Given that sales organizations have only been installed in ten countries, we believe there is a possibility of substantial new growth by continuing to add new markets.

Net revenue. The company derives its revenue from limited manufacturing services and product sales. Net revenue increased $18.7 million from the prior year, to $61.7 million in 20X3. The introduction of the company's products in five new foreign markets contributed to approximately $10 million of this amount. $6 million of the remaining increase was attributable to the rollout of a new line of ceramic knives.

Gross profit. The company's gross profit increased $11.2 million from the prior year, to $37.0 million in 20X3. The gross profit percentage was the same as the preceding year, indicating that the company was able to apply its standard product pricing in the new geographic regions into which it introduced the full suite of products.

Administrative expenses. Selling, general and administrative expenses increased $5.5 million from the prior year, to $26.4 million in 20X3. This represented a reduced proportion of total net revenue, which was caused by the use of more streamlined selling organizations in the new territories into which sales were introduced.

Interest expense. Interest expense increased $3.3 million from the prior year, to $3.6 million in 20X3. This was due to a $27 million increase in company debt, which was needed to fund the additional inventory and receivables required to support the new foreign sales regions. Of this amount of debt, $19 million was used to fund additional inventory, and $8 million was used to fund an increase in accounts receivable. The interest rate charged on the company debt increased from 6.0 percent at the end of 20X2 to 7.4% at the end of 20X3.

Income taxes. The $2.4 million 20X3 income tax provision consists of current tax expense of $2.7 million and a deferred tax benefit of $0.3 million.

The Company's credit facility provides potential total availability of up of $40 million. Loans made under the credit facility will mature and the commitments thereunder will terminate in May 20X8. Actual borrowing availability under the credit facility is determined by a monthly borrowing base collateral calculation that is based on specified percentages of the value of eligible accounts receivable and inventory. Based on that calculation, as of December 31, 20X3, we had actual total borrowing availability under the credit facility of $34.1 million, of which we had drawn down $29.8 million, leaving $4.3 million available for borrowing. Along with an unrestricted cash balance of $2.1 million, we had total cash and available borrowing capacity of $6.4 million as of December 31, 20X3.

The credit facility contains a number of covenants that limit or restrict our ability to dispose of assets, incur additional indebtedness, incur guarantee obligations, prepay other indebtedness, and pay dividends. Our ability to service our indebtedness will require a significant amount of cash. Our ability to generate this cash will depend largely on future operations. Based on our current level of operations and our current business plan, we expect to be able to meet the financial covenants of our credit facility for at least the next twelve months. However, changing business, regulatory and economic conditions may mean that actual results will vary from our forecasts.

We do not have any material off-balance sheet arrangements that have or are reasonably likely to have a current or future effect on our financial condition, changes in financial condition, revenues or expenses, results of operations, liquidity, capital expenditures or capital resources as of December 31, 20X3.

Item 7A. Quantitative and Qualitative Disclosures about Market Risk

This classification of disclosure is intended to reveal the extent to which the results of a business can be impacted by changes in such factors as interest rates, exchange rates, and commodity prices. The SEC has exceptionally detailed reporting requirements in this area, for which only the general requirements are noted in the following bullet points:

- Provide quantitative information about market risk as of the end of the latest fiscal year, subdividing information by instruments entered into for trading purposes and instruments entered into for purposes other than trading. Within these categories, present information for each market risk exposure category, such as for interest rate risk, foreign currency exchange rate risk, commodity price risk, and other relevant market risks. This information may be presented using any one of the following three disclosure alternatives:
  - A tabular presentation, from which a reader can determine future cash flows.
  - A sensitivity analysis that discloses the potential loss in future earnings, fair values, or cash flows based on hypothetical changes in interest rates, foreign currency exchange rates, commodity prices, and so forth over time.
  - A value at risk disclosure that expresses the potential loss in future earnings, fair values, or cash flows of market risk sensitive instruments over a period of time, with a likelihood of occurrence, from changes in interest rates, foreign currency exchange rates, commodity prices, and other relevant market rates or prices. For each category for which value at risk disclosures are made, provide either:

- The average, high and low amounts, or the distribution of the value at risk amounts for the reporting period; or
- The average, high and low amounts, or the distribution of actual changes in fair values, earnings, or cash flows from the market risk sensitive instruments occurring during the reporting period; or
- The percentage or number of times the actual changes in fair values, earnings, or cash flows from the market risk sensitive instruments exceeded the value at risk amounts during the reporting period

- Describe the company's primary market exposures, how these exposures are managed (noting objectives, strategies, and any instruments used), and changes in the company's primary market risk exposures.

For example:

In the normal course of business and consistent with established policies and procedures, we employ a variety of financial instruments to manage exposure to fluctuations in the value of foreign currencies and interest rates. It is our policy to utilize these financial instruments only where necessary to finance our business and manage such exposures; we do not enter into these transactions for trading or speculative purposes.

We are exposed to foreign currency fluctuations, primarily as a result of our international sales, product sourcing and funding activities. Our foreign exchange risk management program is intended to lessen both the positive and negative effects of currency fluctuations on our consolidated results of operations, financial position and cash flows. We use forward exchange contracts and options to hedge certain anticipated but not yet firmly committed transactions as well as certain firm commitments and the related receivables and payables, including third-party and intercompany transactions. We have, and may in the future, also use forward contracts to hedge our investment in the net assets of certain international subsidiaries to offset foreign currency translation adjustments related to our net investment in those subsidiaries. Where exposures are hedged, our program has the effect of delaying the impact of exchange rate movements on our consolidated financial statements.

The timing for hedging exposures, as well as the type and duration of the hedge instruments employed, are guided by our hedging policies and determined based upon the nature of the exposure and prevailing market conditions. Generally, hedged transactions are expected to be recognized within 12 to 18 months. Hedged transactions are principally denominated in Euros, British Pounds and Japanese Yen.

Our earnings are also exposed to movements in short- and long-term market interest rates. Our objective in managing this interest rate exposure is to limit the impact of interest rate changes on earnings and cash flows and to reduce overall borrowing costs. To achieve these objectives, we maintain a mix of bank loans and fixed rate debt of varying maturities and have entered into interest rate swaps for a portion of our fixed rate debt.

We monitor foreign exchange risk, interest rate risk and related derivatives using a variety of techniques including a review of market value, sensitivity analysis, and value-at-risk (VaR). Our market-sensitive derivative and other financial instruments are foreign currency forward contracts, foreign currency option contracts, interest rate swaps, fixed interest rate U.S. Dollar denominated debt, and fixed interest rate Japanese Yen denominated debt.

We use VaR to monitor the foreign exchange risk of our foreign currency forward and foreign currency option derivative instruments only. The VaR determines the maximum potential one-day loss in the fair value of these foreign exchange rate-sensitive financial instruments. The VaR model estimates assume normal market conditions and a 95% confidence level. There are various modeling techniques that can be used in the VaR computation. Our computations are based on interrelationships between currencies and interest rates. These interrelationships are a function of foreign exchange currency market changes and interest rate changes over the preceding one year period. The value of foreign currency options does not change on a one-to-one basis with changes in the underlying currency rate.

The VaR model is a risk analysis tool and does not purport to represent actual losses in fair value that we will incur, nor does it consider the potential effect of favorable changes in market rates. It also does not represent the full extent of the possible loss that may occur. Actual future gains and losses will differ from those estimated because of changes or differences in market rates and interrelationships, hedging instruments and hedge percentages, timing and other factors.

The estimated maximum one-day loss in fair value on our foreign currency sensitive derivative financial instruments, derived using the VaR model, was $0.9 million and $0.5 million at December 31, 20X3 and 20X2, respectively. The VaR increased year-over-year as a result of an increase in the total notional value of our foreign currency derivative portfolio combined with a longer average duration on our outstanding trades at December 31, 20X3. Such a hypothetical loss in the fair value of our derivatives would be offset by increases in the value of the underlying transactions being hedged.

Details of third-party debt and interest rate swaps are provided in the following table. The table presents principal cash flows and related weighted average interest rates by expected maturity dates.

	Expected Maturity Date						
(Dollars in millions)	20X3	20X4	20X5	20X6	20X7	Thereafter	Total
Foreign Exchange Risk							
Japanese Yen debt – Fixed rate							
Principal payments	$0.2	$0.3	$0.3	$0.3	$0.5	$1.2	$2.8

(Dollars in millions)	Expected Maturity Date						
	20X3	20X4	20X5	20X6	20X7	Thereafter	Total
Average interest rate	3.5%	4.8%	4.8%	5.0%	5.0%	5.0%	
Interest Rate Risk							
Japanese Yen debt – Fixed rate							
Principal payments	$0.2	$0.3	$0.3	$0.3	$0.5	$1.2	$2.8
Average interest rate	3.5%	4.8%	4.8%	5.0%	5.0%	5.0%	
U.S. Dollar debt – Fixed rate							
Principal payments	$1.0	$0.8	$0.8	$0.7	$0.7	$2.3	$6.3
Average interest rate	4.5%	6.0%	6.2%	6.5%	6.7%	5.9%	

Item 8. Financial Statements and Supplementary Data

Item 8 may be considered the core of the Form 10-K, since it includes the financial statements and the notes related to those statements, as well as the report of the public accounting firm that examined the financial statements. The requirements for the production of financial statements and their related footnotes go well beyond the scope of this book (see the latest annual edition of the author's *GAAP Guidebook* for comprehensive coverage of this topic). In the following bullet points, we make note of several presentation issues related to the financial statements:

- The balance sheet shall be presented as of the end of each of the last two fiscal years
- The income statement shall be presented for each of the last three years
- The statement of cash flows shall be presented for each of the last three years
- The statement of retained earnings shall be presented for each of the last three years

Item 9. Changes in and Disagreements with Accountants on Accounting and Financial Disclosure

A clear area of concern for the reader of a company's financial statements is when the company switches its auditors. The change could be triggered by a disagreement over the presentation of information in the financial statements, which could mean that company management wants to take an unusually aggressive approach to certain topics. The SEC ensures that these matters are illuminated by requiring the following presentation of information:

- If the independent accountant resigned or was dismissed during the two most recent fiscal years, disclose the following information:

- o Whether the accountant resigned, declined to stand for re-election or was dismissed, as well as the date of this occurrence.
- o Whether the accountant's report on the financial statements for either of the past two years contained an adverse opinion or a disclaimer of opinion, or was qualified or modified as to uncertainty, audit scope, or accounting principles, and also note the nature of each adverse opinion, disclaimer of opinion, modification, or qualification.
- o Whether the decision to change accountants was recommended or approved by the audit committee or the board of directors.
- o Whether there were disagreements with the former accountant on any matter of accounting principles or practices, financial statement disclosure, or auditing scope or procedure. If so, describe these disagreements, whether the board or audit committee discussed the matter with the accountant, and whether the company has authorized the accountant to respond fully to the inquiries of the successor accountant concerning the subject matter of the disagreements; if not, note the nature of and reason for any limitations.

- If a new independent accountant has been engaged, identify the new accountant and note the date of the engagement. Also disclose the following information:

  - o If the company consulted the newly engaged accountant regarding the application of accounting principles to a specific transaction, or the type of audit opinion that might be rendered, or there was a matter that was the subject of a disagreement, then:

    - Identify the issues
    - Describe the views of the new accountant
    - State whether the former accountant was consulted regarding these issues, and if so, provide a summary of the former accountant's views

There are additional non-reporting requirements under which the new accountant is requested to provide a letter, stating whether it agrees with the statements made by the company, and any issues over which it does not agree.

Item 9A. Controls and Procedures

The SEC requires that a company disclose the conclusions of its principal executive and principal financial officers regarding the effectiveness of the company's disclosure controls and procedures. There should be an accompanying report that contains the following:

- A statement of management's responsibility for establishing and maintaining adequate internal control over the financial reporting of the company.

- A statement identifying the framework used by management to evaluate the effectiveness of the company's internal control over financial reporting.
- Management's assessment of the effectiveness of the company's internal control over financial reporting, including a statement as to whether the internal control over financial reporting is effective (disclosures of material weaknesses in the company's internal control over financial reporting must be disclosed).
- The registered public accounting firm's attestation report on the company's internal control over financial reporting, if the company is an accelerated filer or a large accelerated filer.
- Any change in the company's internal control over financial reporting that occurred during the company's last fiscal quarter that has materially affected, or is reasonably likely to materially affect, the company's internal control over financial reporting.

The following example contains several elements of the preceding SEC requirements:

The company maintains a set of disclosure controls and procedures, designed to ensure that information required to be disclosed by the company in reports that it files or submits under the Exchange Act is recorded, processed, summarized or reported within the time periods specified in SEC rules and regulations. Management necessarily applies its judgment in assessing the costs and benefits of such controls and procedures, which, by their nature, can provide only reasonable assurance regarding management's control objectives. The company's management, including the chief executive officer and the chief financial officer, does not expect that our disclosure controls and procedures can prevent all possible errors or fraud. A control system, no matter how well conceived and operated, can provide only reasonable, not absolute, assurance that misstatements due to error or fraud will not occur or that all control issues and instances of fraud, if any, within the company have been detected. Judgments in decision making can be faulty and breakdowns can occur because of simple errors or mistakes. Additionally, controls can be circumvented by the individual acts of one or more persons. The design of any system of controls is based in part upon certain assumptions about the likelihood of future events, and while our disclosure controls and procedures are designed to be effective under circumstances where they should reasonably be expected to operate effectively, there can be no assurance that any design will succeed in achieving its stated goals under all potential future conditions. Because of the inherent limitations in any control system, misstatements due to possible errors or fraud may occur and not be detected.

The company's management, with the participation of the chief executive officer and chief financial officer, has evaluated the effectiveness of the company's disclosure controls and procedures as of December 31, 20X3. Based on that evaluation, the company's chief executive officer and chief financial officer concluded that the company's disclosure controls and procedures were effective as of December 31, 20X3.

The company's independent registered public accounting firm, Ernst & Young LLP, is appointed by the audit committee. Ernst & Young LLP has audited and reported on the consolidated financial statements of Ninja Cutlery and the company's internal control over financial reporting, each as contained in this Form 10-K.

During the year ended December 31, 20X3, including the quarter ended December 31, 20X3, our management completed corrective actions to remediate the material weakness identified in our 20X2 Form 10-K. Specifically, the following actions were taken with respect to the following identified material weakness: The company did not maintain sufficient resources in the corporate tax function to provide for adequate and timely preparation and review of various income tax calculations, reconciliations, and related supporting documentation. To resolve this issue, we implemented the following improvements:

- Hired two additional tax managers
- Changed the reporting of the tax function to the corporate controller
- Installed new tax management software and provided training in its use to the tax staff
- Formalized policies and procedures for the main reporting tasks

Item 10. Directors, Executive Officers and Corporate Governance

The disclosure of background information about the directors and executive officers of an organization is extensive. The SEC requires that the following information be provided in regard to the directors and executive officers of an organization, as well as certain corporate governance issues:

- List the names and ages of all company directors and all persons nominated to become directors. Also indicate all positions and offices with the company held by each of these people. List each person's term of office as a director, and any periods during which he or she has already served in this role. Also note any arrangement under which the person is or was to be selected as a director or nominee.
- List the names and ages of all executive officers of the company and all persons chosen to become executive officers. Note all company positions held by these persons. List each person's term of office as an officer, and the period during which each individual has served in this role. Also note any arrangement under which the person is or was to be selected as an officer.
- Identify all significant employees, such as production managers or research scientists, who are expected to make significant contributions to the business. Also note their backgrounds to the same extent as the executive officers.
- State the nature of any family relationship between any director, executive officer, or person nominated to become a director or executive officer.
- Note the business experience during the past five years of each of the preceding individuals, including their principal occupations and employment, the name and principal business of any entity in which such work was carried on, and whether these entities were a parent, subsidiary or other af-

filiate of the company. Also describe the specific experience, qualifications, or other attributes that led to a person serving as a director of the company. Also for directors, indicate other directorships held.

- Describe any of the following events that occurred during the past ten years and that are material to an evaluation of the ability or integrity of any director or executive officer:
  - o Bankruptcy by the individual or a business of which the person was an executive officer
  - o A criminal conviction or a named subject of a pending criminal proceeding, other than minor offenses
  - o Any court orders enjoining a person from participating in the securities industry in various roles, or violations of federal securities or commodities laws, or mail or wire fraud
- Identify each person who was a director, officer, beneficial owner of more than 10 percent of any class of the company's equity securities that failed to file a Form 3, 4, or 5 on a timely basis. For these individuals, state the number of late reports, the number of transactions not reported on a timely basis, and any known failure to file a form.
- Disclose whether the company has adopted a code of ethics that applies to the entity's principal executive officer, principal financial officer, and principal accounting officer. If not, explain why there is no applicable code of ethics.
- Describe any material changes to the procedures by which shareholders can recommend nominees to the board of directors.
- State whether the company has a separately-designated standing audit committee, and identify each committee member. If the entire board of directors is acting as the audit committee, reveal this situation.
- Disclose that there is at least one financial expert serving on the audit committee, or that there is no such person on the committee, and why no such person is on the committee. If so, disclose the name of the financial expert and whether the person is independent.

The following is a condensed example of several of the preceding disclosure requirements:

The names, ages, year first elected and current titles of each of the executive officers of the company as of December 31, 20X3 are set forth next.

Name	Age	Year First Elected Executive Officer	Title
Gerald Evans	62	19X8	Chief executive officer
Bruce Nolan	59	19X8	President
Allison Vincent	43	20X9	Chief financial officer
Robert Tomberlin	59	19X8	Chief operating officer
Robert Miller	38	20X1	Senior vice president
Stephanie Honor	31	20X7	Chief product designer

Additional information regarding the backgrounds of the executive officers is as follows:

Gerald Evans was elected chief executive officer of the company in October 19X8. He was previously the chief product manager at Sharper Products from 19X0 to 19X8.

Bruce Nolan was elected president of the company in October 19X8. He was previously employed as the vice president of marketing at Sharper Products from 19X0 to 19X8.

Allison Vincent was elected chief financial officer in 20X9. She was previously a senior manager at Ernst & Young from 19X4 to 20X5, and previously served as the controller of Ninja from 20X6 to 20X8.

Robert Tomberlin was elected the chief operating officer in 19X8. He was previously the production manager at Sharper Products from 19X2 to 19X8.

Robert Miller was elected to the senior vice president position in 20X1. He was previously the sales manager at the Lethal Sushi restaurant chain from 19X8 to 20X0.

Stephanie Honor was appointed to the chief product designer position in 20X1. She was previously the chief metallurgist at Katana Blades from 20X3 to 20X7.

There is no family relationship between any of the above-named persons, or between any of such persons and any of the directors of the company.

The Company has adopted a Code of Conduct that applies to its principal executive officer, principal financial officer and controller, among others.

Item 11. Executive Compensation

The amount of disclosure required for executive compensation has grown substantially in recent years, having now reached the point where this can be the second-largest disclosure area outside of the management's discussion and analysis of financial condition and results of operation. The SEC mandates the following disclosures:

- Discuss the compensation of the executive officers, including the objectives of their compensation plans, what the programs are designed to reward, each element of compensation, the reasons for paying each element, how the amount of each element is determined, how the elements fit into the company's overall compensation objectives, and whether the company has considered the results of the most recent shareholder advisory vote on executive compensation.
- Provide a summary compensation table that shows all elements of the compensation of the named executive officers of the company for each of the last three years. The table should include the following columns:
  - Name and principal position of each person listed
  - The applicable fiscal year
  - The dollar value of the base salary
  - The dollar value of the cash and non-cash bonus earned
  - The aggregate grant date fair value for awards of stock
  - The aggregate grant date fair value of option awards
  - Non-equity incentive plan compensation
  - The change in pension value and non-qualified deferred compensation
  - All other compensation, such as perquisites
- Provide a summary of grants of plan-based awards in a table that shows each grant of an award made to an executive officer in the last fiscal year. The table should include the following columns:
  - Name of the executive officer
  - The grant date for equity-based awards
  - The dollar value of the estimated future payout
  - The number of shares of stock to be paid out
  - The number of shares of stock granted that were not required to be disclosed in the preceding columns
  - The number of securities underlying options that were not required to be disclosed in the preceding columns
  - The per-share exercise price of the options granted in the fiscal year
  - If the preceding exercise price was below the market price on the grant date, list in another column the closing market price on the date of the grant
  - The grant date fair value of each equity award

- Provide a narrative description of any material factors needed to understand the information disclosed in the preceding tables. This may include, for example, terms of employment agreements and the nature of any option repricing.
- Provide a summary of outstanding equity awards as of the end of the last fiscal year. The table should include the following columns:
  - Name of the executive officer
  - The number of securities underlying unexercised options that are exercisable
  - The number of securities underlying unexercised options that are unexercisable
  - The number of shares underlying unexercised options awarded under an equity incentive plan that have not been earned
  - The applicable exercise or base price for the preceding items
  - The expiration date for each of the preceding items
  - The total number of shares that have not vested
  - The aggregate market value of shares that have not vested
  - The total number of shares awarded under any equity incentive plan that have not vested and that have not been earned, and the number of shares underlying each such unit
  - The aggregate market or payout value of the shares under any equity incentive plan that have not vested and that have not been earned
- Provide a summary table containing option exercises and similar instruments, and each vesting of stock during the last fiscal year for the executive officers. The table should include the following columns:
  - Name of the executive officer
  - The number of securities for which the options were exercised
  - The aggregate dollar value realized upon exercise of the options or similar instruments
  - The number of shares of stock that have vested
  - The aggregate dollar value realized upon the vesting of stock or such similar transaction
- Provide a summary table containing pension benefits. The table should contain the following columns:
  - Name of the executive officer
  - Name of the plan
  - The number of years of service credited to the executive officer under the plan
  - The actuarial present value of the executive officer's accumulated benefit under the plan
  - The dollar amount of any payments and benefits paid to the executive officer during the last fiscal year

- Provide a summary table containing nonqualified defined contribution and other nonqualified deferred compensation plans. The table should contain columns for the following information:
    - Name of the executive officer
    - The dollar amount of aggregate executive contributions during the last fiscal year
    - The dollar amount of aggregate company contributions during the last fiscal year
    - The dollar amount of aggregate interest or other earnings accrued during the last fiscal year
    - The aggregate dollar amount of all withdrawals by and distributions to the executive during the last fiscal year
    - The dollar amount of the total balance in the executive's account at the end of the fiscal year

- For each contract, agreement, or plan that provides for payments to an executive officer as part of a termination or change in control of the business, provide the following information:
    - The circumstances under which a payment or other benefit would be triggered
    - A quantification and description of the estimated payments and benefits that would be provided in each circumstance, and who would provide these items
    - The determination of payments and benefits under the different circumstances
    - The conditions or obligations applicable to the receipt of payments or benefits, such as the use of non-compete agreements, and the duration and provisions of these agreements
    - Other material factors regarding each contract, agreement, or plan

- Provide a summary table containing the compensation of the directors for the last fiscal year. The table should contain columns for the following information:
    - The name of each director
    - The aggregate dollar amount of all fees earned as a director
    - The aggregate grant date fair value for awards of stock
    - The aggregate grant date fair value for awards of options
    - The dollar value of all earnings for services performed during the fiscal year pursuant to non-equity incentive plans, and all earnings on any outstanding awards
    - The aggregate change in the actuarial present value of the director's accumulated benefit under all defined benefit and actuarial pension plans, and the above-market or preferential earnings on compensation that is deferred on a basis that is not tax-qualified

- o All other compensation for the fiscal year that could not be reported in any other columns, such as perquisites, discounted stock purchases, insurance premiums, and consulting fees.
- o The dollar value of total compensation for the covered fiscal year.

> **Note:** Executive officers are considered to be the principal executive officer, principal financial officer, and the three most highly compensated individuals after the principal executive officer and financial officer.

In the interests of brevity, a substantially reduced example of these disclosures follows:

The company's named executive officers (NEOs) are: Gerald Evans, Chief Executive Officer (CEO); Bruce Nolan, President; Allison Vincent, Chief Financial Officer (CFO); Robert Tomberlin, Chief Operating Officer (COO); and Robert Miller, Senior Vice President (SVP).

The compensation committee adopted and implemented a new executive compensation program design for the NEOs in 20X3. The primary objective of the new design was to increase the amount that an executive's compensation is specifically tied to the operational and financial performance of the company. The following changes incorporate this new objective:

- The CEO was granted long-term equity incentives of which 80% are performance-based restricted stock units (RSUs) and 20% are time-based restricted stock units. The performance units only vest if threshold levels of certain operational and financial metrics are met during a three-year performance measurement period;
- All other NEOs were granted similar long-term equity incentives, using a 50/50 ratio of performance-based to time-based restricted stock units; and
- A new formulaic annual incentive cash bonus program was established based on the levels of achievement of three operational and financial metrics.

The company believes the changes made to its annual incentive cash bonus and long-term equity incentive programs for 20X3 represent a significant step toward enhancing its executive pay structure and further aligning its NEOs' pay opportunities with the interests of its long-term shareholders.

The company's executive compensation program is designed to reward its officers, including the NEOs, for creating long-term value for Ninja's shareholders. This approach allows the company to incentivize its executives for delivering value to shareholders while reducing or eliminating certain compensation if performance goals are not achieved. Ninja competes for the same talent against all companies in the New York area, and, therefore, a primary objective of its compensation program is to attract, retain and challenge executive talent.

The company's compensation program is comprised of elements common in the industry and each individual element serves an important purpose toward the total compensation package. The primary elements of the 20X3 executive compensation package are base salary, annual incentive cash bonus, and long-term equity incentives, as noted in the following table:

Component	Type of Payment/Benefit	Purpose
Base salary	Fixed cash payment with NEO generally available for annual increase	Attract and retain talent; designed to be competitive with comparable companies
Annual incentive cash bonus	Annual cash payments based on performance	Pay for performance tied to success in achieving annual revenue increase, total return on assets, and net profits after tax
Long-term equity incentives	3-year cliff vested performance RSUs	Align NEO compensation with that of long-term shareholders; performance RSUs vest at levels corresponding to the achievement of the three-year total shareholder return

Base salary provides our NEOs with a base level of income and is based on an individual's responsibility, performance assessment, and career experience. We have historically set base salaries for our officers within the third quartile of the competitive market to attract and retain the best talent, and base salary adjustments are made from time to time as a result of our review of market data.

The following table shows the percentage increase in base salaries for our NEOs, along with the actual base salaries of our NEOs for 20X2 and 20X3.

Named Executive Officer	20X2 Salary	20X2 Percentage of Salary Increase	20X3 Salary	20X3 Percentage of Salary Increase
Gerald Evans, CEO	$820,000	3%	$845,000	3%
Bruce Nolan, President	600,000	3%	618,000	3%
Allison Vincent, CFO	550,000	3%	567,000	3%
Robert Tomberlin, COO	460,000	3%	474,000	3%
Robert Miller, SVP	400,000	3%	412,000	3%

The 20X3 annual cash incentive bonus program is based on our pay for performance philosophy. For 20X3, the annual target cash bonus is stated as a percentage of base salary. The target award levels were set, in part, based on discussions with an independent compensation consultant regarding industry trends and competitive compensation data for similar executive positions of our peers. The following table displays for each NEO their target bonus opportunity and the calculation of their potential annual cash bonus, incorporating an actual achievement rate of 38% of the targeted performance levels.

Named Executive Officer	20X3 Target as Percentage of Base Salary	20X3 Annual Target Bonus	20X3 Annual Cash Bonus Potential Based on 20X3 Performance (38% of Target)
Gerald Evans, CEO	100%	$845,000	$321,000
Bruce Nolan, President	80%	494,000	188,000
Allison Vincent, CFO	60%	340,000	129,000
Robert Tomberlin, COO	60%	284,000	108,000
Robert Miller, SVP	60%	247,000	94,000

Long-term equity incentive awards are a critical element in our executive compensation design and are the largest component of an executive's potential compensation. To set the target level amount of long-term equity incentives, our compensation committee utilized position-specific marketplace data, comparing our 20X2 long-term incentive target for our NEOs to the market median provided by an independent compensation consultant. This marketplace data identified that the 20X2 long-term incentive targets for our NEOs were lower than the median of our peer group and led the compensation committee to increase the target for long-term incentives by 20% for each NEO. The following summarizes the 20X3 long-term incentive targets as a percentage of the NEO's base salary:

Named Executive Officer	Approved 20X3 Long-Term Incentive Target as a Percentage of Base Salary
Gerald Evans, CEO	400%
Bruce Nolan, President	300%
Allison Vincent, CFO	200%
Robert Tomberlin, COO	200%
Robert Miller, SVP	200%

The new performance RSUs granted to our NEOs will measure performance over a three-year performance period. Each NEO's performance RSU award payout opportunity ranges from zero to 200% of target depending on the level of performance, with performance levels above target intended to reward for overachievement. The compensation committee approved the following table of weightings and performance levels:

Metric	Threshold Performance (50% of Target)	Target Performance (100% of Target)	Challenge Performance (200% of Target)
3-year total shareholder return	> 25th Percentile	> 50th Percentile	> 75th Percentile

To determine payout levels, at the end of the three-year performance period, the performance metric will be compared to actual performance to determine the number of shares earned by each NEO. Performance below the threshold level will result in no credit awarded. Performance at or above the threshold level will result in computing the pro rata percentage points achieved. The compensation committee will certify the performance results.

The following table sets forth certain summary information regarding compensation paid or accrued by the company to or on behalf of the company's CEO, CFO, and each of the three most highly compensated executive officers of the company other than the CEO and CFO, who were serving as an executive officer at the end of the last fiscal year, for the fiscal years ended December 31 of 20X1, 20X2, and 20X3.

Name and Position	Year	Salary	Bonus	Stock Awards	All Other Compensation	Total
Gerald Evans, CEO	20X3	$845,000	$321,000	--	$25,000	$1,191,000
	20X2	820,000	279,000	410,000	25,000	1,534,000
	20X1	795,000	318,000	795,000	20,000	1,928,000
Bruce Nolan, President	20X3	618,000	188,000	--	43,000	849,000
	20X2	600,000	162,000	300,000	38,000	1,100,000
	20X1	582,000	204,000	582,000	12,000	1,380,000
Allison Vincent, CFO	20X3	567,000	129,000	--	21,000	717,000
	20X2	550,000	110,000	275,000	18,000	953,000
	20X1	534,000	155,000	534,000	--	1,223,000
Robert Tomberlin, COO	20X3	474,000	108,000	--	72,000	654,000
	20X2	460,000	92,000	230,000	60,000	842,000
	20X1	446,000	129,000	446,000	49,000	1,070,000
Robert Miller, SVP	20X3	412,000	94,000	--	--	506,000
	20X2	400,000	80,000	200,000	--	680,000
	20X1	388,000	113,000	388,000	20,000	909,000

The table below and the discussion that follows reflect the amount of compensation payable to each NEO upon the occurrence of the different circumstances of change of control, termination without good cause, or termination for good reason under each NEO's employment agreement and the company's change of control severance plan. The amounts shown assume that such termination was effective December 31,

20X3. The actual amounts to be paid out can only be determined at the time of each executive's separation from the company.

Named Executive Officer	Cash Payments	Benefit Cost	RSU Equity Acceleration	Total
Gerald Evans, CEO				
Change of control	$2,535,000	$30,000	$1,205,000	$3,770,000
Termination for good reason	845,000	10,000	1,205,000	2,060,000
Termination without good cause	1,690,000	30,000	1,205,000	2,925,000
Bruce Nolan, President				
Change of control	1,854,000	30,000	882,000	2,766,000
Termination for good reason	618,000	10,000	882,000	1,510,000
Termination without good cause	1,236,000	30,000	882,000	2,148,000
Allison Vincent, CFO				
Change of control	1,701,000	30,000	809,000	2,540,000
Termination for good reason	567,000	10,000	809,000	1,386,000
Termination without good cause	1,134,000	30,000	809,000	1,973,000
Robert Tomberlin, COO				
Change of control	1,422,000	30,000	676,000	2,128,000
Termination for good reason	474,000	10,000	676,000	1,160,000
Termination without good cause	948,000	30,000	676,000	1,654,000
Robert Miller, SVP				
Change of control	1,236,000	30,000	588,000	1,854,000
Termination for good reason	412,000	10,000	588,000	1,010,000
Termination without good cause	824,000	30,000	588,000	1,442,000

When calculating the compensation payable under all three of the preceding scenarios, the same formula applies to each NEO, which is:

- Upon a change of control, the individual is paid three times his or her ending annual salary, plus one year of medical insurance coverage, and all outstanding RSUs are immediately vested.
- Upon a termination for good reason, the individual is paid his or her ending annual salary, plus four months of medical insurance coverage, and all outstanding RSUs are immediately vested.
- Upon a termination without good cause, the individual is paid two times his or her ending annual salary, plus one year of medical insurance coverage, and all outstanding RSUs are immediately vested.

Item 12. Security Ownership of Certain Beneficial Owners and Management and Related Stockholder Matters

The SEC wants the shareholders of a business to know the share ownership of the executive officers and directors of a business, as well as the identities of the principal shareholders. The reporting requirements are:

- For any shareholders of more than 5% of any class of the company's voting securities, reveal the following information in tabular format:

  o Class of securities held
  o Name and address of owner
  o Amount and nature of ownership
  o Percent ownership of class of securities

- For any directors and executive officers, reveal the following information in tabular format:

  o Class of securities held
  o Name of owner
  o Amount and nature of ownership
  o Percent of ownership of class of securities

Also describe any arrangements that may subsequently result in a change in control of the company.

The following is an abbreviated example of the type of reporting that the SEC expects to see:

The following tables give information concerning the beneficial ownership of Ninja's common stock as of January 20, 20X4 by all directors, director nominees, all directors and executive officers as a group, and the persons who are known to Ninja to be the owners of more than five percent of the outstanding common stock of Ninja Cutlery.

Executive Officer and Directors

| Name | Shares Owned | | Shares Subject to Options Exercisable within 60 Days | Shares Underlying Restricted Stock Units | Total Beneficial Ownership |
	Sole Voting and Investment Power	Shared Voting and Investment Power			
Albert Cowling	40,000	--	--	45,000	85,000
Bronson Davis	120,000	--	40,000		160,000
Ephraim Foss	78,000	5,000	--	72,000	155,000
Garland Hill	12,000	--	20,000		32,000
Ichabod James	400,000	200,000	--		600,000
Kevin Land	200,000	13,000	--	10,000	223,000
All as a group	850,000	218,000	60,000	127,000	1,255,000

Principal Stockholders

Name and Address	Amount and Nature of Beneficial Ownership	Percent of Class
Mango Farms Trust 111 Main Street, Milpitas CA	8,000,000 (1)	20.00%
Nederland Family Trust 45 Brook Lane, Newbury MA	6,500,000 (1)	16.25%
Orehouse Mining Development Trust 300 Central Ave., Elko NV	4,000,000 (1)	10.00%

(1) Based on Schedule 13G filings with the Securities and Exchange Commission. These entities have sole voting and dispositive power of the shares owned by them.

Item 13. Certain Relationships and Related Transactions, and Director Independence

If there have been any transactions with related parties, they are to be disclosed. The SEC provides the following supporting commentary in regard to the level of detail that should be disclosed:

- Make note of any transaction since the beginning of the last fiscal year, or currently proposed, in which the company is or shall be a participant, and the amount involved is at least $120,000, and where a related person has a direct or indirect material interest. The following information is to be disclosed:

    o The name of the related person and the basis of the relationship
    o The related person's interest in the transaction, including the person's position or relationship with the entities involved in the transaction
    o The dollar value of the transaction
    o The dollar value of the amount of the related person's interest in the transaction
    o If there is indebtedness, the largest aggregate amount of principal outstanding during the disclosure period, the ending balance on the last practicable date, the principal paid and interest paid during the disclosure period, and the interest rate
    o Other information related to the transaction or person that is material to investors

- Describe the company's policies and procedures for the review, approval, or ratification of any related party transaction, as well as any transactions not requiring such review, or where a review was not followed.

For example:

> The board of directors has adopted a written policy for the review of transactions involving more than $120,000 in any fiscal year in which the company is a participant and in which any director, executive officer, holder of more than 5% of Ninja's outstanding shares or any immediate family member of any of these persons has a direct or indirect material interest. Directors, 5% shareholders and executive officers are required to inform the company of any such transaction promptly after they become aware of it, and the company collects information from directors and executive officers about their affiliations and the affiliations of their family members so the company can search its records for any such transactions. Transactions are presented to the board for approval before they are entered into or, if this is not possible, for ratification after the transaction has been entered into. The board approves or ratifies a transaction if it determines that the transaction is consistent with the best interests of the company, including whether the transaction impairs the independence of a director. The policy does not require review of the following transactions:
>
> - Employment of executive officers approved by the compensation committee
> - Charitable contributions to entities where a director is an executive officer of the entity, if the amount is less than $250,000 and less than 5% of the annual contributions received by the entity
> - Compensation of directors approved by the board
> - Ordinary banking transactions identified in the policy
> - Transactions in which all shareholders receive benefits proportional to their shareholdings
> - Transactions with entities where the related party's sole interest is as a non-executive officer, employee, or trustee of the entity.
>
> During fiscal year 20X3, there were no transactions requiring disclosure with related parties of the company.

Item 14. Principal Accountant Fees and Services

It is necessary to disclose the amounts paid to the company's auditors for their audit and other services. The SEC defines these disclosures as follows:

- Under the *audit fees* caption, the aggregate fees billed for each of the last two years for professional services rendered by the principal accountant for the audit of the company's annual financial statements and review of its quarterly Form 10-Q.
- Under the *audit-related fees* caption, the aggregate fees billed for each of the last two years for assurance and related services by the principal accountant

that are reasonably related to the performance of the audit or review of the company's financial statements. Describe the nature of these services.

- Under the *tax fees* caption, the aggregate fees billed for each of the last two years for professional services rendered by the principal accountant for tax compliance, tax advice, and tax planning. Describe the nature of these services.
- Under the *all other fees* caption, the aggregate fees billed for each of the last two years for products and services provided by the principal accountant. Describe the nature of these products and services.

For example:

The following table presents fees paid for professional services rendered for the audit of the company's annual financial statements for 20X3 and 20X2 and fees paid for other services provided by our independent auditor in those years:

	20X3	20X2
Audit fees (1)	$287,000	$272,000
Audit-related fees (2)	43,000	56,000
Tax fees (3)	91,000	87,000
All other fees (4)	20,000	15,000
Totals	$441,000	$430,000

(1) Fees for services associated with the annual audit (including internal control reporting), reviews of quarterly reports on Form 10-Q and accounting consultations.
(2) Fees for employee benefit plan audits and certain attestation services not required by statute or regulation.
(3) Primarily fees for tax compliance in various international markets.
(4) Fees for miscellaneous advisory services.

The Form 10-Q

A publicly-held company is required to issue the Form 10-Q to report the results of its first, second, and third fiscal quarters. The Form 10-Q includes not just the financial statements, but also a number of disclosures. The following table itemizes the more common disclosures. We do not provide examples of these disclosures, since they are essentially a sub-set of the information already described in the preceding section for the Form 10-K.

Selection of Form 10-Q Disclosures

Item Header	Description
Part I	
Item 1. Financial statements	Make all disclosures required by GAAP, including descriptions of: • Accrued liabilities • Acquisitions • Discontinued operations • Fixed assets • Income taxes • Related party transactions • Segment information • Stock options
Item 2. Management's discussion and analysis (MD&A)	Describe opportunities, challenges, risks, trends, future plans, and key performance indicators, as well as changes in revenues, the cost of goods sold, other expenses, assets, and liabilities.
Item 3. Quantitative and Qualitative Disclosures about Market Risk	Quantify the market risk at the end of the last fiscal year for the company's market risk-sensitive instruments.
Item 4. Controls and Procedures	Generally describe the system of internal controls, testing of controls, changes in controls, and management's conclusions regarding the effectiveness of those controls.
Part II	
Item 1. Legal Proceedings	Describe any legal proceedings currently involving the company, and its estimate of the likely outcome of those proceedings.
Item 1A. Risk factors	A thorough listing of all risks that the company may experience. It warns investors of what could reduce the value of their investments in the company.
Item 2. Unregistered sales of equity securities and use of proceeds	Describe any equity securities sold during the period that were not registered.

Item Header	Description
Item 3. Defaults upon senior securities	Describe any material default in the payment of principal, interest, or any other material default not cured within 30 days.
Item 4. Mine safety disclosures	If applicable, discuss mine safety laws, and the types of warnings and penalties that occurred during the reporting period.
Item 5. Other information	Any information required to be disclosed under the Form 8-K during the period, but not otherwise reported in this Form.
Item 6. Exhibits and financial statement schedules	Item 601 of Regulation S-K requires that a business attach a number of exhibits to the Form 10-Q, including (but not limited to): • Code of ethics • Material contracts • Articles of incorporation • Bylaws • Acquisition purchase agreements

Tip: Maintain a record of the questions asked during earnings calls, and see if any of them could have been addressed within the MD&A section (Item 2). This can form the basis for an increased amount of MD&A material in the next Form 10-Q.

The Form 10-Q must be filed within 40 days of the end of the fiscal quarter if the company is either a large accelerated filer or an accelerated filer. If that is not the case, it must be filed within 45 days of the end of the fiscal quarter.

Information to be Incorporated by Reference

It can be quite onerous for the accounting staff to repetitively state information in these reports that is already addressed elsewhere in the reports or in other SEC filings. This is a particular problem when a disclosure changes, and so must be updated in numerous places in the reports, with the attendant risk of missing an update. According to the SEC, it is acceptable to incorporate information by reference, subject to the following provisions:

- Financial statements incorporated by reference shall satisfy the requirements of the form or report in which they are incorporated. Financial statements or other financial data required to be given in comparative form for two or more fiscal years or periods shall not be incorporated by reference unless the material includes the entire period for which the comparative data is given.
- Information in any part of the report may be incorporated by reference in answer to any other item of the report.

- Copies of any information or financial statement incorporated into a report by reference shall be filed as an exhibit to the statement or report, with certain exceptions; in particular, information filed on a Form 8-K (see the Form 8-K Reporting chapter) need not be filed as an exhibit.
- Material incorporated by reference shall be clearly identified in the reference by page, paragraph, and caption or otherwise.
- When only certain pages of a document are incorporated by reference and filed as an exhibit, the document from which the material is taken shall be clearly identified in the reference.
- A statement shall be made that the specified matter is incorporated by reference at the place in the report where the information is required.
- Do not incorporate matter by reference in any case where doing so would render the report incomplete, unclear or confusing.

The incorporation of information by reference is to be encouraged, since it can result in a significant reduction in the amount of labor required to produce reports for the SEC.

Summary

This chapter has only addressed the contents of the annual and quarterly reports, and the speed with which they must be filed. For information about which parties must approve these reports prior to filing and how the reports are to be filed with the SEC, see the Closing the Books chapter.

Though the disclosure requirements noted in the Form 10-K section may seem inordinately detailed, they are actually highly compressed versions of the actual SEC regulations, and do not include the many pages of instructions and clarifying examples that accompany the SEC requirements. The complete SEC requirements are listed in the Code of Federal Regulations, Title 17, Parts 210 and 229. It is advisable to regularly review the source documents for these requirements, since the SEC periodically updates them (usually with additional reporting requirements).

Small company reporting requirements are somewhat reduced from those noted in this chapter, though the changes cannot be considered substantial. These reduced requirements are noted in the Code of Federal Regulations, near of the bottom of the main reporting requirements for each topic.

Chapter 9
Form 8-K Reporting

Introduction

The accountant might think that the filing requirements of the SEC stop with the quarterly Form 10-Q and annual Form 10-K. This is not the case. In addition, any material events that arise during the year must be filed on the Form 8-K. Depending on the activity level of a business, this could mean that reports are being filed on a weekly basis with the SEC. In this chapter, we cover the contents of the Form 8-K, and the amount of time allowed in which to file the report.

The Form 8-K

The Form 8-K is by far the most commonly-issued SEC filing. A public company uses it to disclose a broad range of material events that impact the business. The following rules apply to the Form 8-K:

- This report must be filed within four business days of the underlying event
- If the event occurs on a weekend or holiday, the four-day filing period begins on the next business day

The following table itemizes the types of disclosures that can appear in a Form 8-K, with selected examples provided.

Types of Form 8-K Disclosures

Item Header	Description
Item 1.01. Entry into a material definitive agreement	Refers to an agreement not made in the ordinary course of business. Disclose the agreement date, the names of the parties, and the general terms of the agreement. For example:
	On [date] the Company entered into an agreement with the New York City Port Authority to take over its ferry service to Staten Island. Under the terms of the agreement, the Company will provide ferry service on a cost-plus 5% profit basis for the next four years.

Item Header	Description
Item 1.02. Termination of a material definitive agreement	Refers to the non-standard termination of an agreement not made in the ordinary course of business. Disclose the termination date, the general terms of the agreement, the circumstances of the termination, and any termination penalties. For example: On [date] the Company terminated its agreement dated [date] to be acquired by Mega Corporation. The parties' acquisition application had been rejected by the European Union, and further negotiations with that entity made it clear that no adjustment to the proposed acquisition agreement would result in a positive outcome.
Item 1.03. Bankruptcy or receivership	If the business enters bankruptcy or receivership, identify the proceeding, the name of the court, the date when jurisdiction was assumed, and the identity of the receiver. There are additional disclosures regarding reorganization plans. For example: On [date] the Company filed a voluntary petition for bankruptcy relief under Chapter 11 of the United States bankruptcy code in the United States Bankruptcy Court, Western District of Missouri (case number 974356). Company management will continue to operate the Company as debtors-in-possession under the jurisdiction of the court. The bankruptcy filing is attached to this report.
Item 1.04. Mine safety – reporting of shutdowns and patterns of violations	Disclose the receipt of an imminent danger order issued under the Federal Mine Safety and Health Act, noting the date of receipt of the order, the category of the order, and the name and location of the mine involved in the order. For example: On [date], the Company received an imminent danger order issued by the Mine Safety and Health Administration under section 107(a) of the Federal Mine Safety and Health Act of 1977 at the Royally Rich mine in Cripple Creek, Colorado. The order was issued upon observation that two miners were not wearing fall protection while working on the elevated head pulley of a feed conveyor. The miners were standing in the feed hopper of the conveyor and were approximately 25 feet above ground level. The miners had been trained in the use of fall protection and harnesses were available to them, however the miners were not wearing harnesses at the time of the observation. No one was injured as a result of the incident and the order was terminated.
Item 2.01. Completion of acquisition or	Disclose the date of asset acquisition or disposition, describe the assets, and identify the counterparty. Also note the nature and amount of consideration involved. Further, note the source of funds for an acquisition, if there is a material relationship between the company

Item Header	Description
disposition of assets	and the source of funds. For example:
	On [date], the Company accepted for payment and began paying for all shares validly tendered and not properly withdrawn pursuant to the offer on or prior to the offer's expiration, and shortly thereafter, the merger was completed, with no stockholder vote required to consummate the merger. The Company has become a wholly owned subsidiary of Delta Corporation. As a result, a change of control of the Company occurred.
Item 2.02. Results of operations and financial condition	Disclose material non-public information regarding the company's results of operations or financial condition if it was publicly announced or released by someone acting on behalf of the company. For example:
	On [date], the Company issued a press release announcing its financial results for the quarter ended June 30, 20X1 and held a live audio webcast to discuss such results. In connection with this webcast, the Company is furnishing to the Securities and Exchange Commission the following documents attached as exhibits to this Current Report on Form 8-K and incorporated herein by reference to this Item 2.02: the earnings release attached as Exhibit 99.1 hereto, the conference call script attached as Exhibit 99.2 hereto and the webcast slides attached as Exhibit 99.3 hereto.
Item 2.03. Creation of a direct financial obligation	If the company enters into a material, direct financial obligation, disclose the date when the obligation began, describe the transaction, note the amount and terms of the obligation, and other material issues. If the company becomes directly or contingently liable for a material amount under an off-balance sheet arrangement, disclose the same information, as well as the material terms whereby it may become a direct obligation, the nature of any recourse provisions, and the undiscounted maximum amount of any future payments. For example:
	On [date], the Company and Banco International entered into a revolving credit agreement with an aggregate borrowing capacity of up to $40 million, including a $20 million sublimit for letters of credit. The agreement has a one-year term that may be extended for additional one-year periods subject to the consent of the lenders. The Company is required to repay in full all outstanding revolving loans under the agreement on the last business day of each June and December. All proceeds will be used by the Company for working capital, capital expenditures and other general corporate purposes. The Company's obligations under the

Item Header	Description
	agreement are secured by a first priority lien on substantially all of the tangible and intangible assets of the Company. In addition, the agreement contains covenants limiting the Company's ability to create or incur specified liens on its properties.
Item 2.04. Triggering events that accelerate or increase a direct financial obligation	If there was a triggering event that altered a direct financial obligation and the effect is material, disclose the date of the event, describe it, note the amount of the obligation, and the payment terms. For example: Effective [date], the Company paid all holders of its convertible debentures for accrued interest payable through June 30, 20X1. The Company did not pay the holders the principal amount of $100,000 due on the debentures at June 30, 20X1, all of which remain outstanding. The Company will continue to accrue additional interest on the principal amount at the rate set forth in the debentures until the principal amount is paid in full. The Company expects to pay all accrued interest due and the principal amount to all outstanding holders of the debentures after completing substitute financial arrangements, though there can be no assurance of the timing of receipt of these funds and amounts available from these substitute arrangements.
Item 2.05. Costs associated with exit or disposal activities	If the company commits to an exit or disposal plan, disclose the date of the commitment, describe the course of action, and estimate the range of costs for each major type of cost and in total. For example: On [date], the Company approved a restructuring plan that includes staff reductions and the consolidation of certain leased facilities. The Company expects to substantially complete these efforts by the end of its first quarter of fiscal 20X2. The Company anticipates incurring pre-tax restructuring charges of $9 million to $12 million, all of which would result in cash expenditures and of which $7 million to $9 million would be for one-time employee termination benefits and $2 million to $3 million would be for facilities-related costs. The Company is taking these actions to re-balance staffing levels to better align them with the evolving needs of the business. While the Company is reducing its staffing levels in the near-term, the Company will increase staffing in areas where there is increased demand and opportunity.
Item 2.06. Material impairments	If the company concludes that there is a material impairment charge, disclose the date of this conclusion, describe the impaired assets, and the facts and circumstances leading to the conclusion. Also note the

Item Header	Description
	estimated amount of the impairment charge. For example: On [date], the Company filed a Form 8-K related to its 20X0 announcement of a global program to transition its product line. In connection with this transition, the Company indicated that it would record non-cash impairment charges, primarily associated with the write-off of inventory and lease residuals of older equipment that the Company will stop selling as it transitions to the new generation of fully digital equipment. Results of operations for the fourth quarter of 20X1 will include a non-cash pre-tax impairment charge of approximately $170 million.
Item 3.01. Notice of delisting or failure to satisfy a continued listing rule	If the company has received notice that it does not satisfy a rule for continued listing on an exchange, disclose the date when any notice was received, the applicable rule not being satisfied, and actions the company will take in response to the notice. If the company has submitted an application to delist from an exchange, disclose the action taken and the date of the action. For example: On [date], in connection with the consummation of the merger, the Company notified the NASDAQ Stock Market ("NASDAQ") of its intent to remove its shares from listing on NASDAQ and requested that NASDAQ file a delisting application with the SEC to delist and deregister the shares. On [date], NASDAQ filed with the SEC a Notification of Removal from Listing and/or Registration under Section 12(b) of the Securities Exchange Act of 1934, as amended (the "Exchange Act"), on Form 25 to delist and deregister the shares.
Item 3.02. Unregistered sales of equity securities	If the company sells unregistered securities, state the date of sale and the title and amount of the securities sold. Also name the principal underwriters and the names of the persons to whom the securities were sold. Also note the aggregate offering price and the amount of any discounts or commissions paid. Also describe any terms under which the securities are convertible into company stock. For example: On [date], the Company filed a Form 8-K related to a merger with ABC Corporation. In connection with the merger, the Company issued and sold an aggregate of 45,000 shares of its common stock to three former stockholders of ABC, which shares will vest, and the forfeiture restrictions of such shares will lapse, over a period of three years. The shares were sold at a price equal to $14.25 per share. The Company issued such shares of its common stock in reliance upon Section 4(a)(2) of the Securities Act of 1933, as amended, as a transaction by an

Item Header	Description
	issuer not involving any public offering. The purchasers of the securities represented their intentions to acquire the securities for investment.
Item 3.03. Material modifications to rights of security holders	If there has been a material modification to the rights of security holders, disclose the modification date, the name of the affected class of securities, and the effect on the rights of the security holders. For example: On [date] the board of directors of the Company approved an amendment to the Company's Certificate of Incorporation increasing the number of authorized shares of common stock from 100,000,000 to 1,000,000,000. The board of directors believes that it is advisable and in the best interests of the Company to have available additional authorized but unissued shares of common stock in an amount adequate to provide for the Company's future needs. The unissued shares of common stock will be available for issuance from time to time as may be deemed advisable or required for various purposes, including the issuance of shares in connection with financing or acquisition transactions.
Item 4.01. Changes in registrant's certifying accountant	Disclose whether the company's existing independent accountant has resigned or been dismissed. Also disclose whether a new independent accountant has been engaged. For example: The Company, pursuant to the approval of its stockholders holding a majority of its outstanding shares, dismissed International Auditors on August 31, 20X2, as the independent certified accountant of the Company. The Company did not have any disagreements with International Auditors on any matter of accounting principles or practice, financial statement disclosure, or auditing scope or procedure for the Company's fiscal years ended October 31, 20X1, or October 31, 20X0. International Auditor's report in the Company's financial statements for the fiscal years ended October 31, 20X1 and October 31, 20X0 did not contain an adverse opinion or a disclaimer of opinion, and no such report was qualified or modified as to audit scope or accounting principles. The Company delivered a copy of this Form 8-K to International Auditors on September 1, 20X2 and requested that a letter addressed to the Securities and Exchange Commission be provided within ten (10) days stating whether or not it agrees with the statements made in response to this Item and, if not, stating the respects in which it does not agree.

Item Header	Description
Item 4.02. Non-reliance on previously issued financial statements or a related audit report or completed interim review	If the company concludes that previously issued financial statements contain errors and so should not be relied upon, disclose the date when this conclusion was reached and identify the financial statements and periods that cannot be relied upon. Also note the facts underlying this conclusion, and state whether the issue has been discussed with the company's independent accountant. For example: On March 15, 20X2, the Audit Committee of the Board of Directors of the Company concluded that the financial statements contained in the Company's Annual Reports on Form 10-K for the fiscal years ended on December 31, 20X1 and December 31, 20X0 should no longer be relied upon due to the combined effect of financial statement errors that the Audit Committee believes are material and are primarily attributable to the corporate policy related to the recognition of bill-and-hold revenue. The Company intends to file as soon as practicable restated financial statements for fiscal 20X1 and 20X0 in the Company's Annual Report on Form 10-K. The Audit Committee of the Company has discussed the matters disclosed in this Form 8-K pursuant to this Item 4.02 with the Company's independent registered public accounting firm, Major Auditors. Management is assessing the effect of the restatement on the Company's internal control over financial reporting and disclosure controls and procedures and will report its conclusion regarding the Company's internal control over financial reporting and the effectiveness of its disclosure controls and procedures in the 20X2 Form 10-K.
Item 5.01. Changes in control of registrant	If there is a change in control of the company, disclose the identity of the persons who acquired control, the date of the change in control, the basis of the control, the amount of consideration used by the acquiring person, the sources of funds used, the identity of the persons from whom control was assumed, and any arrangements between the old and new control groups. For example: On [date], Mr. Smith, the sole shareholder of the Company, consummated a sale of 30,000,000 shares of the Company's common stock to Widget Company for an aggregate purchase price of $27,000,000 in cash. Following the closing of the share purchase transaction, Widget owns a 100% interest in the issued and outstanding shares of the Company's common stock. Widget is owned and controlled by Mr. Louis Miller.

Item Header	Description
Item 5.02. Departure of directors or certain officers; election of directors; appointment of certain officers; compensatory arrangements of certain officers	If a director has resigned or will not stand for re-election due to a disagreement with the company, disclose the date of the resignation or refusal to stand for election, the positions held by the director, and describe the circumstances. If the director has sent written correspondence to the company concerning this matter, attach it to the Form 8-K. If a senior manager of the company resigns from the company or is terminated, disclose the date of the event. If a new senior manager is hired, disclose the person's name, position, and date of appointment, and compensation arrangements. For example: Effective [date], Paul Arundel was engaged by the Company as Chairman of the Board pursuant to the terms of an executive employment agreement. Mr. Arundel replaces Steven Jones as Chairman of the Board. Mr. Jones remains as a director. Under the Agreement, Mr. Arundel will have direct responsibility working in conjunction with the Company's Chief Executive Officer over Company operations. The initial term of Mr. Arundel's employment is three years. Mr. Arundel's base salary is $200,000 per year. He is to receive a signing bonus of $50,000 and is entitled to a quarterly bonus of up to $25,000 based on recognized revenues for the applicable quarter and additional bonuses at the discretion of the compensation committee.
Item 5.03. Amendments to articles of incorporation or bylaws; change in fiscal year	If the company amends its articles of incorporation or bylaws, disclose the effective date of the amendment, and describe the alteration. If the company changes its fiscal year, disclose the change date, and the date of the new fiscal year end. For example: By unanimous written consent effective [date], the Board of Directors of the Company determined to change its fiscal year end from September 30th to December 31st. The change is intended to align the Company's fiscal periods more closely with the seasonality of its business and to improve comparability with industry peers.
Item 5.04. Temporary suspension of trading under registrant's employee benefit plans	When a director or officer of the company is subject to a blackout period for an equity security, disclose the reasons for the blackout period, a description of those transactions to be suspended, the class of securities subject to the blackout, and the expected beginning and ending dates of the blackout period. For example: On [date], the Company initiated a blackout period event with respect to participants in The Newsome Bank 401(k) Plan & Trust, during which participants will be temporarily unable to direct or diversify investments in their individual accounts, including investments in the Company's common stock, or obtain distributions or loans from the Plan. The blackout

Item Header	Description
	period began December 30, 20X1 and is scheduled to end the week of February 15, 20X2.
Item 5.05. Amendments to the registrant's code of ethics, or waiver of a provision of the code of ethics	If there has been an amendment to or waiver of the company's code of ethics, disclose the date and nature of the event. If a waiver is involved, also state the name of the person to whom the waiver was granted. For example: On [date], the Company's Board of Directors adopted a code of business conduct and ethics, a copy of which is annexed as Exhibit 14.01.
Item 5.06. Change in shell company status	If the company was a shell company, and has ceased being classified as a shell, disclose the material terms of the transaction. For example: Upon completion of the Merger on February 10, 20X1 as reported in Item 2.01, the Company ceased being a shell company, as defined in Rule 12b-2.
Item 5.07. Submission of matters to a vote of security holders	If any matters have been submitted to shareholders for a vote, disclose the date of the meeting, whether it was a special or annual meeting, the names of the directors elected, and a summarization of each matter voted upon at the meeting. Also state the number of votes cast for, against, and withheld on each voting matter, as well as by individual director (if there is a director election). For example: On [date], the Company held its annual meeting of stockholders in Denver, Colorado. As of March 31, 20X1, the Company's record date, there were a total of 35,000,000 shares of common stock outstanding and entitled to vote at the annual meeting. At the annual meeting, 33,500,000 shares of common stock were represented in person or by proxy and, therefore, a quorum was present. A vote for one director was acted upon by stockholders at the annual meeting. The final voting results for the election of Mr. Brian Jones are as follows: • For – 29,250,000 • Against – 3,400,000 • Abstain – 100,000 • Broker non-votes – 750,000
Item 5.08. Shareholder director nominations	If the company did not hold an annual meeting in the preceding year, or if the date of this year's meeting is more than 30 days from the date of the preceding year's meeting, disclose the date by which a nominating shareholder must submit notice on Schedule 14N, so that the company can include any director nominations by shareholders in its proxy materials. For example: On February 15, 20X1, the Company announced that it will

Item Header	Description
	hold its 20X1 annual meeting of stockholders on April 21, 20X1. Because the new annual meeting date has advanced by more than 30 days from the anniversary date of the Company's 20X0 annual meeting of stockholders, in accordance with Rule 14a–5(f) under the Securities Exchange Act of 1934, the Company is informing stockholders of such change. Because the annual meeting will be held more than 30 days from the anniversary date of the 20X0 annual meeting, the deadline for stockholder nominations or proposals for consideration at the annual meeting set forth in the Company's 20X0 proxy statement no longer applies. Accordingly, if a stockholder intends to nominate a candidate for election to the Board or to propose other business for consideration at the annual meeting to be included in the Company's proxy statement relating to the annual meeting must be received by the Company at its principal executive offices no later than the close of business on February 21, 20X1. In addition, the proxy solicited by the Board of Directors for the annual meeting will confer discretionary authority to vote on any stockholder proposal presented at the annual meeting if the Company does not receive notice of such proposal prior to February 21, 20X1.
Item 6.01. ABS informational and computational material	Disclose any informational and computational material for asset-backed securities.
Item 6.02. Change of servicer or trustee	If a servicer or trustee has resigned or been replaced, or if a new servicer has been appointed, disclose the date and nature of the event. For a new servicer, describe the material terms of the agreement and the servicer's duties.
Item 6.03. Change in credit enhancement or other external report	If the depositor becomes aware of any material enhancement or support that was previously applicable for any class of asset-backed securities, and which has been terminated other than by contract expiration or the completion by all parties of their obligations, disclose the date of termination, the identity of the parties providing enhancement or support, the terms and conditions of the enhancement or support, the circumstances of the termination, and any early termination penalties.
Item 6.04. Failure to make a required distribution	If distributions are not made to the holders of asset-backed securities by the required date, disclose the nature of the failure.

Item Header	Description
Item 6.05. Securities Act updating procedure	If any material pool characteristic of an offering of asset-backed securities differs by more than five percent from the prospectus description at the time of issuance, disclose the characteristics of the actual asset pool.
Item 6.06. Static pool	The required disclosure concerns a special situation involving an offering of asset-backed securities, which would otherwise be disclosed in a prospectus.
Item 7.01. Regulation FD disclosure	The company may elect to disclose information under the provisions of Regulation FD (Fair Disclosure). For example: On June 15, 20X1, members of management of the Company will deliver a presentation at the ___ Conference in San Francisco, California. The presentation will include a slide presentation, a copy of which is being furnished as Exhibit 99.1. The Company will also make the presentation available on its website at ___.
Item 8.01. Other events	The company can, at its option, disclose any information that is not specifically identified elsewhere in the Form 8-K. This is typically only done if the company believes that the information will be of importance to the holders of its securities. For example: As a result of worsening economic conditions for the Company's investment in Bacon Holdings, a Canadian transportation and logistics company, based on preliminary estimates, the company expects to record an impairment charge of between $10 million to $15 million to write down the value of its investment in Bacon. Bacon was purchased by the Company in 20X0 for $60 million. The non-cash impairment charge will be reported with 20X1 fourth-quarter and full-year results. The charge is based on an impairment review of goodwill and other intangible assets recorded from the acquisition.
Item 9.01. Financial statements and exhibits	Attach the financial statements, pro forma financial information, and any other exhibits filed along with the Form 8-K.

The information presented in the preceding table, including the examples, was only intended to give an overview of the types of presentations that could be made in a Form 8-K. In reality, the presentations made would be more substantial, possibly including the text of underlying agreements or contracts.

Corporate counsel is usually responsible for the text to be included in each Form 8-K filing, and may work with the corporate controller to devise report presentations that involve accounting-related activities.

Summary

Depending on the types of activities in which a business is engaged, it is quite possible that Form 8-K filings will exceed all other types of SEC filings combined. The accountant should not downplay the importance of Form 8-K filings. This means that a detailed system of notifications should be constructed to ensure that all possible material events are forwarded expeditiously from all parts of the company to corporate counsel, who can then decide which items need to be reported to the SEC. Several controls related to this system of notifications are described in the Accounting and Finance Controls chapter.

Chapter 10
Insider Securities Reporting

Introduction

Certain holders of company securities are required by the SEC to report their holdings of those securities to the SEC, as well as changes to their holdings. In this chapter, we note which persons fall under these requirements, which SEC forms are used to fulfill the filing requirements, and several related matters.

Forms 3, 4 and 5

The SEC requires corporate insiders to file periodic reports with the SEC, disclosing their holdings in the company and any changes in that ownership. Corporate insiders are considered to be:

- Officers
- Directors
- Beneficial owners

The company officer is defined by the SEC as follows:

> [The]…president, principal financial officer, principal accounting officer (or, if there is no such accounting officer, the controller), and vice president of the company in charge of a principal business unit, division, or function (such as sales, administration or finance), any other officer who performs a policy-making function, or any other person who performs similar policy-making functions for the company.

A beneficial owner must also file reports. This is considered to be anyone who has a direct or indirect interest in the equity securities of a business, and who owns more than 10% of a class of the company's registered equity securities. This definition does not apply to brokers, banks, or employee benefit plans. Examples of beneficial owners are immediate family members if they share the same household. To arrive at the 10% figure, include any outstanding stock appreciation rights, options, and warrants. Options and warrants are to be included even if their exercise prices are currently above the market price (and so are unlikely to be exercised).

> **Note:** In this chapter, when we refer to a corporate insider, the term includes the officers, directors, and beneficial owners of company shares.

A corporate insider as defined in the preceding classifications must file the following reports, as indicated in the following table.

Form 3, 4, 5 Filing Requirements

Form Number	Form Title	Description
Form 3	Initial Statement of Beneficial Ownership of Securities	File when the company is registering equity securities for the first time (by the date when the registration statement is declared effective), or file within 10 days of a person becoming an officer, director, or beneficial owner. Lists company securities held.
Form 4	Statement of Changes in Beneficial Ownership	File within two business days of a change in ownership. Lists changes in company securities held. Direct and indirect ownership changes are reported on separate lines of the form. If the person acquires securities amounting to no more than $10,000, it is not necessary to file this form. The filing requirement continues for six months after a person has stopped being an officer or director of the issuer.
Form 5	Annual Statement of Changes in Beneficial Ownership of Securities	File when reporting any transactions that should have been reported earlier on a Form 4. Due 45 days after the end of the fiscal year. Is intended to be a summarization form to be filed at year-end, on which are noted all additional transactions for which a person was exempt from filing on a Form 4. The form should be filed within 45 days of the fiscal year-end of the business.

The Form 4 is the most frequently filed of the three forms, since there may be a large number of individual transactions requiring documentation over the course of a year, especially if a person actively buys or sells the company's securities.

The key information required on all three of these forms is approximately the same, and includes the following items:

- Title of security
- The amount and price at which securities were acquired or disposed of
- If a derivative security, the conversion or exercise price
- The amount of securities beneficially owned
- Whether securities ownership is direct or indirect; if indirect, state the nature of the ownership

The intent of these filings is to disclose to the public any changes in corporate ownership by insiders, which can be used to infer how insiders feel about the prospects of the business, based on their stock purchase and sale activity.

The issuing entity is not responsible for filing these forms, but must indicate in its annual proxy statement if it has knowledge of missing or untimely filings.

> **Note:** Corporate insiders are responsible for filing these forms, but the company frequently does so on their behalf, to ensure that the filings are made in a timely manner.

SEC Filing Codes

A corporate insider who must report information to the SEC can only do so with SEC filing codes. These codes are granted by the SEC, and are used as access codes to submit reports. The four SEC filing codes are:

- *Central index key (CIK).* This is a unique number that identifies the person or entity submitting a report. It is a public code.
- *Password.* This is a unique code that identifies a person as being authorized to submit a report. This is a confidential code.
- *CIK confirmation code (CCC).* This is a unique code used with the CIK noted above as part of a report submission. Its lower-case format is eight characters, where at least one is a special character and one is a number. This is a confidential code.
- *PMAC.* This is a unique code that is intended to authorize a password change. The format is similar to the CIK code just noted. This is also a confidential code.

To apply for these codes, an applicant must enter his or her name, address, phone, and e-mail address on an SEC form, have it notarized, and submit it to the SEC. The following table contains examples of what the codes look like that are then issued to the applicant by the SEC:

EDGAR Access Code	
[Recipient Name]	
CIK:	0123456789
Password:	bb@e8hge
CCC:	kjj4#fol
PMAC:	*yu3cozt

If a corporate insider needs to update any personal information or change passwords, he or she can do so on the Filer Management website maintained by the SEC on its www.sec.gov site.

Related Topics

Thus far, the concern of the public company accountant has been with the proper reporting of securities ownership on behalf of certain corporate insiders. In addition, the accountant, or at least corporate counsel, should be aware of the rights of the company in regard to short-swing profits by corporate insiders.

A short-swing profit is either the sale-and-purchase or purchase-and-sale of the issuer's equity securities that results in a profit during a six-month period. When there are short-swing sales, the SEC allows either the issuer or the owner of any issuer security acting on behalf of the issuer to initiate a lawsuit to recover the profits. There is a two-year limitation on such a lawsuit, starting on the date when the insider realized the short-swing profit.

An insider is still subject to the short-swing profit rule under the following two circumstances:

- If the individual leaves his or her position and then earns a short-swing profit within the next six months.
- If the individual has purchased the issuer's equity and is then promoted to an officer position, but prior to the sale of the securities.

The company could also warn its corporate insiders that they are prohibited by the SEC from selling company shares short. Short selling refers to the practice of selling securities owned by a third party, with the intent of buying the shares later and at a presumably lower price, and then returning the shares to the third party owner. Instead, the SEC requires that corporate insiders first buy and hold the company's securities for at least 20 days.

Summary

It is customary for a company to file Forms 3, 4, and 5 on behalf of its officers and directors. If the company elects to do this, the process should be under a formal procedure where the officers and directors commit to forward their securities transactions to corporate counsel on a timely basis. They should also give the company a power of attorney, under which the company is authorized to issue these filings on their behalf.

If individuals instead decide to create these filings by themselves, it is prudent for corporate counsel to discuss the filing requirements with them, as well as the dates by which these filings are to be made. Otherwise, the persons involved could be in violation of the SEC's reporting rules.

Chapter 11
Non-GAAP Reporting

Introduction

A problem for the accountant is dealing with situations in which GAAP accounting results in unusually poor financial results, when the underlying fundamentals of the organization are not really that bad. If so, there will be a temptation to explain matters to the investment community by altering the type of financial measures reported. For example, management might want to report earnings before certain additional charges, rather than the usual net profit figure. The SEC deals with these situations by allowing such reporting, but only if they are reconciled to the normal GAAP financial measures. This chapter addresses the SEC requirements for non-GAAP reporting, as well as how to apply policies and procedures to ensure that the SEC requirements are consistently applied.

The Disclosure of Non-GAAP Information

Some publicly-held companies want to present the best possible version of their results to the investment community, and do so by selectively disclosing only the better portions of their actual financial results. Such information is considered to be a *non-GAAP financial measure* by the SEC, which defines such information as follows:

> A non-GAAP financial measure is a numerical measure of a registrant's historical or future financial performance, financial position or cash flows that:
>
> (i) Excludes amounts, or is subject to adjustments that have the effect of excluding amounts, that are included in the most directly comparable measure calculated and presented in accordance with GAAP in the statement of income, balance sheet or statement of cash flows (or equivalent statements of the issuer); or
>
> (ii) Includes amounts, or is subject to adjustments that have the effect of including amounts, that are excluded from the most directly comparable measure so calculated and presented.
>
> A non-GAAP financial measure does not include operating and other financial measures and ratios or statistical measures calculated using exclusively one or both of;
>
> (i) Financial measures calculated in accordance with GAAP; and
>
> (ii) Operating measures or other measures that are not non-GAAP financial measures.

The result of issuing non-GAAP financial measures can be misleading, when compared to the actual results reported under GAAP. To mitigate the effects of this misleading information, the SEC's Regulation G requires certain additional disclosures. The following text is taken from the Regulation:

a. Whenever a registrant … publicly discloses material information that includes a non-GAAP financial measure, the registrant must accompany that non-GAAP financial measure with:

   1. A presentation of the most directly comparable financial measure calculated and presented in accordance with GAAP; and
   2. A reconciliation … of the differences between the non-GAAP financial measure disclosed or released with the most comparable financial measure or measures calculated and presented in accordance with GAAP.

b. A registrant, or a person acting on its behalf, shall not make public a non-GAAP financial measure that, taken together with the information accompanying that measure and any other accompanying discussion of that measure, contains an untrue statement of a material fact or omits to state a material fact necessary in order to make the presentation of the non-GAAP financial measure, in light of the circumstances under which it is presented, not misleading.

Regulation G also contains limited exemptions for certain foreign issuers of securities or in relation to proposed business combinations.

In summary, the SEC requires that any non-GAAP financial measures disclosed by a company must be accompanied by a reconciliation to a financial measurement that has been calculated using GAAP, and it should not be misleading. This means that non-GAAP financial measures can still be released; it is up to the reader of the presented information to examine the accompanying reconciliation and decide if the non-GAAP information is relevant to his or her investing needs.

An example of how Regulation G may be used to construct an information release is noted in the following example.

EXAMPLE

The reported net loss of Hegemony Toy Company was strongly impacted by the recognition of a $500,000 impairment charge against our goodwill asset. We believe that an adjusted net income measure more closely represents our actual performance, because it excludes the one-time, non-cash impairment charge. We define adjusted net income as the net income or loss of the company, less the impact of impairment charges.

Adjusted net income is not a financial performance measurement under GAAP. Adjusted net income has material limitations and should not be used as an alternative to such GAAP measurements as net income, cash flows from operations, investing, or financing activities, or other financial statement data contained within the financial statements. Because the adjusted net income figure is not defined by GAAP, and can be compiled in many ways, it may not be comparable to other similarly titled performance measurements issued by other companies.

The following table presents a reconciliation of Hegemony's adjusted net income to our net loss during fiscal year 201X.

	For the Year Ended December 31, 201X
Adjusted net income	$400,000
Impairment charge	(500,000)
Net loss	$(100,000)

Tip: Someone disclosing information may make public a non-GAAP financial measure through a speech or other form of oral presentation. If so, prepare a reconciliation of the non-GAAP measure to a GAAP measure on the company's website, and mention the web page location during the presentation. Alternatively, issue a Form 8-K in advance that contains this information.

Practical Application of Non-GAAP Financial Measures

Non-GAAP reporting is generally not advised. The problem is that managers tend to use it to rectify what they perceive to be short-term differences in GAAP results versus what they believe to be the "true" performance of the business. When these non-GAAP measures are continually included in the financial reporting and presentations of a business, it creates a perception in the investment community that the management team is always placing the best possible "spin" on financial results.

If non-GAAP reporting is to be used at all, it should only be applied to those rare cases where GAAP reporting appears to be causing a long-term imbalance between the reported results of a business and its underlying cash flows. For example, the long-term charging of intangible assets to expense that is related to an acquisition could be causing long-term losses, even though the organization is clearly generating positive cash flows. In this situation, settle upon a standard non-GAAP financial measure, and be prepared to use it consistently over a long period of time.

Non-GAAP Financial Measure Policies and Procedures

This section contains a number of policies and procedures that can be used to develop tight control over the use of non-GAAP financial measures in a company's reporting to the public.

Non-GAAP Financial Measure Policies

If management agrees that it is generally not advisable to report non-GAAP information, consider creating a policy whose intent is to restrict the situations in which such reporting can be used. A sample policy might be:

It is only allowable to report non-GAAP financial measures when both of the following criteria are met:

- Doing so results in a notable improvement in the quality of information provided to the investment community; and
- The improved reporting quality is expected to continue for several years.

The use and discontinuance of non-GAAP measures must be approved in advance by the disclosure committee. In addition, the audit committee must be notified in advance of these changes.

The intent of this policy is to keep an organization from adopting short-term non-GAAP reporting, as well as to narrow the circumstances under which such reporting is considered useful.

Another policy may be needed to deal with those situations in which non-GAAP financial measures are included in an oral presentation. The SEC requires that a reconciliation of these measures to GAAP be provided, either through posting on the company website or through a Form 8-K filing. The safer approach is to file a Form 8-K, since a website page may be hidden deep in the file structure of the site or inadvertently deleted. The following policy deals with this situation:

When a non-GAAP financial measure is to be included in an oral presentation to the public, the related non-GAAP to GAAP reconciliation must be included in a Form 8-K and filed at the same time as the presentation, or immediately thereafter.

A final risk to be addressed is that someone could include a non-GAAP financial measure in an oral presentation without warning anyone on the disclosure committee. If so, there will be no indication that a Form 8-K should be filed with the SEC, so that the company will not be in compliance with Regulation G. The following policy deals with this situation by requiring that the text of all oral presentations be vetted by the disclosure committee prior to use:

The text of all oral presentations to the public must be submitted to the disclosure committee for review at least three business days prior to the presentation date.

The date requirement is included in the policy in order to give the committee sufficient time to conduct a review of the text. From a practical perspective, the committee may not be able to conduct a formal meeting on such short notice, in which case the text of oral presentations can instead be submitted to the company controller, who checks the text for non-GAAP financial measures. Corporate counsel does not have a sufficient knowledge of GAAP to conduct this review.

Non-GAAP Financial Measure Procedures

There are several procedures that could be used to maintain tight control over the use of non-GAAP financial measures. The first of these procedures involves the use of the following approval form for the dissemination of non-GAAP financial measures. The form is intended to provide structure to the process of determining which non-GAAP financial measures shall be issued. The basic procedural steps are:

1. Note whether the form is intended to begin or halt the use of a non-GAAP financial measure, as well as the date on which the action is planned.
2. If the intent is to begin using the non-GAAP measure, indicate on the form the nature of the proposed measure, why the company should report it, the reporting duration, and how the measure is to be reconciled back to GAAP. Also, list on the form those SEC filings in which the measure is to be included on a recurring basis.
3. If the intent is to stop using the non-GAAP measure, instead list the reason why the measure is no longer needed in the "reason" block. There is no need to complete the other text blocks.
4. Obtain the approval signatures of every member of the disclosure committee.
5. Send copies of the completed form to everyone noted at the bottom of the form; in particular, a copy must be sent to the controller, since this person must ensure that the non-GAAP financial measure is either included in or excluded from the indicated SEC filings, as noted on the form.

Non-GAAP Financial Measure Approval Form

☐ Start request ☐ Stop request Trigger date: _____

Proposed Non-GAAP Financial Measure: EBITDA	Reason: Eliminates amortization related to ABC acquisition	Duration: Through the 10 year amortization period
Reconciliation to GAAP: Net profit + interest + taxes + depreciation + amortization		Added to these filings: 10-K, 10-Q

Approvals:

Corporate Counsel: _____
CFO: _____
Controller: _____

Filing: Copies to corporate counsel, IRO, and controller. Original in minutes of the disclosure committee.

It can also be useful to include a processing step in the procedure for the production of each SEC filing. This step covers two activities, which are:

1. Review the minutes of the disclosure committee to see if there are any changes to the approved group of non-GAAP financial measures.
2. Ensure that any new measures are included in or excluded from the relevant SEC filing.
3. If a non-GAAP financial measure is ongoing, compare its calculation to what was used in the immediately preceding SEC filing, to ensure that the calculation is consistent.

This process can be simplified by maintaining a report that lists the essential information about each approved non-GAAP financial measure. Referring to this report is easier than continually having to refer back to the original minutes of the disclosure committee. A sample report, using the information stated in the preceding approval form, is:

Sample Summary Report for Approved Non-GAAP Financial Measures

Non-GAAP Measure	Trigger Date	Filing Inclusion	Reconciliation
EBITDA	6/30/x2	10-K, 10-Q	Net profit + interest + taxes + depreciation + amortization

Another procedure can be used to determine whether the business is reporting approved non-GAAP financial measures in a consistent manner. This procedure can be used by the internal audit staff on an occasional basis. The procedure steps are:

1. Obtain copies of all approved and current Non-GAAP Financial Measure Approval forms from the minutes of the disclosure committee.
2. Match the forms to the SEC filings in which the non-GAAP financial measures are supposed to be included. Verify that the measures are included; if not, report an exception. If the measures are included, verify that the GAAP reconciliations are consistently applied in all filings; if not, report an exception.
3. Scan the indicated filings to see if any non-GAAP financial measures are included that were not approved; if so, report an exception.
4. Obtain copies of the Non-GAAP Financial Measure Approval forms related to the most recently terminated non-GAAP measures. Match the forms to the SEC filings in which the measures are no longer supposed to be reported. If present, report an exception.
5. Review all exceptions with the company controller.
6. Schedule a review date, on which all reported exceptions are to be investigated to see if they have been corrected on a prospective basis.

Summary

If non-GAAP financial measures are to be reported, be sure to apply them consistently across all forms of communication, such as 8-K filings, analyst calls, press releases, and the company website. The SEC might take notice if the presentation is not consistently applied, and require the company to standardize its use of the information. Given the annoyance of having to achieve this high level of reporting consistency, it is best to minimize the use of these financial measures entirely.

Chapter 12
Fedwire Payments

Introduction

Many of the reports that a publicly-held entity must file with the SEC can be filed with no fee payable to the SEC, such as the Forms 10-Q, 10-K, and 8-K. Other filings, such as the S-1, S-2, and S-3 stock registrations, require examination work by the SEC staff, and so a fee is payable to the SEC. The amount payable is stated within the "Calculation of Registration Fee" section located near the top of the applicable SEC form. The SEC will not begin its examination of these latter types of filings until the related payment has been received, so a company typically issues the required payment as expeditiously as possible, which is through the Fedwire system. In this chapter, we describe the Fedwire system and how the SEC is to be paid through it, as well as the less common approach of paying by check.

Fedwire

The Fedwire system is operated by the Federal Reserve System (Fed) in the United States. Fedwire is a same-day gross settlement system, where funds are immediately transferred to the recipient. The system settles payments with a simultaneous same-day credit to the account of the payee's bank and a debit to the account of the payer's bank. The Fed guarantees all payments made through the Fedwire system. The Fedwire system is primarily used for high-value payments, because the per-transaction fee is quite high, and so is cost-prohibitive for smaller payments. Also, once funds have been shifted to the payee and confirmed by the Fed, they cannot be recalled without the permission of the payee.

The following exhibit shows the process flow when a payment is made using the Fedwire system.

Fedwire Process Flow

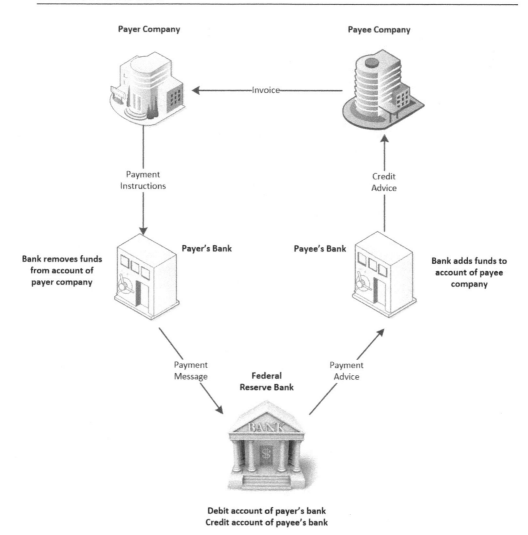

The basic process flow with the Fedwire system is for a company to send payment instructions to its bank, which removes the funds from the company's account and sends the payment instructions to the Fed. The Fed transfers the cash from the Fed account of the payer's bank to the Fed account of the payee's bank. The payee's bank then credits the bank account of the payee.

Fedwire Payment Instructions

If a company wishes to ensure the immediate receipt by the SEC of a payment for a filing, it should send the SEC a wire transfer using the Fedwire system. The recipient bank that handles wire transfer payments on behalf of the SEC is currently

U.S. Bank, based in St. Louis. The essential information to include in the wire transfer instructions is as follows:

- The American Bankers Association number, which is 021030004
- The receiving bank's name, which is TREAS NYC
- The U.S. Treasury account number designated for SEC filers, which is 850000001001
- The receiving account name, which is Securities and Exchange Commission
- The central index key (CIK) assigned to the filer (as discussed in the preceding Insider Securities Reporting chapter)

A sample transaction that incorporates this information is:

Transaction dollar amount	$5,000.00
Receiving bank ABA number	021030004
Receiving bank name	TREAS NYC
Receiving account number	850000001001
Receiving account name	Securities & Exchange Commission
CIK number	CIK0123456789

Wire transfers will be processed by U.S. Bank during its normal business hours, which are from 8:30 a.m. to 6 p.m., Eastern Time. Wire transfers received after closing time will be processed the next business day.

Tip: There is no need to establish an account at U.S. Bank in order to remit filing fees to the SEC; a wire transfer from the company's own bank is sufficient.

When a wire transfer is sent to the SEC, be sure to obtain the reference number associated with the transfer. This identifier can be used to trace where the funds were sent, in case the SEC is having trouble locating the funds.

Check Payments

In those rare situations when an organization is not in a rush to have a filing examined by the SEC, it may instead choose to pay by check. If so, make the check payable to the Securities and Exchange Commission. On the face of the check, note the following information:

- SEC account number: 152307768324
- The CIK number to which the payment is to be applied

The address to which checks are to be sent varies, depending on the mode of delivery. If a payment is sent via the United States Postal Service, mail to the following address:

Securities & Exchange Commission
P.O. Box 979081
St. Louis, MO 63197-9000

If a check is instead being sent via a common carrier (such as FedEx or UPS), mail to the following address:

U.S. Bank
Government Lockbox 979081
1005 Convention Plaza
SL-MO-C2-GL
St. Louis, MO 63101

Summary

The Fedwire system is nearly always used to pay the SEC. Payments are usually related to securities registrations, on which an organization has placed a high priority. Sending payments by check can seriously delay the date by which the SEC will agree to review these filings. Consequently, it is useful to have the Fedwire payment procedure in place and tested before a registration document is ready for filing.

The SEC periodically changes the bank through which it accepts payments, so before submitting a payment, check the SEC website to see if the payment instructions have changed.

Chapter 13
The Initial Public Offering

Introduction

When the owners of an organization want the business to be publicly-held, they must first prepare for and undergo the initial public offering (IPO) process, which is an expensive and time-consuming ordeal. This chapter contains a high-level review of the IPO, and also notes the reasons both in favor of and against engaging in this process.

Reasons for and Against an IPO

There are several reasons why the owners of a business may want to take it public through an IPO. The first is the perception that the owners can more easily sell their shares, or at least have the option to do so through a stock exchange. Second, being publicly held makes it easier to raise funds with which to operate the business or pay for acquisitions. Third, the absence of restrictions on the sale of shares tends to increase their price. Fourth, the increased ease with which a company can sell shares tends to reduce its proportion of debt to equity, which can reduce the risk of its financial structure. Another reason is prestige – taking a company public is considered by some to be the capstone of one's professional career. Also, the awarding of stock options has more meaning in a public company, since they can eventually be sold on a stock exchange. Finally, there is some evidence that the management team of a public company receives higher compensation than they would in a similar private company, so managers tend to be in favor of going public.

While these reasons may seem compelling, there are a number of other excellent reasons for *not* going public. First, it requires significant new expenditures for the services of auditors and securities attorneys, as well as additional in-house accounting, internal audit, and investor relations personnel. The cost of directors and officers liability insurance will also increase (possibly by several multiples of the prior amount). These incremental expenses may be large enough to eliminate the profits of a smaller organization. Also, the multitude of public company activities will take up some of the time of the management team, such as attendance at shareholder meetings, analyst meetings, earnings calls, and road shows. Further, the new owners of the business may demand that the company focus more attention on the immediate generation of profits, rather than the pursuit of longer-term goals. Also, there is a risk that required public disclosures might shift some competitive advantage to other players in the industry. In addition, there is some risk that the original owner will be forced out as part of an unfriendly takeover, which would have been impossible if the company had remained private. Further, investment bankers charge a high fee for raising capital through stock offerings, which a smaller business might find exorbitant. Finally, there are always alternatives to selling stock on the open market to raise funds, and which may be less expensive than doing so through an initial or secondary stock issuance.

In addition to the problems just pointed out with being public, smaller firms may also suffer from stock manipulation. When there are few registered shares outstanding, it is relatively easy for dishonest shareholders to create transactions that rapidly alter the stock price and allow them to sell out at a profit.

In short, there are a number of arguments both in favor of and against going public. Smaller companies will likely find that the cost of compliance with securities laws will erase a large part of their profits, and so may elect to remain private. A larger firm with more revenues will probably find that these costs only reduce profits by a relatively small amount, so that the overall benefits of being public outweigh those of being private.

Preparation for the IPO

A company should be preparing for an IPO several years before the actual event takes place. By doing so, the organization will have the appropriate system of controls and proper governance structures demanded by auditors, stock exchanges, the SEC, and the investment community. It may also be necessary to alter the asset base of the business, as well as to strip away low-growth or unprofitable business segments. The necessary changes are outlined in the following bullet points:

- *Auditors.* The company's auditors must be registered with the Public Company Accounting Oversight Board (PCAOB). Many auditors choose not to pay the fees or engage in the extra compliance activities required by the PCAOB, so it is entirely likely that the company will have to switch auditors. This also means that the fees paid for the annual audit will increase, since the larger and more sophisticated audit firms are the only ones registered with the PCAOB.

- *Advisors.* The company's advisors in many areas may not be accustomed to the demands of the public markets. This could mean that new advisors must be found to assist with risk management, taxes, controls, and other functional areas. In particular, the company's audit firm must maintain a high level of independence from the company in a public environment, and so can no longer provide certain services to the company, such as preparing tax provisions and assisting with the development of internal controls.

- *Asset reduction.* The investment community rewards companies that can operate lean, with a minimal asset base. Otherwise, a company needs more equity to fund its assets, which means that it must sell more shares, which in turn reduces the earnings per share that it generates. Reducing assets can require many actions, such as outsourcing manufacturing to eliminate fixed assets, tightening the credit policy to minimize accounts receivable, and having employees work from home in order to reduce facility investments.

- *Board of directors.* The existing board of directors may be comprised of company managers or friends of the owners. A higher level of governance can be achieved by replacing this group with a set of more independent directors who are willing to place the interests of investors ahead of the requirements of the managers. It can be useful to invest in a high-profile group of directors who sit on a number of boards, and so are experienced in public company governance.

- *Closing speed.* A publicly-held company is required to file financial reports with the SEC within a relatively short time period following the end of each fiscal quarter and year. If the accounting department is accustomed to a leisurely closing process, it may be necessary to impose a more regimented closing process that mandates specific release dates for the financial statements, along with the completion of disclosures to be included with the quarterly financial statements. This process includes having the necessary schedules prepared for the auditors, so that they can conduct their quarterly reviews and year-end audits.

- *Committees.* Part of the IPO process involves being listed on a stock exchange, which can greatly increase the amount of trading in a company's shares. Each stock exchange imposes its own governance requirements on those entities trading their shares on the exchange. This typically means that there must be an audit committee and compensation committee; both must meet regularly and record meeting minutes.

- *Growth focus.* Investors are much more willing to pay a high price for the shares of a company when it has a proven record of achieving a high rate of growth, year after year. Ideally, the growth should be concentrated in areas where the market has been rewarding other companies with high price/earnings multiples. To achieve this growth rate, review the various components of the business several years in advance of the IPO and eliminate those parts that have declining or tepid growth. Also, invest heavily in those parts of the business with the highest growth prospects. This can be a difficult task, especially if the owners are attached to the original core part of the business, which may no longer be growing.

- *Legal review.* The legal structure of the company, its contracts, and board minutes could all contain issues that could derail an IPO at the last minute. To ensure that all legal issues are discovered and corrected well in advance, hire a high-quality securities law firm well in advance of the IPO, and have them conduct a thorough investigation.

- *Management team.* The management team of a publicly-held business is expected to behave in a professional manner, create and adhere to a coherent strategic plan, and generally operate the business to benefit its shareholders. It is entirely possible that some members of the management team cannot meet these expectations, and so should be replaced. If so, conduct replacements far enough in advance of the IPO that the new managers are fully settled into their jobs.

- *Personal transactions.* In a closely-held business, the owners commonly mix their personal affairs with those of the business. For example, they may run personal vacation spending though the accounts payable system, or require the business to guarantee the loans of other businesses that are separately run by the owners. All of these personal transactions must be stripped away from the company well before the IPO, so that they do not appear in the financial statements for the two preceding years that must be presented to investors as part of the IPO.

- *Profitability.* It is not always possible for a high-growth business to report outsized profits, since it may be necessary to spend an inordinate amount supporting the high rate of growth – on new product development, new staff additions, product rollouts in new regions, and so forth. Nonetheless, there must still be a certain amount of attention to the bottom line, to keep prospective investors from believing that the company is suffering from runaway expenses. This means there should be a strong system of cost controls in place, perhaps supported by periodic consulting or benchmarking reviews to locate any areas in which costs can be further reduced.

- *Research and development (R&D).* If the company is competing based on its products, be sure to invest in a strong R&D group several years in advance. By doing so, there is a greater chance that the business will have a broader product line by the IPO date that is clearly differentiated from other products in the marketplace. This is a major concern. If a company has only developed a single unique product, and especially one with a limited lifespan, the organization cannot present a valid case to investors for why they should purchase its shares in an IPO.

- *Revenue threshold.* It is much easier to sell shares in an IPO to a small number of large investors, such as pension funds. These institutional investors will only buy shares if the company is sufficiently large to foster an active market for its stock. This means that the management team needs to grow the business to the point where its expected market capitalization will be at least $100 million. This is not an easy feat, and will likely require years of concentrated effort to achieve.

- *Stock options.* A review of the company's system of compensation may reveal a need to create a pool of stock options for future distribution to the staff. If so, it is easier to gain approval to set aside these options before the company goes public.

The multitude of requirements noted here should make it abundantly clear that several years (or more) of preparation are needed before a business is sufficiently ready to attempt an IPO.

A particular concern when ramping up to an IPO is tracking the point at which the number of shareholders exceeds 2,000 (recently increased from 500 under the JOBS Act), or when there are more than 500 accredited investors. When that number is reached, a company is a de facto public entity, which then triggers SEC reporting requirements – even if management had no immediate intent of becoming a public company. This issue can arise even when a company has only issued shares to a small number of individuals, since those people could sell their shares on secondary markets, thereby multiplying the number of shareholders. This situation is most common when a business is clearly successful, and so there is a perception in the investment community that its shares are particularly valuable – thereby making it easy for current shareholders to cash out for substantial amounts.

> **Tip:** Tightly restrict share issuances in the period leading up to an IPO. Also place restrictions on the re-sale of shares, such as prohibiting transfers until an IPO, or the retirement or disability of the shareholder. Also consider mandating a right of first refusal for the company.

One way to avoid having a company inadvertently go public is to only issue *phantom stock* to employees. These contrivances require a standardized calculation to determine the value of the company (such as a revenue or earnings multiple), and pay employees in cash when they want to "cash in" their phantom shares. This approach limits the number of actual shareholders to a very small group, but could require the organization to make large payouts to redeem the phantom stock.

In short, think long and hard before issuing shares to anyone during the initial years of a business – those shares have a way of being distributed further than was the original intent.

The Initial Public Offering

The following discussion of the IPO process represents the *approximate* flow of activities. In reality, there is some timing overlap between events. We have also clustered together some actions to improve the narrative flow. The intent is to give a sense of how the process works, rather than an exact series of perfectly sequenced steps.

When the board of directors believes that a company is ready to make the step from being a private company to a public company, it hires one or more underwriters to assist the entity in going public. An underwriter uses its contacts within the investment community to sell the company's shares to investors.

The choice of which investment bank to use as an underwriter depends upon a number of factors, such as the prestige of the bank, whether it has prior experience in the company's industry, the size of its contacts within the investor community, and its fee. A larger and more prestigious firm usually charges a higher fee, but also has a greater ability to sell the entire amount of a company's offering of securities.

> **Tip:** Obtain references from candidate underwriters and call the CFOs of those companies to obtain an understanding of the actual level of support that each candidate provides, as well as its expertise and willingness to continue to support the company.

The selected underwriter may enroll the efforts of additional underwriters to assist it in selling shares. This is more likely to be the case for a larger IPO, where it is more difficult to place all the shares that the company wants to sell.

> **Tip:** It is better to hire the services of an underwriter that has previously been a *managing underwriter*, which means that it has experience in managing the IPO process. If a bank has only been part of an underwriting syndicate, it may lack the requisite amount of experience.

The company negotiates the terms of a letter of intent with its preferred underwriter. The following are among the key elements of the letter of intent:

- *Fee*. The primary fee of the underwriter is a percentage of the total amount of funds collected. In addition, there are a variety of legal, accounting, travel, and other costs that it may pass through to the company for reimbursement.
- *Firm commitment or best efforts*. The underwriter will either agree to a *firm commitment* or a *best efforts* arrangement. Under a firm commitment deal, the underwriter agrees to buy a certain number of shares from the company, irrespective of its ability to sell those shares to third parties. This is preferable if the company is targeting raising a certain amount of cash. Under a best efforts deal, the underwriter takes a commission on as many shares as it can sell. If an underwriter insists on a best efforts deal, it indicates that there is some risk of not being able to sell the targeted number of shares.
- *Overallotment*. The underwriter may want the option to purchase additional shares from the company at a certain price within a set time period after the IPO date, which it can then sell to investors at a profit.

The underwriter will first engage in a detailed due diligence review of the company. The intent of this review is to ensure that the company is correctly representing itself to the investment community. The underwriter team will examine the company's financial statements and accounting records, contact business partners, investigate the backgrounds of the management team, and a great deal more. This level of investigation is needed to ensure that the information later presented in the company's filings with the SEC is correct. If a material point is missed, the underwriter could be liable, so this investigation is quite detailed. The underwriter may ask the company's auditors for a *comfort letter*, which declares that there is no indication of false or misleading information in the company's financial statements, and that the presented information is in compliance with the applicable accounting standards.

A legal firm is then hired that specializes in SEC filings to complete a registration statement. As noted in the preceding section, this firm may have been hired several years earlier, to prepare the company for its IPO.

The registration statement is mandated by the SEC, and contains a detailed review of the company's financial and operational condition, risk factors, and any other items that it believes investors should be aware of before they buy the company's stock. The primary categories of information in a registration statement are:

- Summary information and risk factors
- Use of proceeds
- Description of the business
- Financial statements
- Management's discussion and analysis of the business
- Compensation of key parties
- Related party transactions

There are a large number of additional categories of information, as well. As a result, the registration statement can be a massive document. Since the company's auditors and attorneys must review it several times and in great detail, it is also a very expensive document to create. We discuss this document at length in the Registration Statements chapter.

Once the SEC receives the registration statement, its staff has 30 days in which to review the document – which it will, and in excruciating detail. The SEC's in-house accountants and attorneys look for inconsistencies and errors in the registration statement as well as unclear or overblown statements, and summarize these points in a comment letter, which it sends to the company. Some of the comments made by the SEC involve substantive issues, such as the nature of the revenue recognition methodology used by the company, and which may call for a restatement of the company's financial statements. Other comments may note minor typographical issues, such as a missing middle initial in the name of a board member. The SEC does not impose a materiality convention on its staff for reviews – *all* parts of the registration statement are subject to review, no matter how minor the resulting changes may be.

The company responds to all of the SEC's questions and updates its registration statement as well, and then sends back the documents via an amended filing for another review. The SEC is allowed 30 days for each iteration of its review process. The SEC staff is in absolutely no hurry to assist a company with its IPO; consequently, this question-and-answer process may require a number of iterations and more months than the management team would believe possible.

Tip: High-end securities attorneys are extremely expensive, and totally worth the money, since they can minimize the number of question-and-answer iterations with the SEC, thereby accelerating the process of going public.

The underwriter supervises the creation of a road show presentation, in which the senior management team is expected to present a summary of the company and its investment prospects to prospective investors. These investors are likely to be mostly institutional investors, such as the managers of pension funds. The bankers and management team will go through a number of iterations to polish the presentation.

The management team and its investment bank advisors embark on a road show, which spans several weeks and takes them to a number of cities to meet with investors. If investors are interested in buying the company's stock, they tell the bankers how many shares they want to buy, and at what price.

> **Tip:** Do not sell fewer than one million shares during the initial public offering. Otherwise, there will not be a sufficient number of shares available to create an active market. Also, most stock exchanges require that at least one million registered shares be outstanding.

At this time, the company also files an application with the stock exchange on which it wants its stock to be listed. The stock exchange verifies that the company meets its listing requirements and then assigns it a ticker symbol. In addition, if it does not already have one, the company hires a stock transfer agent to handle the transfer of shares between parties. The company's legal staff will also submit filings to the securities agencies of those states in which the company anticipates selling shares (see the following Blue Sky Laws section).

From the period when the company files a registration statement with the SEC to the date when the SEC declares the registration statement effective, the federal securities laws limit the amount of information that the company can release to the public. This is known as the *quiet period*, and the intent is to keep from overheating investor expectations prior to sale of the stock, which could lead to an unwarranted bubble in the stock price. During the quiet period, no information should be released that would cause investors to change their stock holdings. For example, the following topics should be avoided in any releases to the public:

- Progress toward achieving company goals
- New sales made or contracts signed
- Major new product offerings
- Major new partnership deals
- Changes in the management team

This does not mean that all information is suppressed. A company can continue to publish factual business information that it has already been releasing on a regular basis, as long as the information is intended for recipients other than in their capacity as investors.

> **Tip:** The safest approach to dealing with information releases during the quiet period is to have corporate counsel give final approval of all information releases during this time period.

When the SEC is satisfied with the latest draft of the registration statement, it declares the filing to be "effective." The management team and its bankers then decide upon the price at which the company will sell its shares. A key determinant is the price at which institutional investors are most likely to buy shares, since they usually comprise a large part of the initial block of shares sold. Underwriters want to set the initial share price slightly low, so that there is more likely to be a run-up in the first trading day that they can publicize. Also, a slightly low price makes it easier to create an active aftermarket in the stock, since other investors will be interested in obtaining and holding the stock to realize additional gains.

> **Tip:** The underpricing of shares is most common in an IPO. If management wants to obtain the highest price per share, consider selling fewer shares during the IPO and more shares in a secondary offering, when the amount of underpricing is less extensive.

The underwriter traditionally likes to set the initial price of a share at somewhere between $10 and $20. Doing so may require a stock split or reverse stock split, depending on the number of shares currently outstanding. For example:

- A company has an initial valuation of $100 million, and has one million shares outstanding. To offer shares at an initial price of $20, there must be a five-for-one stock split that brings the number of shares outstanding to five million shares. Thus, a $100 million valuation divided by five million shares equals $20 per share.
- A company has an initial valuation of $80 million, and has 20 million shares outstanding. To offer shares at an initial price of $16, there must be a four-for-one reverse stock split that brings the number of shares outstanding to five million. Thus, an $80 million valuation divided by five million shares equals $16 per share.

The company then sends the registration statement to a financial printer. The printer puts the final stock price in the document, and uploads it to the SEC.

In those cases where there is more demand for shares than are to be sold, the underwriter is forced to allocate shares among its customers. The bankers will likely allocate more shares to their best customers, and may be somewhat more inclined to reduce allocations to those customers who are less likely to hold the stock for a reasonable period of time.

The underwriter sells the shares to the investors that it has lined up. The underwriter collects cash from the investors, takes out its commission, and pays the remaining proceeds to the company at a closing meeting. The underwriter is typically paid about five percent of the amount of the total placement, though this can involve a sliding scale where a larger placement results in an aggregate fee that is substantially lower. Conversely, bankers may not be interested in handling a smaller placement without charging a correspondingly higher fee.

The company is now listed on a stock exchange, has registered shares that are being traded among investors, and has presumably just received a large amount of cash for its efforts.

Blue Sky Laws

The state governments individually enacted blue sky laws to prevent securities dealers from committing fraud through the sale of fake securities to investors. The "blue sky" name is derived from being able to "sell the sky" to an investor without the restrictions of any regulations.

In essence, blue sky laws mandate that securities being offered for sale for the first time be qualified by the state regulatory commission, and registered with the state. Further, the terms and prices of the securities must follow the statutory guidelines imposed by the state. These guidelines are usually modeled on the Uniform Securities Act of 1956, for which the main provisions are:

- *Reason for existence.* The securities issuer is engaged in business. It is not bankrupt or in an organizational state, nor is it a blind pool, blank check, or shell company that has no purpose for being in existence.
- *Price.* The security is priced at a reasonable level in comparison to its current market price.
- *Unsold allotment.* The security is not related to any unsold allotments given to a securities dealer who has underwritten the security.
- *Asset base.* The issuer owns a minimum amount of assets.

Consequently, it is not possible for a securities dealer to market a company's stock for sale, unless the stock conforms to both state and SEC regulations. If a security is sold that does not conform to state blue sky laws, the following comment applies (as taken from section 410(a) of the 1956 Act):

> "Any person who offers or sells a security is liable to the person buying the security from him, who may sue… to recover the consideration paid for the security, together with interest at six percent per year from date of payment, [court] costs, and reasonable attorney's fees, less the amount of income received on the security, upon tender of the security, or for damages if he no longer owns the security."

The onerous penalties of the 1956 Act are a major concern for securities dealers, since its provisions may require them to buy securities back from investors. Since a buy back would only happen if securities had lost some or all of their value, the buyback could bankrupt a securities dealer. Given the ramifications of this penalty, securities dealers are very careful to ensure that blue sky laws are always followed.

An issuing entity is exempt from the blue sky laws if its securities are listed on a national stock exchange, such as the NASDAQ or New York Stock Exchange. For businesses listed in this manner, states issue a "manual exemption," which (despite the name) automatically allows securities to be sold within their borders. This exemption was initiated under the National Securities Markets Improvement Act of 1996.

The exemption is not so clear if an issuer's securities are only available for sale in the over the counter (OTC) market. If an issuer registers with one of the credit rating agencies and renews the registration each year, the majority of state governments will allow a registration exemption. This registration is a lengthy filing that includes the issuer's financial statements, the names of the executive officers of the business, and a description of what the entity does. Despite the presence of this registration facility, some states continue to require registration directly with them; these states are Alabama, California, Georgia, Illinois, Kentucky, Louisiana, New York, Pennsylvania, Tennessee, Virginia, and Wisconsin.

The content of blue sky laws vary by state. Consequently, if a company intends to sell its securities in a specific state, it should obtain legal advice in that state, to ensure that the local regulations are being followed. Also, anyone participating in a road show should be able to answer questions about the company's blue sky status, since this question is commonly asked by investors and brokers.

Summary

The requirements for going public are not especially onerous for a larger organization, but can be profoundly expensive and time-consuming for a smaller business. This means that the owners of smaller entities are well advised to delay the IPO process until their organizations have increased in size, and so can more easily absorb the requirements of an IPO while still operating the core functions of the business.

This chapter has described the process involved in having an initial set of shares registered with the SEC. This is only the first step on the long road of being a publicly-held entity, which also involves dealing with a stock exchange, managing the expectations of the investment community, and maximizing the stock float of the business. For more information about these additional activities, see the author's *Investor Relations Guidebook*.

Chapter 14
The Reverse Merger

Introduction

Though the traditional path to being publicly-held is the initial public offering, there is a way to back into this role, which is the reverse merger. This chapter describes the reverse merger concept, the circumstances in which it makes sense to engage in a reverse merger (or not), and other considerations related to the selection and price of a merger candidate.

> **Related Podcast Episode:** Episode 33 of the Accounting Best Practices Podcast discusses acquiring a public shell company. It is available at: **accounting-tools.com/podcasts** or **iTunes**

The Reverse Merger Concept

A company uses a reverse merger when it wants to avoid the expense of an initial public offering, and instead buys a company that is already publicly-held. In most cases, the company being purchased is nothing more than a shell company that has been inactive for several years. A shell company is an entity with no operations and minimal assets. By owning the public company, the buyer can now register stock for sale to the public, though it must now have its financial statements audited and issue regular reports to the SEC. Its shares will probably initially be available for trading on the over-the-counter (OTC) market, though it can apply to have its shares traded on a formal stock exchange.

The basic transaction flow for a reverse merger is that a private company gains control of a public shell company, with the shell structured to be the parent company and the buyer's company becoming its subsidiary. The owners of the private company exchange their shares in the private company for shares in the public company. They have now gained control over a majority of the stock of the shell.

The legal structure used for this merger is called a reverse triangular merger. The process flow for a reverse triangular merger is:

1. The shell company creates a subsidiary entity.
2. The newly-formed subsidiary merges into the private company that is buying the shell.
3. The newly-formed subsidiary has now disappeared, so the private company becomes a subsidiary of the shell company.

The reverse triangular merger is used to avoid the cumbersome shareholder approval process that is normally required for an acquisition. Though the shareholders of the private company must still approve the deal, it is only the shareholder of the new subsidiary that must approve the deal on behalf of the shell company – and the only shareholder of the new subsidiary is its parent company.

The reverse triangular concept is particularly useful, because it allows a private company to continue operating as a going concern and without a change in control of the entity. Otherwise, the business might suffer from the loss of any contracts that would automatically expire if either of those events were to occur.

> **Note:** It is easier to complete a reverse merger with a shell company whose shares only trade on the over-the-counter market, rather than on a formal exchange. The reason is that stock exchange rules typically require the approval of the shareholders of the shell company. Thus, it may make sense for a shell company to delist from an exchange prior to engaging in a reverse merger.

Other than the use of the reverse triangular merger concept, the reverse merger follows the normal set of steps used for any acquisition. The acquirer conducts due diligence on the shell, and the attorneys for both sides negotiate a purchase agreement. However, there is one additional requirement, and it is an onerous one – the filing of a Form 8-K with the SEC within four business days of the reverse merger. This filing contains many of the items found in a full-scale prospectus for an initial public offering, and so is a major production. It includes several years of audited financial statements, a comparative analysis of results over several periods, related party transactions, and so forth. This Form 8-K filing should be the source of considerable dread by the accounting staff of the acquiring business, since the four-day filing requirement makes it difficult to issue this document with the complete suite of required information.

Advantages and Disadvantages of the Reverse Merger

There are a number of advantages associated with the reverse merger concept, which are:

- *Speed*. A reverse merger can be completed in just a few months.
- *Time commitment*. If a company were to follow the tortuous path of an initial public offering, the management team would be so distracted that there would be little time left to run the business. Conversely, a reverse merger can be accomplished with such minimal effort that management barely notices the change.
- *No underwriters*. There is no need to engage the services of an underwriter, which means that their multi-million dollar fees can be entirely avoided. An underwriter is not needed, since no shares are being sold as part of a reverse merger.
- *Timing*. If the buyer is not immediately intending to use the shell to raise money from the public, it can take the reverse merger path even in weak stock market conditions.

- *Tradable currency.* Being public means that the stock issued by the combined entity is a more tradable form of currency than the stock of a private company, which makes it easier for an acquirer to engage in stock-for-stock transactions. Also, the shares of a public company are frequently valued higher than those of a private one (because the stock is more tradable), so the public company that engages in stock-for-stock purchases can do so with fewer shares. However, issued shares must still be registered if the recipient wants to sell them, which can be an involved process. Also, if the market for the company's stock is not large, it may be difficult for the recipients of its shares to sell them over a relatively short period of time.
- *Liquidity.* The reverse merger path is sometimes pushed by the current shareholders of a business, because they want to have an avenue for selling their shares. This is a particular concern for those shareholders who have been unable to liquidate their shares by other means, such as selling them back to the company or selling the entire business.
- *Dilution.* In an IPO, the underwriter wants the company to sell more stock than it really needs to, since the underwriter earns more money by collecting more cash from stock sales on behalf of the company. This dilutes the ownership of the original shareholders. In a reverse merger situation, the company typically raises only the amount of cash it needs, thereby limiting the amount of shareholder dilution.
- *Stock options.* Being public makes the issuance of stock options much more attractive to the recipients. If they elect to exercise their options, they can then sell the shares to the general public, while also obtaining enough cash to pay for taxes on any gains generated from the options.

Against these advantages are arrayed several disadvantages, which are:

- *Cash.* A company may not achieve an immediate cash inflow from the sale of its stock, as would be the case if it had taken the path of an initial public offering. Instead, a stock offering may be delayed until a later date.
- *Cost.* Even the lower-cost reverse merger approach still requires a large ongoing expenditure to meet the requirements of being public. It is difficult for an active business to spend less than $500,000 per year for the auditors, attorneys, controls, filing fees, investor relations, and other costs needed to be a public entity. In the author's experience, the actual figure is closer to $800,000 for the first year of operations, after which annual costs can be reduced into the $400,000 to $500,000 range.

> **Tip:** Do not engage in a reverse merger unless senior management is fully committed to making the necessary expenditures needed for a public company, such as extra accounting staff and more attention to control systems. Otherwise, the CFO and controller will be so harried that they will be rendered ineffective for all normal activities.

- *Liabilities*. There is a risk associated with buying the liabilities that still attach to the old public company shell. This risk can be ameliorated by acquiring only a shell that has been inactive for a number of years. The seller is rarely willing to personally commit to any representations and warranties regarding liabilities, so the acquirer is taking on these risks.
- *Stock price*. When a company goes public through a reverse merger, the sudden rush of selling shareholders puts immediate downward pressure on the price of the stock, since there are more sellers than buyers. When the stock price drops, this makes any stock options issued to employees less effective, since they will not profit from exercising the options. Also, if the company intends to use its stock to make acquisitions, it will now have to issue more shares to do so.
- *Thinly traded*. There is usually only a minimal amount of trading volume in the stock of a public shell company – after all, it has been sitting quietly for several years with no operational activity, so why should anyone trade its stock? Also, immediately following the purchase of the shell, the only stock that is trading is the original stock of the business, since no other shares have yet been registered with the SEC. It takes time to build trading volume, which may require active public relations and investor relations campaigns, as well as the ongoing registration of additional stock.

Tip: A good way to keep too much downward pressure from impacting the stock price is to impose waiting periods on the holders of company stock, so that there are no surges of sell orders hitting the market as soon as the company becomes publicly-held.

This lengthy list of problems with reverse mergers keeps many companies from engaging in them. In particular, take note of the annual cost of being public, and the issue with thinly-traded stock. The cost should completely block smaller companies from taking this path, while the lack of a market for the stock offsets the main reason for being public, which is having tradable stock.

The Price of a Shell

If a company wishes to purchase a public shell company, it should contact the local legal community to determine who has shells for sale. Shell companies are frequently acquired or fronted by attorneys who are responsible for maintaining them, usually for a number of years.

The price of a shell will certainly vary based on supply and demand, but the following factors also impact its price:

- *Assets*. Most shells have a small cash balance to pay for accounting and legal fees, but some have larger cash balances that will boost the price.
- *Liabilities*. If there are liabilities on the books of the shell, the buyer needs to take them into account. Some are valid, and will reduce the purchase

price. Other liabilities are so old that no one is actively trying to collect them. The attorney managing a shell has usually settled all liabilities already, perhaps by convincing creditors to accept equity in the shell as payment.

- *Legal and other issues.* If there have been legal issues in the past or other unresolved liabilities, and especially environmental liability problems, then these issues will seriously impact the price. However, a price reduction is not worth the risk associated with these issues, so a buyer would be better served by spending more to buy a cleaner shell.
- *Reporting status.* If the shell has continued to report its results to the SEC on a regular basis, this calls for less work by the acquirer to bring the reporting status of the entity up-to-date, so current reporting yields a more valuable shell.
- *Shareholders.* The foundation of an active market in a company's stock is a large number of shareholders, so if the shell has several thousand shareholders, it is considered more valuable than one with just a few. However, depending on the age of the shell, many of these shareholders may be inactive or have bad addresses, which make them less valuable to the buyer.

Tip: If there are potential legal issues or liabilities, the buyer can ask for an indemnification clause in the purchase agreement, so that the seller must reimburse the buyer for any liabilities settled after the purchase date.

These factors make it difficult to pin down a price for a shell. Generally, most shells sell for well under $1,000,000, with some clean shells selling for less than half that amount. The seller usually wants some stock in the acquiring company, as well.

Shell Due Diligence

Even though there may appear to be nothing about a shell company to review, the acquirer must *always* engage in due diligence, especially if there are to be no representations and warranties associated with the deal. There are admittedly fewer due diligence tasks to pursue than in a normal acquisition, since the shell has no operations. Nonetheless, the acquirer should investigate the following items:

- *Assets.* Though unlikely, there may be some non-cash assets still owned by the shell. If so, review them to see if they have any value, or can be profitably disposed of.
- *Auditors.* Have the financial statements of the shell been audited, and has the audit been conducted by auditors who are registered with the Public Company Accounting Oversight Board?
- *Board minutes.* Review the board minutes to search for any issues that may require additional investigation.
- *Contracts.* Are there any contracts that the company entered into when it was an operating entity that are still in force?

- *Historical business.* What was the original business of the company underlying the shell? Is there any reason to believe that the nature of the business makes it more likely that there will be undocumented liabilities?
- *Liabilities.* Search for any undocumented liabilities of the shell.
- *Litigation.* Have any lawsuits been filed against the shell, or has anyone threatened to do so?
- *Personnel.* Review the histories of anyone currently involved with the management or sale of the shell. Any prior lawsuit relating to shells is a major red flag.
- *SEC filings.* Review the shell's most recent filings with the SEC to see if it is a current filer.
- *SEC investigations.* See if the SEC has ever conducted investigations of the company, and the results of those investigations.
- *Shareholders.* Review the list of current shareholders. If there are many small shareholders, the acquirer may need to engage in a reverse stock split to flush them out of the shareholder records. For example, a number of shareholders own fewer than 100 shares of company stock. They can all be eliminated by enacting a 100-to-1 stock split, so that each one now holds less than one share. The company sends them a payment for these residual amounts, and they are no longer shareholders.
- *Shares.* Pay particular attention to the records of stock issuances and repurchases, and verify that the net amount outstanding matches the detailed stockholder list.
- *Structure.* Examine the certificate of incorporation and bylaws.
- *Trading patterns.* Has there been much trading volume recently in the shell's tradable stock? If so, it may indicate the presence of insider trading in anticipation of selling the shell to the acquirer.

This list is far shorter than the due diligence list needed for an operating entity, because it is targeted at those few aspects of a shell company that can cause problems for the acquirer. The acquirer should investigate all of the items noted here, since any one of them could uncover a serious issue.

Nearly every item in this due diligence list is related to legal issues. Therefore, it would be appropriate to have an all-lawyer team conduct the due diligence. These attorneys should have specific experience in due diligence investigations. Also, give the team sufficient time to investigate the shell thoroughly; mandating a one-day investigation presents a considerable risk of missing a problem.

A strong indicator of problems in a shell is missing documentation. This could simply be sloppy record keeping by the shell administrator, but a true professional understands that there has been plenty of time to "scrub" the shell and have everything laid out perfectly for an acquirer. Consequently, if contracts, shareholders votes, board minutes, and so forth are missing, it is time to look at other shells.

Trading Volume

One of the larger problems with a reverse merger is that the acquirer wants to use its publicly-traded stock to acquire other businesses, but there is only a minimal market for the stock. The trouble is that the shell company was not reporting its results for years, so no one has any interest in the stock. Also, the only trading has been in the shares that were tradable prior to the reverse merger, and there may be few of those shares in circulation. Further, institutional investors are usually barred by their own internal investment rules from buying stock in companies that are not listed on a stock exchange, or which sell below a certain minimum price point. This means that the owners of an acquisition target may not accept a stock payment because it would then be nearly impossible to sell the shares. In short, an acquirer who has bought a shell company needs to build the trading volume of its stock in order to make stock-for-stock purchases attractive to its acquisition targets.

It is not easy to increase trading volume. Here are several techniques for improving the situation:

- *Analyst coverage.* It is nearly impossible to gain analyst coverage of a new reverse merger company. It is possible, however, to pay for such coverage (as long as the payment is disclosed). The resulting analyst reports may generate some interest in the stock.
- *Investor relations.* The company should hire an investor relations firm and its own investor relations officer. They are both responsible for spreading news about the company throughout the investor community.
- *Road shows.* The senior management team should periodically go on road shows, where they talk about the firm to brokers and investors.
- *Create a message.* The investor relations people need to craft a message about the company that investors understand, and which they are willing to buy into. This message should be consistently applied over time, with the company's actions adhering to its statements.
- *Report consistent results.* The company does not want to startle the investment community with unexpected jumps and drops in its reported results. Instead, the senior management team and its advisors must use all of the communication tools at its disposal to convey its expectations for the company's results in the near term, so that actual reported results are usually close to the expectations that the company has established in the marketplace.
- *List on an exchange.* Gaining a listing on any stock exchange will probably increase trading volume, with higher volumes being associated with larger and more reputable stock exchanges. Each exchange has its own listing requirements, which typically involve some mix of shareholder, revenue, profit, and asset volumes that may be difficult for a smaller business to achieve in the near term. However, if the company has a consistent pattern of growth, it may eventually gain entry into a stock exchange.

A company may engage heavily in all of the preceding activities and still see little improvement in its trading volume. This is particularly likely when a company is in an industry that the investment community does not feel is "hot" at the moment. If so, the company could elect to reposition itself with a new strategic direction that would attract more investor attention.

Summary

One of the main subjects of this book is public company finance, which means that we explain ways to obtain financing. The reverse merger concept presents only a convoluted path to gaining additional financing, since one must first obtain a public shell company and then submit a registration statement to the SEC in order to sell additional shares. The more direct path to additional financing is an initial public offering, where shares are sold as part of the going-public process. Consequently, the reverse merger concept, despite its initially lower cost, is not the best way for a business to obtain additional financing.

Chapter 15
Registration Statements

Introduction

Ideally, investors want to have their shares registered, so that the shares are freely tradable. This status greatly reduces the risk to investors, who can immediately sell their shares for cash. However, the registration process is both expensive and time-consuming for a company, which must produce a large amount of carefully-formatted information for the SEC to peruse.

In this chapter, we describe the contents of the most comprehensive registration filing, the Form S-1, and also note the circumstances under which the less-onerous Form S-3 can be filed. We also make note of the Form S-8, which can be used to register shares issued to employees under an employee benefit plan.

Related Podcast Episode: Episode 93 of the Accounting Best Practices Podcast discusses stock registrations. It is available at: **accountingtools.com/podcasts** or **iTunes**

Form S-1

Investors are always the most interested in buying registered stock. A company that wants to sell registered stock must file a registration statement with the SEC. The Form S-1 registration statement is an extremely detailed document that describes a company's financial and operational condition, as well as other matters. Given its comprehensive nature, companies try to avoid filing an S-1, preferring instead the Form S-3, which is only available to companies that are considered seasoned public companies (see the following section for more information). If a company has only recently gone public, or has gone public by purchasing a public shell company, it will likely have to use an S-1 filing.

If a company has no alternative to an S-1 filing, it must set aside a substantial amount of staff time to complete the Form. The key points to be addressed in the document are noted in the following table.

Selected Form S-1 Disclosures

Item Header	Description
Item 3. Summary information, risk factors and ratio of earnings to fixed charges	Provide a summary of the information in the prospectus. Also include the mailing address and telephone number of the principal executive offices. In addition, discuss the most significant factors that make the offering speculative or risky. If the business is registering debt securities, show a ratio of earnings to fixed

Item Header	Description
	charges.
Item 4. Use of proceeds	State the principal purposes for which the net proceeds from the securities to be offered are intended to be used and the approximate amount intended to be used for each purpose.
Item 5. Determination of offering price	Where common equity is being registered for which there is no established public trading market or where there is a material disparity between the offering price of the common equity being registered and the market price of outstanding shares of the same class, describe the various factors considered in determining the offering price.
Item 6. Dilution	Where common equity securities are being registered and there is a substantial disparity between the public offering price and the effective cash cost to officers, directors, promoters and affiliated persons of the common equity acquired by them in transactions during the past five years, or which they have the right to acquire, include a comparison of the public contribution under the proposed public offering and the effective cash contribution of these individuals.
Item 7. Selling security holders	If any of the securities to be registered are to be offered for the account of security holders, name each such security holder, indicate the nature of any position, office, or other material relationship which the selling security holder has had within the past three years with the company, state the amount of securities of the class owned by the security holder prior to the offering, note the amount to be offered for the security holder's account, and (if one percent or more) the percentage of the class to be owned by such security holder after completion of the offering.
Item 8. Plan of distribution	State the name of the managing underwriter, the nature of the underwriter's obligation to take the securities, the manner of distribution, the basis upon which the securities are to be offered, the amount of distribution compensation, and related matters.
Item 9. Description of securities to be registered	Describe for the securities being registered their dividend rights, voting rights, conversion rights, interest and maturity (depending on the type of security), and so forth.
Item 10. Interests of named experts and counsel	If an expert is named in the registration statement as having prepared or certified any part of it, was employed on a contingent basis, or has a substantial interest in the company or was connected with the company as a promoter, managing underwriter, voting trustee, director, officer, or employee, describe the nature of the contingent basis, interest, or connection.

Item Header	Description
Item 11. Information with respect to the registrant	Describe the general development of the business, financial information about its segments and geographic regions, property holdings, legal proceedings, market information for the company's securities, financial statements, management's discussion and analysis of the business, disagreements with accountants, market risk, directors and executive officers, executive compensation, securities ownership, and many other matters. This is typically the largest part of the filing.
Item 11A. Material changes	Describe any material changes in the affairs of the business since the end of the latest fiscal year for which audited financial statements were included in the latest Form 10-K, and which have not been described in a subsequent Form 10-Q or Form 8-K.
Item 12. Incorporation of certain information by reference	If information located in other documents is being referenced in the Form S-1 filing, specific disclosure must be made of the location of this information in the other documents.
Item 12A. Disclosure of Commission position on indemnification of Securities Act liabilities	Describe the indemnification provisions relating to directors, officers and controlling persons of the company against liability arising under the Securities Act, along with a statement in the following form: "Insofar as indemnification for liabilities arising under the Securities Act of 1933 may be permitted to directors, officers or persons controlling the registrant pursuant to the foregoing provisions, the registrant has been informed that in the opinion of the Securities and Exchange Commission such indemnification is against public policy as expressed in the Act and is therefore unenforceable."
Item 13. Other expenses of issuance and distribution	Furnish an itemized statement of all expenses in connection with the issuance and distribution of the securities to be registered, other than underwriting discounts and commissions. If any of the securities to be registered are to be offered for the account of security holders, indicate the portion of such expenses to be borne by these security holders.
Item 14. Indemnification of directors and officers	State the general effect of any statute, charter provisions, bylaws, contract or other arrangements under which any controlling persons, director or officer of the registrant is insured or indemnified in any manner against liability which he may incur in his capacity as such.
Item 15. Recent sales of unregistered securities	Furnish information for all securities of the company sold within the past three years which were not registered, including the dates of sale and amounts sold, underwriter names, the type of

Item Header	Description
	exemption claimed, and the use of the proceeds.
Item 16. Exhibits and financial statement schedules	Furnish any exhibits referenced in the main text of the registration filing, including financial statement schedules. See the Exhibits to Registration Filings section for more information.

Completing the form properly requires the services of the company's auditors and securities attorneys, as well as their assistance when the SEC sends back several iterations of questions about the information in the form. It is likely that a number of months will pass before the SEC declares the form effective, which means that the stock listed in the form is now registered, and can be sold without restriction.

Form S-3

Whenever possible, a company tries to avoid the grief of an S-1 filing by instead using the Form S-3 for a securities registration. The great benefit of the S-3 is that a business can incorporate large blocks of information by reference. In particular, all information already filed in a company's Forms 10-K, 10-Q, and 8-K can be incorporated by reference.

Only an entity with the following characteristics is qualified to file a Form S-3 instead of a Form S-1:

- It is organized under the laws of the United States and has its principal business operations in the United States or its territories.
- It already has a class of registered securities.
- It has been filing periodic reports with the SEC for at least the past 12-month period.
- It has not failed to pay any dividend or sinking fund installment on preferred stock, and has not defaulted on any material debt repayment or lease payment.
- The aggregate market value of the voting and non-voting common equity held by non-affiliates of the company is at least $75 million. If a company does not meet this criterion, it can still register securities using the Form S-3, provided that it can meet the following three additional criteria:
  - The aggregate market value of the securities sold by the company during the preceding 12 months does not exceed one-third of the aggregate market value of the voting and non-voting common equity held by non-affiliates of the company; and
  - The company is not a shell company, and has not been a shell company for the past 12 months; and
  - The company has at least one class of common equity securities listed on a national securities exchange.

These requirements make it clear that the Form S-3 is only to be used by larger entities that have already been publicly-held for some time, and which have a substantial base of recurring filings with the SEC. Thus, a smaller business or one that has gone public through a reverse merger with a shell company will either have to use the Form S-1 to register stock, or resort to the sale of non-registered stock.

Form S-8

By filing a Form S-8 with the SEC, a business can register those securities that it has awarded to its employees under the terms of an employee benefit plan. The plan can be used to register a number of issuances of securities, such as:

- Common stock
- Restricted stock units
- Stock options
- Stock purchases allowed under an employee stock purchase program

The following individuals can all have their securities registered with a Form S-8 filing:

- Employees of the issuer
- Family of employees, if they receive securities through an employee gift
- Directors of the issuer
- Officers of the issuer
- General partners of the issuer
- Consultants providing services to the issuer

In the last case, securities issued to consultants can only be registered under the Form S-8 if the services provided by the consultants are not related to the sale of securities by the issuer.

The Form S-8 is especially useful for the following reasons:

- The form is considered effective as soon as the issuer files it, which is much faster than the usual registration process.
- The form requires little time to complete, in comparison to the vastly more elaborate Form S-1 that is used for other types of securities registrations.

The Form S-8 would be used more frequently, but it is restricted to those organizations that:

- Are publicly held; and
- Which have been timely in submitting their reports to the SEC for the past 12 months; and
- Which have not been classified as a shell company for at least the preceding 60 days.

In summary, the Form S-8 is much easier to use than other securities registration methods, but it is mostly applicable to shares issued to employees under employee benefit plans, which limits its use.

Exhibits to Registration Filings

The SEC requires that a number of exhibits be attached to registration filings, which can greatly expand the volume of information supplied. The following table shows the exhibit requirements, which vary based on the type of registration form being filed.

Exhibit Table for Registration Statements

Exhibit	Form S-1	Form S-3	Form S-8
Underwriting agreement	×	×	×
Plan of acquisition, reorganization, arrangement, liquidation, or succession	×	×	
Articles of incorporation	×		
Bylaws	×		
Instruments defining the rights of security holders	×	×	×
Opinion regarding legality	×	×	×
Opinion regarding tax matters	×	×	
Voting trust agreement	×		
Material contracts	×		
Statement regarding computation of per share earnings	×		
Statement regarding computation of ratios	×	×	
Letter regarding unaudited interim financial information	×	×	×
Letter regarding change in certifying accountant	×		
Subsidiaries of the registrant	×		
Consents of experts and counsel	×	×	×
Power of attorney	×	×	×
Statement of eligibility of trustee	×	×	
Invitations for competitive bids	×	×	
Additional exhibits	×	×	×

Brief descriptions of the exhibits noted in the preceding table are stated in the following bullet points:

- *Underwriting agreement.* Includes every underwriting contract with a principal underwriter under which the securities being registered are to be distributed.
- *Plan of acquisition, reorganization, arrangement, liquidation or succession.* Any of these stated plan types, but only if they contain information that is material to an investment decision and which is not otherwise disclosed.
- *Articles of incorporation.* Those articles of incorporation of the company, as currently in effect. If the articles are amended, a complete copy must be filed as an exhibit to the next registration statement or periodic report filed by the company.
- *Bylaws.* The bylaws of the company, as currently in effect. If the bylaws are amended, a complete copy must be filed as an exhibit to the next registration statement or periodic report filed by the company.
- *Instruments defining the rights of security holders.* This can include separate documents defining the rights of security holders, as well as the relevant portions of the articles of incorporation or bylaws of the company.
- *Opinion regarding legality.* An opinion from counsel regarding the legality of the securities being registered, indicating whether they will, when sold, be legally issued, fully paid and non-assessable, and, if debt securities, whether they will be binding obligations of the company.
- *Opinion regarding tax matters.* An opinion of counsel or a certified public accountant, or a revenue ruling from the Internal Revenue Service, supporting any tax matters and consequences to the shareholders as described in the filing. This exhibit is only necessary when the tax consequences are material to an investor.
- *Voting trust agreement.* Any voting trust agreements and related amendments.
- *Material contracts.* Every contract not made in the ordinary course of business which is material to the company, and is to be performed in whole or in part at or after the filing of the registration statement, or was entered into not more than two years before the filing.
- *Statement regarding computation of per share earnings.* A statement noting in reasonable detail the computation of per share earnings, unless the computation can be clearly determined from the material contained in the registration statement.
- *Statement regarding computation of ratios.* A statement setting forth in reasonable detail the computation of any ratio of earnings to fixed charges, any ratio of earnings to combined fixed charges and preferred stock dividends or any other ratios which appear in the registration statement.
- *Letter regarding unaudited interim financial information.* If applicable, this is a letter from the independent accountant, acknowledging awareness of the

use in the registration statement of a report on unaudited interim financial information.

- *Letter regarding change in certifying accountant.* A letter from the company's former independent accountant regarding its concurrence or disagreement with the statements made by the company in the current report concerning the accountant's resignation or dismissal as the company's principal accountant.
- *Subsidiaries of the registrant.* A listing of all subsidiaries of the company, the state or other jurisdiction of incorporation of each one, and the names under which they do business.
- *Consents of experts and counsel.* All of the written consents obtained from experts and counsel as part of the filing, which must be dated and manually signed.
- *Power of attorney.* If any name is signed on the registration statement under a power of attorney, file as an exhibit a manually signed copy of the power of attorney.
- *Statement of eligibility of trustee.* A statement regarding the eligibility and qualification of each person designated to act as trustee.
- *Invitations for competitive bids.* If the registration statement covers securities to be offered at competitive bidding, file as an exhibit any form of communication which is an invitation for competitive bid.
- *Additional exhibits.* Any document which is incorporated by reference in the filing, and which is not otherwise required to be filed.

The volume of exhibits to be filed for the Form S-1 as opposed to the Form S-3 should clarify the need to avoid an S-1 filing to the greatest extent possible. The work load is substantially smaller when the S-3 can be used instead.

Shelf Registration

A business engages in a shelf registration when it registers a new issuance of securities with the SEC, where the issuance is to be made sometime during the next three years. This approach means that a company has pre-approved securities in hand, which it can issue on short notice. A shelf registration is especially useful when issuing debt securities, since the time period during which the market rate of interest is low may be very short, and a company will want to issue the debt securities just as the interest rate bottoms out.

The SEC's Rule 415 governs shelf registrations. In brief, a shelf registration can be accomplished by filing a Form S-3, though only larger firms qualify to use this approach. A Form S-1 filing can also be employed, though only when the company intends to issue the underlying securities on an "immediate, continuous, or delayed basis," with all sale transactions concluded within the next two years.

Normally, a company cannot issue securities related to a shelf registration until the registration has been declared effective by the SEC. However, a shelf registration can be declared effective as soon as it is filed, according to Rule 462(e), but only when the issuer is a *well-known seasoned issuer* (WKSI). An issuer qualifies as a WKSI if:

- The market value of its stock owned by non-affiliates is at least $700 million; or
- The entity has issued at least $1 billion of non-convertible securities during the last three years, other than common equity, for cash.

A WKSI can only have securities declared effective on the filing date if the following circumstances apply:

- The registration statement is being used to register additional securities of the same class as was included in an earlier registration statement that was declared effective by the SEC; and
- The new registration statement is filed prior to the time confirmations are sent or given; and
- The new registration statement registers additional securities in an amount and at a price that together represent no more than 20% of the maximum aggregate offering price noted in the registration statement.

Registration Statement Effectiveness

Once a registration statement has been completed, it is filed with the SEC. The statement is assigned by the SEC to their staff, which reviews the document to see if the information it contains complies with SEC regulations. If so, the statement is declared effective; at that point, the securities listed in the statement are registered, and so can be sold.

It can be quite difficult to convince the SEC to declare a registration statement effective. The SEC staff typically spends one month examining the document, after which it compiles all issues found into a comment letter. The SEC's description of a comment letter is as follows:

> In issuing comments to a company, the staff may request that a company provide additional supplemental information so the staff can better understand the company's disclosure, revise disclosure in a document on file with the SEC, provide additional disclosure in a document on file with the SEC, or provide additional or different disclosure in a future filing with the SEC. There may be several rounds of letters from the SEC staff and responses from the filer until the issues identified in the review are resolved. These letters set forth staff positions and do not constitute an official expression of the SEC's views. The letters are limited to the specific facts of the filing in question and do not apply to other filings.

A comment letter may contain dozens of concerns that the SEC staff raises about issues contained within the registration document. Many may be picayune, at the level of adding a middle initial to the name of a director. Other issues will be major, such as a concern about how revenues or expenses are being recognized. Whatever the issue may be, the company must craft a response that clarifies the company's position, provides additional documentation, or states that the registration document has been altered to comply with the SEC's comments. This letter is then filed with the SEC, which then has another month in which to examine the revised information. This extended period may result in yet another comment letter or a declaration that the registration is effective.

An entity that is not used to dealing with the SEC may find that it must endure a series of comment letters that could last for months, while it sorts through the SEC's opinions of its documentation and gradually polishes the documents to a level that the SEC finds acceptable. A more experienced public company that has already undergone an SEC review may find that only one or two rounds of comment letters will be needed to gain an effectiveness declaration.

The cost required to craft a registration statement is amplified by comment letters, since the company's auditors and securities attorneys will be deeply involved in the creation and revision of all responses to these letters. Consequently, the more cycles of comment letters and responses that a company experiences, the greater the cost required to have its securities registered.

Summary

From the perspective of the accountant, the principal issue in writing a Form S-1 registration document is to not write this document at all. The S-1 requires a great deal of time to assemble, and will call for substantial amounts of time (and billings) by the company's auditors and securities attorneys to perfect. In addition, the inevitable questions from the SEC will result in prolonged reviews that will continually interfere with the work of the accounting staff. Consequently, it is better from an administrative perspective to transition to the Form S-3 as soon as possible, or convince qualified investors to purchase securities under one of the SEC's exemptions. See the Regulation A Stock Sales chapter and the Sale of Unregistered Securities – Regulation D chapter for more information about these alternatives.

Chapter 16
Regulation A Stock Sales

Introduction

The onerous stock registration requirements of the SEC are primarily intended for the sale of large amounts of stock, where a company can see a reasonable tradeoff between the effort of the stock registration and raising a large amount of capital. The tradeoff is not so apparent when a company only wants to raise a smaller amount, which is why the SEC offers an exemption from the stock registration requirements if the amount to be raised is somewhat smaller. In this chapter, we cover the rules under which a stock registration can be avoided under Regulation A.

> **Related Podcast Episode:** Episode 90 of the Accounting Best Practices Podcast discusses Regulation A stock sales. It is available at: **accountingtools.com/podcasts** or **iTunes**

Regulation A Stock Sales

Under Regulation A, a company can issue securities under two tiers. The more essential requirements associated with each tier are noted in the following table.

Regulation A Tiers

	Tier 1	Tier 2
Amount raised per year	$20 million maximum	$50 million maximum
Investment limitations	None	For non-accredited investors, 10% of the greater of income or net worth, per offering
Non-accredited investors allowed	Yes	Yes
Audited financials required	No	Yes
Registration required with SEC	Yes	Yes
Shares freely tradable	Yes	Yes
Ongoing reporting requirements	No	Yes (semi-annual)

The Regulation A exemption is not available to a number of types of companies. They are investment companies, foreign companies, oil and gas companies, public companies, and companies selling asset-backed securities.

If a company qualifies for this exemption, the basic process flow is to issue an SEC-reviewed offering circular to attract investors, then file a Form 1-A with the SEC, then sell shares, and then file a Form 1-Z to document the termination or completion of the offering. If the company is in Tier 2, it must then file a Form 1-K annual report that includes audited financial statements, a discussion of its financial results, and information about its business and management, related-party transactions, and share ownership. A Tier 2 company must also file a Form 1-SA semi-annual report that includes interim unaudited financial statements, as well as a discussion of the company's financial results. Finally, a Tier 2 company must file a Form 1-U within four business days of certain events, such as a bankruptcy, change in accountant, or change in control.

A key feature of Regulation A stock sales is that shares are freely tradable. This might initially appear to be an exceedingly valuable feature for investors. However, because the shares are not being traded on a public exchange, it still may be difficult for investors to sell their shares.

In short, Regulation A is designed to be a moderately streamlined way to raise a reasonable amount of cash. If there is a need to raise larger amounts of cash without going public, the Regulation D exemption (as described in the next chapter) is a better choice.

Solicitations of Interest

If a company is interested in issuing securities, it can deliver to prospective investors a document, scripted broadcast, or oral message to determine if there is any interest in the offering. This delivery can be made under the following conditions:

- The script of the message must first be delivered to the SEC
- The message states:
  - That money will not be accepted
  - That no sales will be made until an offering circular is delivered
  - That any indication of interest made to the company is not an obligation
  - The name of the company's chief executive officer
  - The business and products of the entity

- Sales cannot be made until 20 calendar days after the last delivery of the document or broadcast

If the delivered information is in the form of a document, it is permissible to include a returnable coupon that indicates an interest in the proposed offering, and which includes the name and contact information of a prospective investor.

Form 1-A

As noted earlier, a company selling stock under both tiers of Regulation A must file the Form 1-A before it begins selling stock. Creating this form is not a minor endeavor, since the topics it must address include the following:

- Proof of eligibility to take advantage of Regulation A

- Risk factors for investors investing in the offering
- Plan for distributing the securities
- Identification of any selling shareholders
- How the business plans to use the proceeds from the securities issuance
- Description of the business
- Description of significant properties owned by the business
- Management's discussion and analysis of financial condition and results of operations (see the Annual and Quarterly Reporting chapter for more information)
- Names of company directors, executive officers and significant employees
- Compensation paid to directors and executive officers
- Security ownership of management and a selection of its security holders
- Material interests of management in certain types of recent transactions
- Characteristics of the securities being offered
- Financial statements
- Exhibits, including the underwriting agreement, charter and bylaws of the business, rights of the security holders, subscription agreement, voting trust agreement, certain contracts, certain acquisition or reorganization plans, escrow agreements, and consents.

In the interests of brevity, not all topics were included in the preceding list; incidental or boilerplate items were excluded.

Even the briefest perusal of the contents of Form 1-A should make it clear that this report is not a minor undertaking, since it contains the essential requirements of a full registration filing. In fact, the SEC states on its instructions for completing the form that the estimated completion time is more than 600 hours. However, the Form 1-A does not require the company's financial statements to be audited. If the entity does not have its financials audited already, this can represent a significant cost reduction.

The Form 1-SA is a semi-annual report that is used to notify the SEC of the ongoing financial results and financial position of the issuing company. The report must contain management's discussion and analysis of the financial condition and results of operations of the company, as well as the following financial statements:

- An interim consolidated balance sheet as of the six-month period covered by the report, as well as a balance sheet as of the end of the preceding fiscal year.
- An interim consolidated statement of income for the six-month interim period covered by the report, as well as for the corresponding period of the preceding fiscal year.
- An interim statement of cash flows for the six-month interim period covered by the report, as well as for the corresponding period of the preceding fiscal year.

- Footnote disclosures as needed to ensure that the financial statements are fairly presented and not misleading.

This reporting requirement only applies to Tier 2 companies, as described in the preceding Regulation A Tiers table.

Summary

Regulation A provides for a relatively high cap on the amount of funding that can be raised directly from investors, making this a reasonable option for many businesses. However, those who have bought securities under Regulation A will likely press for the company to go public and be listed on a stock exchange. Otherwise, the investors will have a difficult time selling their shares to third parties. Consequently, the use of Regulation A can avoid the immediate need to go public, but may create more pressure to do so later.

Chapter 17
Sale of Unregistered Securities – Regulation D

Introduction

The requirements for registering shares are so onerous that a company may want to explore other alternatives that can bring in needed funds with less effort. One option is the sale of restricted stock under Regulation D to accredited investors. This approach is commonly used by businesses not willing to go public just yet, but can also be employed by organizations that have already gone public. In this chapter, we describe the essential requirements of a Regulation D stock offering, the nature of an accredited investor, and how a Regulation D sale is used as part of a private investment in public equity (PIPE) transaction.

> **Related Podcast Episode:** Episode 89 of the Accounting Best Practices Podcast discusses Regulation D stock sales. It is available at: **accountingtools.com/podcasts** or **iTunes**

Regulation D Stock Sales

Regulation D provides an exemption from the normal stock registration requirement. This is an exceedingly useful exemption, since unregistered shares can be sold to investors with a minimal amount of reporting to the SEC. Thus, the administrative aspects of registering shares are almost entirely eliminated.

The detailed aspects of Regulation D are described in the SEC's Rules 504, 505, and 506. In general, to sell shares under Regulation D, a company must follow these rules:

- Only sell shares to accredited investors (as described in a later section).
- Investors cannot be contacted through a general solicitation, such as advertising or free seminars open to the public.
- If shares are sold over a long time period, prove that all sales are covered by Regulation D (rather than being separate offerings). This can be done by documenting a financing plan, selling the same type of stock to all investors, showing that all shares are sold for the same type of consideration, *and* by proving that the sales are being made for the same general purpose.

Because of the inability to advertise a stock sale, companies usually turn to investment bankers, who contact their clients to see who is interested in buying shares. The bankers impose a fee for this service, which is a percentage of the amount of funds generated.

If a prospective investor is interested in buying shares, the company sends them a boilerplate questionnaire to fill out, in which they state that they are accredited investors. This form provides the company with legal protection, in case the SEC questions whether the stock issuance is protected by Regulation D. The questions posed by this questionnaire typically include the following:

- *Knowledge and experience.* The investor has sufficient knowledge of and experience in financial matters to be able to properly evaluate the merits and risk of the stock offering.
- *Restricted nature of shares.* The investor understands that the securities are restricted, and so cannot be sold until they have been registered.
- *Ability to invest.* The investor affirms that his/her total commitment to unregistered investments is not out of proportion to his/her net worth. Further, the investor has sufficient liquidity to provide for personal needs, and does not expect a change in liquidity that will require the sale of these securities at a later date.
- *Personal ownership.* The investor will hold the securities for his/her personal account, not with the intent of selling them to a third party.
- *Questions asked.* The investor affirms that he/she can question the company concerning the securities prior to purchasing them, and that these questions have been asked prior to the purchase.
- *Completeness of information.* The investor affirms that the information he/she provides in this questionnaire is complete and accurate.
- *Accredited investor qualifications.* The questionnaire also includes yes/no affirmations of each line item in the definition of an accredited investor, as described in a following section. This information is used to determine whether a prospective investor falls within the definition of an accredited investor, and so can purchase shares from the company under Regulation D.

Investors then send their money to an escrow account that is maintained by a third party, until such time as the total amount of funding meets the minimum requirement set by the company. The investment banker extracts its fee from the escrowed funds, the company collects its cash, and the company's stock transfer agent sends stock certificates to the investors.

Shares issued under Regulation D are not initially registered, which means that a restriction statement appears on the back of each certificate. This statement essentially prohibits the shareholder from selling to a third party. A sample statement is:

> The shares represented by this certificate have been acquired for investment and have not been registered under the Securities Act of 1933. Such shares may not be sold or transferred or pledged in the absence of such registration unless the company receives an opinion of counsel reasonably acceptable to the company stating that such sale or transfer is exempt from the registration and prospectus delivery requirements of said Act.

This restriction on the resale of stock is usually a concern for all but the most long-term investors. Accordingly, investors like to see one or more of the following guarantees being offered by a company:

- *Piggyback rights*. The company promises to include their shares in any stock registration statement that it may eventually file with the SEC. This is a near-universal inclusion in a Regulation D offering, since it does not impose an immediate obligation on the company.
- *Registration promise*. The company promises to file a registration statement with the SEC by a certain date. If the company is currently privately held, this promise essentially requires it to become publicly held, along with the various ongoing SEC filing requirements that are part of being a public company. A more onerous agreement will even require the company to issue additional stock if it does not obtain SEC approval of the registration statement by a certain date.

The downside of using a Registration D stock sale is that investors typically want something extra in exchange for buying unregistered stock. This may take the form of a reduced price per share. In addition, investors may demand warrants, which are a formal right to buy additional company stock at a certain exercise price.

EXAMPLE

Hegemony Toy Company sells 10,000 shares of its common stock for $10.00, along with 10,000 warrants to buy additional shares of the company for the next three years at $10.00 per share. The price of the company's stock later rises to $17.00, at which point the investor uses his warrant privileges to buy an additional 10,000 shares at $10.00 each. If he can then have the shares registered and sells them at the $17.00 market price, he will pocket a profit of $70,000 on his exercise of the warrants.

A company is paying a steep price if it issues warrants and then experiences a sharp increase in its stock price, since the recipient of the warrants will eventually buy shares from the company at what will then be an inordinately low price. If the company had not issued warrants, it would instead be able to later sell shares at the full market price.

If an investor wants one warrant for every share purchased, this is called 100% warrant coverage. If an investor agrees to one warrant for every two shares purchased, this is called 50% warrant coverage. These are the two most common warrant issuance terms, though any proportion of warrants to shares purchased may be agreed to.

An even more serious downside of using Regulation D is when prospective investors insist upon buying preferred stock, rather than common stock. Preferred stock may include a number of oppressive terms, such as favorable conversion rights into common stock, the payment of dividends, and perhaps even override voting privileges concerning the sale of the company or other matters.

Given the number of rights that investors may demand in a Regulation D stock sale, it is best to only use this approach when the company is operating from a position of strength, where it does not have an immediate need for cash.

The Form D Filing

An organization that sells shares under the provisions of Regulation D must file a report with the SEC concerning the sale. This is the Form D, which must be filed by the securities issuer no later than 15 calendar days after the date on which securities were first sold. This date is considered to be when the first investor is irrevocably contractually committed to invest. Examples of first sale dates are:

- When the entity receives a stock subscription agreement from an investor
- When the entity receives a check from an investor to pay for shares

An amendment to this form must be filed annually, if the entity is continuing to sell shares under the offering contained within the original notification. An amendment is also needed if there is a material mistake of fact or error in the preceding filing, or if there is a change in the information provided (with certain exceptions). The main types of information to be described on the Form D are:

- *Identity*. The name and type of entity of the issuer.
- *Contact information*. The location and contact information for the issuer.
- *Related persons*. The executive officer, directors, and promoter of the issuer, as well as their contact information.
- *Industry type*. The industry group in which the issuer is situated.
- *Issuer size*. The revenue range or aggregate net asset value range of the issuer.
- *Exemptions*. The federal exemptions or exclusions claimed, under which the shares are being sold.
- *Investment*. The minimum investment amount to be accepted from investors.
- *Sales compensation*. The identification of anyone receiving compensation as part of the stock sales, and the states in which solicitations are being made.
- *Offering and sales amounts*. The total offering amount, the amount sold, and the amount remaining to be sold.
- *Expenses*. The amounts of any sales commissions and finder's fees to be paid as part of the offering.
- *Use of proceeds*. The uses to which the resulting funds are to be put.

The amount of information required by the Form D is actually relatively small, compared to the much more comprehensive requirements of a formal securities registration document.

The Accredited Investor

An accredited investor qualifies under SEC rules as being financially sophisticated. The SEC definition of an accredited investor is:

1. A bank, insurance company, registered investment company, business development company, or small business investment company;
2. An employee benefit plan, within the meaning of the Employee Retirement Income Security Act, if a bank, insurance company, or registered investment adviser makes the investment decisions, or if the plan has total assets in excess of $5 million;
3. A charitable organization, corporation, or partnership with assets exceeding $5 million;
4. A director, executive officer, or general partner of the company selling the securities;
5. A business in which all the equity owners are accredited investors;
6. A natural person who has individual net worth, or joint net worth with the person's spouse, that exceeds $1 million at the time of the purchase, excluding the value of the primary residence of such person;
7. A natural person with income exceeding $200,000 in each of the two most recent years or joint income with a spouse exceeding $300,000 for those years and a reasonable expectation of the same income level in the current year; or
8. A trust with assets in excess of $5 million, not formed to acquire the securities offered, whose purchases a sophisticated person makes.

This definition comes from Rule 501 of the SEC's Regulation D.

A questionnaire is used to ascertain whether a prospective investor is accredited; elements of this questionnaire were noted earlier in the Regulation D Stock Sales section. The company should go to some lengths to ensure that all investors who intend to buy shares under Regulation D have completed and signed the questionnaire, since this represents the company's only evidence that it has sold shares to accredited investors.

Private Investments in Public Equity

When a publicly-held company's equity is sold to accredited private investors, this is referred to as a private investment in public equity (PIPE). Private investors are usually willing to engage in such a transaction when they are offered a discount from the market price of a company's stock, typically in the range of a 10% to 25% discount. The sale of securities under a PIPE can be structured in a number of ways, including the following:

- Common stock sold at a specific price point
- Common stock sold with warrants having fixed exercise prices
- Common stock sold with warrants having resettable exercise prices
- Common stock sold at a variable price point

- Convertible preferred stock
- Convertible debt

A major advantage of a PIPE is that it is considered a private investment by the SEC under Regulation D, so the shares do not have to be immediately registered with the SEC. Since no registration is required, the offering can be completed quickly and with minimal administrative hassles. A further advantage for the issuing company is that shares are typically sold in large blocks under a PIPE transaction to longer-term and more knowledgeable investors.

However, there are some disadvantages to entering into a PIPE transaction, from the perspective of the company. Consider the following issues:

- *Additional shares*. The company may have to guarantee the issuance of additional shares to PIPE investors if the market price of the shares subsequently falls below a threshold amount.
- *Rapid sell-off*. Unless the company is careful about which investors are allowed to buy shares in a PIPE deal, it may find that the investors sell off their shares as soon as possible after the shares have been registered, thereby driving down the market price of the stock.
- *Registration obligation*. The company is typically obligated to file a registration statement with the SEC shortly after the sale is completed, so that the investors can eventually have the restrictions removed from their stock certificates and can then sell their shares.
- *Short seller manipulation*. If the company is obligated to issue more shares to investors if the stock price declines, short sellers could take advantage of the situation by continually driving down the stock price, which triggers the issuance of more and more shares. This *death spiral PIPE* can even result in majority ownership of the company by the PIPE investors. The scenario can be avoided by specifying a minimum stock price below which no additional compensatory shares will be issued.
- *Warrants*. Investors may demand that they also be granted warrants, so that they can participate in any upside growth in the price of the company's stock.

Summary

The Regulation D option for fund raising is intended for those entities that are not yet willing to go public, or for those entities already reporting to the SEC as publicly-held entities, but which are trying to raise money quickly, without the wait required for a stock registration. We make note of Regulation D as a significant funding option, because it is typically one of the last avenues that an organization will take before it *does* go public, usually at the behest of the investors who bought shares under Regulation D, and now want to have their shares registered.

Chapter 18
The Jumpstart Our Business Startups Act

Introduction

The JOBS Act was passed in 2012, with the intent of making it easier for companies to raise small amounts of capital, both by opening up stock sales to the general public and by reducing the reporting requirements of businesses. In this chapter, we delve into the details of the Act and the subsequent commentary of the SEC on the subject, and also note which elements of it are most likely to succeed and which are less likely to assist in fund raising.

Provisions of the JOBS Act

The Jumpstart Our Business Startups Act became law in 2012 and has since been fully implemented by the Securities & Exchange Commission (SEC). The Act is divided into seven sections, the first five of which are summarized as follows (the final two sections dealt with administrative issues):

Title I – Reopening American Capital Markets to Emerging Growth Companies

The Act applies to an emerging growth company, which is defined as a company that had total annual gross revenues of less than $1 billion during its most recently completed fiscal year. Such an organization does not need to present more than two years of audited financial statements in order for its registration statement for an initial public offering of its common stock to be effective. In addition, the reporting of certain financial information is not required in the reports of the entity to the SEC. Information about the initial sale of these securities can be issued to the public, as noted in the following text from the Act:

> The publication or distribution by a broker or dealer of a research report about an emerging growth company that is the subject of a proposed public offering of the common equity securities of such emerging growth company pursuant to a registration statement that the issuer proposes to file, or has filed, or that is effective shall be deemed... not to constitute an offer for sale or offer to sell a security, even if the broker or dealer is participating or will participate in the registered offering of the securities of the issuer.

> A research report means a written, electronic, or oral communication that includes information, opinions, or recommendations with respect to securities of an issuer or an analysis of a security or an issuer, whether or not it provides information reasonably sufficient upon which to base an investment decision.

An emerging growth company or any person authorized to act on behalf of an emerging growth company may engage in oral or written communications with potential investors that are qualified institutional buyers or institutions that are accredited investors... to determine whether such investors might have an interest in a contemplated securities offering, either prior to or following the date of filing of a registration statement with respect to such securities with the [SEC].

Neither the [SEC] nor any national securities association... may adopt or maintain any rule or regulation prohibiting any broker, dealer, or member of a national securities association from publishing or distributing any research report or making a public appearance, with respect to the securities of an emerging growth company, either (1) within any prescribed period of time following the initial public offering date of the emerging growth company; or within any prescribed period of time prior to the expiration date of any agreement between the broker, dealer, or member of a national securities association and the emerging growth company or its shareholders that restricts or prohibits the sale of securities held by the emerging growth company or its shareholders after the initial public offering date.

In short, Title I is designed to slightly loosen the initial reporting requirements for a smaller business that wants to engage in an initial public offering, while also allowing it a greater degree of freedom in publicizing the prospective sale of its securities to investors.

> **Note:** The SEC has since clarified that it will not classify an asset-backed securities issuer or an investment company as an emerging growth company.

Title II – Access to Capital for Job Creators

The general theme of Title I continues, where the prohibition against the advertising of stock sales is dropped. However, this change only applies to accredited investors, which is a sub-group of investors previously only used for Regulation D offerings (see the Sale of Unregistered Securities – Regulation D chapter). Another allowed group (for advertising purposes) is qualified institutional buyers. The relevant text is:

The [SEC] shall revise its rules... to provide that the prohibition against general solicitation or general advertising... shall not apply to offers and sales of securities... provided that all purchasers of the securities are accredited investors. Such rules shall require the issuer to take reasonable steps to verify that purchasers of the securities are accredited investors...

The [SEC] shall revise [its rules] to provide that securities sold under such revised exemption may be offered to persons other than qualified institutional buyers, including by means of general solicitation or general advertising, provided that securities are sold only to persons that the seller and any person acting on behalf of the seller reasonably believe is a qualified institutional buyer.

Title III – Crowdfunding

The most interesting section of the Act is Title III, which relates to the concept of crowdfunding. In essence, this portion of the Act allows an organization to raise up to $1 million (inflation adjusted) from the investing public, with a cap on the amount of funds that can be raised from each individual. Information about the company must still be issued to the SEC and investors, so this is not necessarily a low-cost method for raising capital. The issuer also bears the risk of having to compensate investors for the amount of their investments plus interest, if the issuer made material misstatements of information as part of its solicitation of funds. The Act also provides limited regulation of the website portals that may be used as intermediaries to sell these securities to the public.

From the perspective of investors, securities can be purchased relatively easily, but cannot be transferred to another party (with certain limitations) for one year from the purchase date.

Being a longer section than the previous two, we will paraphrase its contents[1] as follows, rather than citing specific text:

- The aggregate amount that a company can sell to investors during a 12-month period is $1,070,000.
- The aggregate amount that can be sold to any single investor cannot exceed:
  - The greater of $2,200 or five percent of the annual income or net worth of the investor, if the annual income or net worth of the investor is less than $107,000; and
  - Ten percent of the annual income or net worth of the investor, not to exceed a maximum aggregate amount sold of $107,000, if either the annual income or net worth of the investor is equal to or greater than $107,000

EXAMPLE

An investor has annual income of $150,000 and a net worth of $80,000. The individual can invest the greater of $2,200 or 5% of $80,000. Therefore, the maximum possible investment is $4,000.

An investor has annual income of $200,000 and a net worth of $900,000. The individual can invest 10% of the $200,000 income, which is a $20,000 investment.

- A person acting as an intermediary in a crowdfunding sale of securities must register with the SEC as a broker or a funding portal, who will provide investors with investor-education information, and affirm that investors understand that they are risking the loss of their entire investments, and take steps to reduce the risk of fraud with respect to these transactions. Fraud reduction includes obtaining a background and securities history check on each officer, director, and person holding more than 20 percent of the outstanding

---

[1] The figures noted in this section are inflation-adjusted as of 2017.

equity of the issuing entity. No later than 21 days prior to the first day on which securities will be sold by an issuer, the person must make available to the SEC and to potential investors any information provided by the issuer. Also, the person can only forward funds to the issuer when the aggregate capital raised from all investors equals or exceeds the target offering amount.

- The issuing entity must file the following information with the SEC and other parties:
  - Its name and contact information
  - The names of the directors and officers, and each person holding more than 20 percent of its shares
  - A description of the business and its business plan
  - Its financial condition, for which the requirements differ as follows, depending on the amount of funding raised in the past 12-month period:
    - If $107,000 or less, its income tax return for the most recently completed year, and its financial statements (to be certified by the principal executive officer)
    - If more than $107,000 but not more than $535,000, its financial statements that have been reviewed by an independent public accountant
    - If more than $535,000, its audited financial statements
  - A description of the purpose and intended use of the proceeds from the stock offering
  - The target offering amount, the deadline by which the target is to be reached, and regular updates regarding progress toward that target
  - The price at which the securities are being offered to the public
  - A description of the ownership and capital structure of the issuer
- The company must also make at least annual filings with the SEC and report on the results of operations and its financial statements.
- If there are material misstatements in the company's representations, a person who purchases its securities can take legal action to recover the amount paid plus interest, minus the amount of any income received on the securities (such as dividends).
- The securities sold cannot be transferred by the seller for a period of one year from the date of purchase, unless the securities are transferred back to the issuer, or to an accredited investor, or as part of a registration with the SEC, or to a family member of the buyer.
- The dollar amounts noted in this section are to be adjusted for changes in the Consumer Price Index by the SEC no less frequently than once every five years.
- A person shall be disqualified from selling securities under the provisions of this Act if he or she is subject to an order that bars the person from engaging

in the business of securities, insurance, or banking, or has been convicted of a felony or misdemeanor in relation to the purchase or sale of securities or false filings with the SEC.

- The SEC shall exempt a registered funding portal from the requirement to register as a broker or dealer.

> **Note:** A funding portal is defined as any person acting as an intermediary in a transaction involving the offer or sale of securities for the account of others, that does not offer investment advice, solicit purchases or sales to buy the securities listed on its website, or compensate its employees for soliciting the securities listed on its website, or handle investor funds or securities.

This section of the Act may prove to be of limited use to organizations trying to raise money. These businesses are tightly restricted in terms of the amount of money they can raise, must still provide periodic reports to the SEC and investors, and are liable for any material misstatements made to investors. In addition, if the amount to be raised is greater than $535,000, an organization must produce audited financial statements; given the cost of an audit, many firms may conclude that the real limitation on fund raising is actually $535,000, rather than $1,070,000. Given these limitations, companies may instead use more traditional fund raising methods, such as Regulation D stock sales to accredited investors.

Title IV – Small Company Capital Formation

The Act also provides for an increase in the amount of funding that can be raised under Regulation A within a 12-month period, to $50 million (see the Regulation A Stock Sales chapter for more information). The following additional changes are made:

- The securities are not to be considered restricted, and so may be sold to third parties.
- The issuer can solicit interest in the offering prior to the filing of an offering statement
- The issuer must file audited financial statements with the SEC each year
- The SEC can adjust the offering amount limitation at regular intervals

While these changes certainly make the use of Regulation A securities sales more palatable to issuers, the increased filing requirements associated with the changes would make the owners of a business question whether it would be more cost-effective to simply engage in an initial public offering and sell registered shares.

Title V – Private Company Flexibility and Growth

This section takes an expanded view of the mass of an organization before it is considered to be a publicly-held entity. For this to be the case, an entity must now have assets exceeding $10 million, as well as a class of equity security that is held by at least either 2,000 individuals or 500 accredited investors.

This is a welcome change, which allows a privately-held business to issue shares to a considerably larger number of employees and outside investors without having to worry about being forced into public company reporting requirements.

Summary

Though the crowdfunding concept is interesting, the reduced level of reporting over the requirements for a publicly-held business means that crowdfunding could be subject to abuse. Also, the annual fund raising limitation for a business is so small that crowdfunding is likely to be a viable alternative only for the smallest startup companies. Further, a prospective issuer will likely compare the amount of money to be gained to the level of required information reporting, and conclude that the trade-off is not a reasonable one. In many cases, the Regulation A and Regulation D fund raising options noted in the preceding two chapters present a better trade-off of funds received to offsetting reporting requirements.

Chapter 19
Sale of Unregistered Securities – Rule 144

Introduction

The primary financing intent of a public company is to sell its own shares to investors. In addition, the entity typically endeavors to register the shares of early shareholders in the business, or shares issued to the owners of acquirees. There will be circumstances in which it can be difficult or expensive for the company to register these shares. If so, it needs to provide an alternative path to liquidity for its shareholders. One possibility is provided by the SEC's Rule 144, which is described in this chapter.

> **Related Podcast Episode:** Episode 94 of the Accounting Best Practices Podcast discusses Rule 144. It is available at: **accountingtools.com/podcasts** or **iTunes**

Rule 144 Stock Sales

A company is not always in a position where it can register the shares held by certain investors, since the necessary registrations are expensive and can take a long time to complete. These investors may want to sell their shares in the near term; to do so, they must first have the restrictions removed from their stock certificates. A possible alternative for these investors is the SEC's Rule 144.

Under Rule 144, someone who wants to sell his share holdings to the public must abide by these five conditions:

- *Holding period.* If the issuing company is a public company and is making its regularly-scheduled filings with the SEC, the shareholder must hold the shares for at least six months. The holding period begins when the shareholder bought and paid for the shares.
- *Adequate current information.* The issuing company must be currently fulfilling its filing obligations with the SEC.
- *Trading volume formula.* If the shareholder is an affiliate of the issuing company, the maximum number of shares that can be sold during any three-month period cannot exceed the greater of 1% of the outstanding shares of the same class being sold, or if the class is listed on a stock exchange, the greater of 1% or the average reported weekly trading volume during the four weeks preceding the filing of a notice of sale on Form 144. If shares are only listed over-the-counter, then they can only be sold using the 1% measurement.

> Note: An *affiliate* is a person who can exercise control over the issuer, such as an executive officer, a director, or a large shareholder.

- *Ordinary brokerage transactions.* If the seller is an affiliate of the company, all stock sales made by the seller must be handled as routine trading transactions. Brokers cannot receive more than a normal commission on these sales. The seller and broker are not allowed to solicit orders to buy the shares that are up for sale.
- *Notice of proposed sale.* If the seller is an affiliate of the company, the SEC must be informed of the proposed sale on Form 144 if the sale is for more than 5,000 shares or the aggregate dollar amount is greater than $50,000 in any three-month period. Further, the sale must take place within three months of filing the Form 144. If the shares are not sold, an amended notice must be filed.

If the seller is not an affiliate of the company, and has not been an affiliate for at least three months, the only applicable requirement is that the shares be held for one year from the purchase or receipt date.

Both affiliates and non-affiliates must first have the restriction statement removed from their share certificates before the certificates can be sold. To do this, the issuing company's attorney must send an opinion letter to the company's stock transfer agent, allowing the legend to be removed. To initiate this process, the investor should contact the company (not the attorney or the transfer agent) to inquire about the legend removal procedure. The paperwork that must eventually be sent to the stock transfer agent in order to complete a legend removal is noted in the following Rule 144 Administrative Procedure section.

> **Tip:** If shareholders inquire about using Rule 144, remind them that the related legal opinion is only valid for 90 days, after which they will have to obtain a replacement opinion if any shares designated for sale have not yet been sold.

From the perspective of the investor, the use of Rule 144 is by no means perfect. The following issues may apply:

- If the issuer is no longer filing reports with the SEC, the investor can no longer use Rule 144 to sell shares.
- The volume of stock trades in the market may be low; if so, the sale limitations imposed by Rule 144 can make the sale of an investor's holdings an exceedingly prolonged affair.
- If the typical trading volume in a stock is low, continuing sales of shares under Rule 144 will exert long-term downward pressure on the stock price. If an investor is selling shares over a long period of time, this means that the proceeds from these sales could decline substantially over time.

EXAMPLE

Ambivalence Corporation acquires Creekside Industrial, paying the sole shareholder of Creekside 600,000 shares of Ambivalence common stock for his Creekside shares. This shareholder agreed to the deal while under the impression that Ambivalence would soon go public and register his shares. Since then, Ambivalence has indeed gone public, but the circumstances have not cooperated with a stock registration for the former Creekside owner. Consequently, he decides to sell his shares under Rule 144. Being a significant shareholder, he is considered an affiliate of the company. The shares of Ambivalence are listed in the over-the-counter market. There are currently 7,500,000 shares of Creekside common stock outstanding.

The quarterly sales of stock by this individual are capped at 1% of the 7,500,000 total shares of common stock currently outstanding, which is 75,000 shares. If he sells the maximum number of shares in each quarter, it will take two years to sell all of his shares.

A key part of the process of selling shares under Rule 144 is the determination of whether a restrictive legend can be removed. An investor must work out any issues in this area with the issuer, which has sole discretion in whether legends can be removed. The SEC will not intervene in this matter.

Rule 144 Administrative Procedure

Any investors inquiring about using Rule 144 to sell their shares should use the following procedure to have the restriction removed from their share certificates:

1. Send their stock certificate to their broker, along with a statement regarding the number of shares to be sold.
2. The broker then sends to the issuer's securities attorney the following information:

   - A copy of the stock certificate
   - The name of the investor
   - A statement regarding the number of shares to be sold
   - The address of the broker
   - A copy of the Form 144
   - A representation letter from the broker
   - A representation letter from the investor, stating that the individual acquired and paid for the shares more than one year ago, and that the person has not been an affiliate of the company for at least the last three months

3. The securities attorney examines this information. If acceptable, the attorney prepares an opinion letter and sends it to the broker. A copy is sent to the issuer.
4. Once the opinion letter is received, the broker sends the following information to the issuer's stock transfer agent:

- A copy of the Form 144
- The original stock certificate
- The securities attorney's opinion letter
- A request to have the restriction removed from the stock certificate
- The representation letters of the broker and the investor
- A medallion signature guarantee, which limits the liability of the stock transfer agent
- A handling fee

5. The stock transfer agent examines this information. If acceptable, the agent creates a replacement stock certificate that no longer has a restriction statement on it, and sends the certificate to the broker.

Summary

The handling of the Rule 144 alternative is a relatively simple one from the perspective of the company. It simply advises inquiring investors about how the rule works, and then refers them to the company's securities attorney. The company is not involved in the process from that point onward.

Though Rule 144 appears to give investors a reasonable means for selling their stock, its practical application is limited by the volume of trading in the stock. Thus, even though investors may be allowed to sell their stock, it does not mean that there will be a sufficient number of interested buyers to allow for their sale. This is a particular concern for the holders of large blocks of stock, who may find that they will require years of continuing effort to liquidate their holdings.

Chapter 20
Rule 10b5-1 Stock Sales

Introduction

Though a public company primarily intends to sell stock, it may also give stock to employees through compensation plans, or sell them shares through an employee stock purchase plan. If so, some employees with access to material, nonpublic information (especially in the accounting department!) will have a difficult time selling their shares. They cannot do so if they have such information, since they are then considered to be engaged in insider trading. A possible solution for them is the Rule 10b5-1 stock sale, which is described in this chapter, along with comments regarding how a company can control these types of sales.

> **Related Podcast Episode:** Episode 95 of the Accounting Best Practices Podcast discusses 10b5-1 trading plans. It is available at: **accountingtools.com/podcasts** or **iTunes**

Rule 10b5-1 Stock Sales

A person in a public company may regularly come into contact with material information about the company that has not yet been revealed to the public. If so, they would be engaging in illegal insider trading if they were to buy or sell company stock.

This type of person can take advantage of the SEC's Rule 10b5-1, which allows them to implement a trading plan. The main concept behind a trading plan is that it be set up in advance and then operated without further direction. This means that a person cannot be held liable for insider trading activities, since there is no day-to-day direction of buying and selling activities. To use such a trading plan, compliance with the following issues must be affirmed:

- The person entered into a written trading plan, to be conducted by a third party, prior to being aware of material information that had not been released to the public.
- The plan specifies the prices at which securities will be bought or sold, or a formula for doing so, and the dates within which activities will occur. The plan does not allow for subsequent alterations to the trading instructions.
- The person must be able to prove that all subsequent trading conducted by him or her was as specified in the trading plan.

It is possible to cancel a trading plan once it has been initiated, which means that an insider could legitimately cancel the plan if his or her inside knowledge makes it apparent that continuing with the plan could lead to losses. A series of short-duration trading plans would have a similar effect. In both cases, an insider can keep from incurring much downside risk by engaging in trading plans, while still taking advantage of upswings in the stock price. Despite this advantage, employees are not necessarily able to maximize their returns from stock sales, since they cannot place sell orders with their brokers in response to daily changes in the stock price.

Rule 10b5-1 Administrative Procedure

To enter in a 10b5-1 trading plan, a person should contact his or her broker. Brokers usually have a standard plan format that can be filled out, and which forms the basis for a trading program. These plans typically offer three alternatives for selling stock, which are:

- *Price basis*. State the number of shares to be sold at a minimum price point, and the date range over which the shares are to be sold.
- *Timing basis*. State the date range over which an indicated number of shares are to be sold, irrespective of the market price on those dates.
- *Price and timing basis*. State the final trading date by which a certain number of shares are to be sold, preferably above a designating minimum price.

In addition to selecting one of the preceding options (or some variation thereof), a person must also enter into a trading plan agreement with the broker, which sets forth the following items:

- Identifies the securities to be sold
- The person appoints the broker to be his or her agent
- The person agrees to pay the commissions designated in the agreement
- The person can only make modifications to the selling plan by stating in writing that he or she is not aware of any material, nonpublic information about the company, and that the modifications are not intended to evade the intent of Rule 10b5-1.
- The agreement will be terminated under certain conditions or by the receipt of written notice from the person.
- The person represents that he or she is not aware of any material, nonpublic information concerning the company, that there are no transfer restrictions on the securities to be sold, and that there is no hedging plan to offset the outcome of the prospective stock sales. The person also represents that he or she will not sell additional securities outside of this selling plan that will impact the number of shares that can be sold under Rule 144 (see the Sale of Unregistered Securities – Rule 144 chapter).

When employees engage in trading plans with the intent of selling large quantities of company stock, they should notify corporate counsel, preferably by forwarding a copy of the relevant trading plan. Corporate counsel must then decide whether the amount of stock to be sold is sufficiently material to warrant disclosure to the investment community. If so, a selection of the information in the stock trading plan is included in a Form 8-K, for filing with the SEC.

Another concern for the company is when several employees enter into stock trading plans at roughly the same time, and the plans authorize brokers to begin trading at once. These actions can give outsiders the impression that these individuals have access to material, nonpublic information about the company, and are selling before the (presumably) negative information hits the market. To avoid this perception, a company can require employees to enter into trading plans that have at least a one-month delay; doing so makes it much less likely the employees do indeed have access to material, nonpublic information.

A variation on the last point is to prohibit employees from entering into stock trading plans, except during time periods designated by corporate counsel when all material, nonpublic information has been made public. For example, this may be a brief period immediately following the release of a company's quarterly Form 10-Q or annual Form 10-K. Doing so reduces the likelihood that any additional nonpublic information is available to employees that they could use to gain an advantage in garnering a high sale price for their shares.

An argument can be made that employees abruptly terminating their trading plans have inside knowledge about negative information about the company, and so are acting to keep from selling at a low price. A company can mitigate this impression in the marketplace by prohibiting employees from terminating their trading plans prior to the previously-scheduled termination dates of the plans. However, this prohibition is not overly effective, since a canny employee can simply create a series of short-duration trading plans, and choose not to enact the next plan in line if the stock price declines. A variation is to require that all such trading plans span a long interval, such as a full year, and not be cancellable; doing so eliminates any appearance of attempting to benefit from short-term stock price variations.

A company can also prohibit employees from selling shares outside of their 10b5-1 trading plans. The intent of this requirement is to give employees the full protection of the SEC Rule, so there is less chance that they will be accused of insider trading.

To maximize the protection afforded to employees engaged in stock sales, it can make sense to require all corporate insiders to use a stock trading plan under Rule 10b5-1.

The general intent of the cluster of company rules noted here is to reinforce the perception in the marketplace that an organization's employees only sell their shares when they do not have access to material, nonpublic information. This builds the ethical image of the business, while also giving employees a more robust defense against any charges that they are engaging in insider trading activities.

Tip: Include the preceding requirements in the employee manual, and reinforce these items with employees periodically – especially when they have just received company stock.

Summary

Rule 10b5-1 is really intended for employees, and does not directly involve the company that has issued shares. Nonetheless, it is a common defense against charges of insider trading, so company management should be conversant with how it works and regularly encourage employees to use it. The internal policies noted in the preceding section can be used to bolster the effect of the Rule.

This chapter has been less concerned with public company fund raising, and more interested in a side effect of issuing stock – that of the plight of employees who are trying to sell stock without triggering any insider trading allegations.

Chapter 21
Closing the Books

Introduction

Closing the books for a publicly-held company is considerably more involved than it is for a privately-held company, because several parties have to examine and approve the financial statements, and because the disclosures that accompany the financial statements are substantial. In this chapter, we present an overview of the core steps required to close the books of any business, and then go on to address unique aspects of the closing process that apply to public companies.

> **Related Podcast Episode:** Episode 77 of the Accounting Best Practices Podcast discusses closing the books for a public company. It is available at: **accounting-tools.com/podcasts** or **iTunes**

Basic Steps for Closing the Books

One of the more complex procedures that the accounting staff must follow is the set of activities needed to close the books at the end of each reporting period. The exact number of closing activities and the order in which they are completed will depend upon the complexity of a company's operations and the number of subsidiaries whose results must be consolidated.

This section contains a listing of the key steps to follow to close the books. They are not presented in an exact numerical sequence, since it may be necessary to alter the order of certain tasks, depending upon the structure and procedures of the organization. The closing steps are:

Customer Billings

- Issue recurring invoices to customers.
- Verify that all billable time has been included in the timekeeping system.
- Issue invoices to customers for all services provided and goods shipped through period-end. If the billings are related to customer contracts, first verify that there is sufficient funding to support the invoices.
- Accumulate rebillable expenses and issue invoices for them to customers.
- Reconcile invoices to shipping log.
- Verify that all subcontractor invoices were received and included in customer billings.
- Accrue revenue as applicable.

Accounts Payable

- Notify all employees to submit their expense reports.
- Enter all supplier invoices in the system by the designated cutoff date.
- Enter all employee expense reports.
- Accrue for any material expenses for which the supplier invoice has not yet been received.

Fixed Assets

- Verify that all fixed asset additions and deletions are correctly reflected in the fixed asset register.
- Capitalize interest on applicable projects.
- Record depreciation and amortization expense.
- Record the impairment of applicable fixed assets.

Inventory

- Verify that there was a proper inventory cutoff.
- Count the inventory or run a perpetual inventory report.
- Determine the cost of the ending inventory.
- Allocate overhead to ending inventory and the cost of goods sold.
- Adjust the ending inventory valuation for the lower of cost or market rule.

Journal Entries

- *Allowance for doubtful accounts.* Do not run this calculation early if a large part of company billings are issued at period-end.
- *Accrued revenue.* Only accrue revenue if the amount accrued meets all revenue recognition rules. When in doubt, do not accrue revenue. **[this is a reversing entry]**
- *Accrued royalties.* Accrue the amount of any royalties owed to third parties who own the intellectual property. **[this is a reversing entry]**
- *Accrued supplier billings.* If supplier invoices do not appear in time for the closing date, accrue the expense if it is material. **[this is a reversing entry]**
- *Accrued vacations.* Accrue for any changes in the amount of earned but unused vacation time. This balance can go up or down, depending upon actual vacation usage.
- *Accrued wages.* Accrue the earned but unpaid amount of wages at period-end. It usually makes sense to also accrue for the related amount of payroll taxes. **[this is a reversing entry]**
- *Bonus expense.* Accrue for the incremental amount of bonuses earned in the period.
- *Commission expense.* Accrue for the commission amount earned but not paid in the period. Consider also accruing the related amount of payroll taxes. **[this is a reversing entry]**

- *Depreciation and amortization.* If depreciation and amortization are being calculated with a spreadsheet, verify that the calculations do not run past the useful life of the asset, and that any salvage values are reasonable.
- *Income tax liability.* Adjust the income tax liability. This amount could increase or decrease, depending upon whether there was a gain or a loss, and whether there is a net operating loss carryforward.
- *Interest expense.* Accrue for any interest expense for which a billing has not yet been received from the lender. **[this is a reversing entry]**
- *Reserve for obsolete inventory.* Estimate the amount of obsolete inventory likely to be in the warehouse and adjust the reserve to match the estimate. This can be run at any time during the period.
- *Reserve for sales returns.* If the historical amount of sales returns is immaterial, this entry can be avoided.
- *Reserve for warranty claims.* If the historical amount of warranties is immaterial, this entry can be avoided.

Balance Sheet Reconciliations

- *Bank reconciliation(s).* Access the bank's online account records and reconcile all bank accounts. It is preferable to do so in advance for the bulk of the period's transactions, and then complete the last few days of the reconciliation during the core closing period.
- *Petty cash.* Reconcile the amount of petty cash on hand. This is usually such a small amount that it can be done outside of the core closing period.
- *Accounts receivable (trade).* Match the total in the ending aged accounts receivable report to the trade accounts receivable account in the general ledger.
- *Accounts receivable (other).* Verify that all items remaining in this general ledger account are still unpaid and are valid receivables. Adjust as necessary.
- *Prepaid expenses.* Review this general ledger account to see if any items should be charged to expense.
- *Inventory.* Match the total in the extended ending inventory report to the balance in the inventory account in the general ledger.
- *Fixed assets.* Match the subtotals for each asset classification in the fixed asset register to the corresponding accounts in the general ledger.
- *Accounts payable.* Match the total in the ending aged accounts payable report to the trade accounts payable account in the general ledger.
- *Sales taxes payable.* Most sales taxes are paid in the following month, so there should not be any residual balances from the preceding month (unless payment intervals are longer than one month).
- *Income taxes payable.* The amount of income taxes paid on a quarterly basis does not have to match the accrued liability, but verify that the quarterly payments were made.

- *Accrued liabilities.* Inspect the contents of each accrued liability account in the general ledger and verify that it matches the supporting detail.
- *Notes payable.* The balance in this general ledger account should exactly match the account balance provided by the lender, barring any exceptions for in-transit payments.
- *Equity.* Inspect the contents of each equity account in the general ledger and verify that it matches the supporting detail.

Consolidate Results

- *Convert currencies.* Convert the results forwarded from subsidiaries to the parent company's reporting currency.
- *Map results.* Map the converted subsidiary results to the chart of accounts of the parent company.
- *Eliminate intercompany transactions.* Aggregate the supporting schedule detailing all intercompany transactions and use it to eliminate these transactions from the consolidated results.

Error Checking

- *Journal entry review.* Review all journal entries for incorrect accounts, transpositions, and the incorrect use of reversing flags.
- *Income statement review.* Print a preliminary version of the income statement and review it for obvious errors. This works best if it can be compared to the results of previous periods using horizontal analysis, or compared to budgeted results.
- *Negative cash.* If there is negative cash on the balance sheet, set the cash balance to zero with a journal entry and move the difference to a current liability account.

Preparation of the Financial Statements – Public Company

1. Calculate basic and diluted earnings per share.
2. Add those disclosures required for publicly held companies. This includes segment reporting.
3. Prepare all supporting schedules associated with the SEC-mandated disclosures.
4. Complete the first draft of the Form 10-Q or Form 10-K.
5. Prepare schedules requested by auditors.
6. Support the auditors' review or audit of the financial statements and systems.
7. Obtain officer certifications of the Forms.
8. Obtain audit committee approval of the Form 10-Q (if applicable).
9. Obtain board of directors approval of the Form 10-K (if applicable).
10. EDGARize the applicable Form.
11. Obtain final auditor approval of the EDGARized Form.

12. File the Form with the SEC.

Final Tasks – Period-End

- Mail any customer invoices that have not yet been issued.
- Generate metrics regarding the speed with which the books were closed.
- Update the error tracking database for errors found during the close.
- Update controls based on system flaws found.
- Document any future changes to the closing process.
- Request programming changes from the information technology staff.
- Update the closing procedures, as necessary. This may involve the reallocation of work among the accounting staff if someone is expected to be out of the office during the next closing period.
- Close all activity in the subsidiary ledgers and the general ledger for the closed period and open the next period for the recordation of transactions.
- Update the period-end closing binder with all applicable supporting documentation related to the close. This should include:
  - Master activity list with steps initialed
  - Journal entry support
  - Schedules
  - Account reconciliations
  - Bank reconciliation
- If applicable, also update the period-end closing binder for a public company with the audit committee approval, officer certifications, and auditor-approved copy of the EDGARized Form 10-Q or 10-K filing.

Final Tasks – Year-End

- Update the year-end binder. This should include:
  - Financial statements
  - Trial balance
  - General ledger
  - Subsidiary ledgers
  - Ending inventory report
  - Fixed asset register
  - Fixed asset roll forward
  - Invoice register
  - Ending accounts receivable aging report
  - Ending accounts payable aging report

For a more thorough review of the steps involved in closing the books, see the latest edition of the author's *Closing the Books* book.

In the following sections, we expand upon those portions of the closing process that are specifically targeted at a publicly-held business.

The Public Company Closing Process

A publicly held company is required by the SEC to file a large report concerning its financial condition at the end of each quarter. These are the Form 10-Q (for quarterly filings) and Form 10-K (for annual filings). The contents of both reports are discussed in other chapters.

There are a number of time-consuming steps involved in the production of the Forms 10-Q and 10-K. In fact, though there may be an excellent system in place for producing reliable financial statements within a few days of period-end, the additional steps are so onerous that the accounting department may find it difficult to file the reports with the SEC in a timely manner, even though the filing dates are a number of weeks later.

> **Tip:** If a company is a small one with a minimal public valuation, consider outsourcing the construction of the Forms 10-Q and 10-K to outside specialists. These reports require particular types of knowledge that the accounting staff of a small business is unlikely to have, which makes outsourcing a good option. However, since these specialists are overwhelmed with work from all of their clients following the end of each quarter, the company's reports may be filed near or on the last allowable date.

The additional steps needed to close the books for a publicly held company include all of the following:

1. *Auditor investigation.* The outside auditors must conduct a review of the company's financial statements and disclosures for its quarterly results, and a full audit of its annual results. A *review* is a service under which an auditor obtains limited assurance that there are no material modifications that need to be made to an entity's financial statements for them to be in conformity with the applicable financial reporting framework. An *audit* is the review and verification of an entity's accounting records, as well as the physical inspection of its assets. The auditor then attests to the fairness of presentation of the financial statements and related disclosures. An audit is more time-consuming and expensive than a review. The auditor investigation is the most time-consuming of the public company requirements. The company can reduce the amount of time required for a review or audit by providing full staff support to the audit team, as well as by having all requested information available as of the beginning of the audit or review work.

2. *Legal review.* It would be extremely unwise to issue the financial statement package without first having legal counsel review the statements and (especially) the disclosures to ensure that all required disclosures have been made, and to verify that all statements made are correct and fully supportable. This review is usually completed near or after the end of the work done by the auditors, but can be scheduled slightly sooner if the disclosures should be substantially complete at that time.

> **Tip:** The auditors can waste a considerable amount of time double-checking and triple-checking the accuracy of the disclosures that accompany the financial statements. Doing so delays the closing process, as well as increasing the fees charged by the auditors. To reduce the auditor time spent reviewing the disclosures, have one or more in-house personnel review them in advance.

3. *Officer certification.* Depending upon what type of SEC report is being issued, different company officers are required to certify that the information in the financial statements presents fairly the financial condition and results of operations of the business. Since there are substantial penalties and jail time involved if an officer were to make a false certification, it should be no surprise that the signing officers will want to spend time reviewing the complete set of financial statements and disclosures. This review can be done before the auditors have completed their work, so officer certification does not usually increase the duration of the closing process.

4. *Audit committee and board approvals.* The audit committee must approve every Form 10-Q, and the board of directors must approve every Form 10-K. Given the number of people involved, schedule review and approval meetings well in advance, to be conducted a few days prior to the required filing date of the applicable report. Scheduling the review slightly early should leave enough time to make adjustments, in case anyone expresses concerns during the review, and wants changes to be made prior to filing.

   Issue the complete set of financial statements and disclosures to the audit committee or board members at least one full day in advance of a review and approval meeting, so that they have sufficient time to examine the material.

> **Tip:** It is customary to use conference calls for review and approval meetings, rather than in person; doing so works well if people are located far apart. Also, the company may have an arrangement where audit committee or board members are paid less if they attend meetings by phone, so this approach can save the company money.

5. *EDGARize and file.* Once the Form 10-Q or Form 10-K is complete and fully approved, file it with the SEC. The filing is done using the Electronic Data Gathering, Analysis, and Retrieval (EDGAR) system that is operated by the SEC. The information can be submitted in various formats, but the company will almost certainly have to convert it from the format in which the documents were originally prepared. This means hiring someone to convert the reports to the applicable format, which is a process known as *EDGARizing.* Not only is the conversion specialist responsible for converting the financial statements, but this person also files the statements with the SEC on behalf of the company. The conversion process usually takes one or two days, but also factor in additional time for the auditors to review the

converted format – the auditors must give their approval before the report can be filed with the SEC.

Tip: Spend as much time as possible reviewing the financial statement package in advance before sending it to the EDGARizing firm, because they charge significant fees if the company wants to make subsequent changes to the converted documents.

Of all the issues noted in this section, the largest factor standing in the way of closing the books is likely to be the work schedule of the auditors. If they have other clients scheduled ahead of the company, the review or audit work may not even begin until several weeks after the entity has closed its books in all other respects. Consequently, it is useful to work with the audit partner to move the company to the head of the auditors' work queue. Of course, if the organization is scheduled first by the auditors, this means that the accounting department must also have financial statements and all supporting schedules prepared at a very early date – so be ready before lobbying for a scheduling change.

The Form 10-Q Approval

Before filing with the SEC, the Form 10-Q must be signed by an authorized officer, as well as the principal financial or chief accounting officer.

A *large accelerated filer* is a company having an aggregate market value owned by investors who are not affiliated with the company of a minimum of $700 million. An *accelerated filer* is a company having an aggregate market value owned by investors who are not affiliated with the company of less than $700 million, but more than $75 million. The Form 10-Q must be filed within 40 days of the end of the fiscal quarter if the company is either a large accelerated filer or an accelerated filer. If that is not the case, file it within 45 days of the end of the fiscal quarter.

The Form 10-K Approval

Before filing with the SEC, the Form 10-K must be signed by *all* of the following:

- Principal executive officer
- Principal financial officer
- Controller
- A majority of the board of directors

The Form 10-K must be filed within 60 days of the end of the fiscal year if the company is a large accelerated filer or an accelerated filer, or within 75 days of the end of the fiscal year if the company is an accelerated filer. If the company does not have either designation, file it within 90 days of the end of the fiscal year.

Summary

This chapter has outlined a large number of steps that are needed to close the books. The level of organization required to close the books in this manner may appear to be overkill. However, consider that the primary work product of the accounting department as a whole, and the controller in particular, is the financial statements. If the department can establish a reputation for consistently issuing high-quality financial statements within a reasonable period of time, this will likely be the basis for the company's view of the entire department.

We place particular importance on the prior review of SEC reports by legal counsel. An experienced attorney can spot incorrect or missing disclosures that an auditor might not be aware of. This means blocking out a sufficient amount of time in the closing schedule to ensure that an attorney can complete a thorough review.

A common problem with closing the books of a public company is that it is extremely difficult to reduce the amount of time required to file reports, because it requires the cooperation of many parties outside of the accounting department – and over whom the controller has no control. This means that the group over which the controller *does* have control – the accounting department – must complete the financial statements as expeditiously as possible.

Chapter 22
Accounting and Finance Controls

Introduction

The establishment and maintenance of a proper set of controls is an essential element of accounting and finance in a publicly-held business. The investment community demands an adequate control system to mitigate losses from inadvertent errors and fraud, as well as to ensure that the information presented in the financial statements is correct. In this chapter, we explore the control environment in a publicly-held organization, the nature and types of controls that may be employed, and specific controls that apply to certain types of accounting and financing transactions.

Preventive and Detective Controls

When considering the proper balance of controls used for recording transactions and producing financial statements, consider the types of controls being installed. A *preventive control* is one that keeps a financial statement error from ever occurring. Another type of control is the *detective control*. This control is useful, but only detects an error after it has occurred; thus, its main use is in making management aware of a problem that must be fixed.

A control system needs to have a mix of preventive and detective controls. Even though preventive controls are considered more valuable, they also tend to be more intrusive in the functioning of key business processes. Also, they are installed to address specific control issues that management is already aware of. Management also needs a liberal helping of detective controls, which can be used to spot new types of financial statement errors. Thus, a common occurrence is to throw out a web of detective controls that occasionally haul in a new type of problem, for which management then installs a preventive control.

In short, a mix of the two types of controls is needed, where there may be no ideal solution. Instead, there may be a range of possible configurations within which a controller would consider a control system to be effective. In the Basic Financial Controls section later in this chapter, we describe a number of controls for closing the books, most of which are of the detective variety.

General Controls for Public Companies

Any publicly-held organization is required to bolster its existing suite of financial statement controls with the participation of the following three groups:

- Outside auditors
- Audit committee

- Chief executive officer (CEO)

If a company is publicly-held, its auditors are required to review its financial statements for the first, second, and third quarters of its fiscal year. The auditors must complete many audit steps before they will allow the financial statements to be issued, and those audit steps are essentially a massive cluster of detective controls.

Since the Form 10-Q cannot be issued without the permission of the auditors, there is no rush to release the financial statements. Thus, there is no tradeoff between the speed of release and the quality of the financial statements; instead, the auditors will work through their review procedures as fast as possible, but are primarily concerned with the quality of the final product.

Despite the presence of the auditors, do not consider them to be a backstop for any failed or missing internal controls. Instead, have a sufficient system of controls already in place for the auditors not to find *any* problems with the financial statements. A better way to use these reviews is to carefully examine any reports by the auditors of exceptions found, and then institute new controls to mitigate those issues.

A requirement of being publicly-held is to have an audit committee, which is a sub-group of the board of directors. This group must formally vote in favor of all quarterly and annual financial statements before they are released in the Forms 10-K and 10-Q. A diligent audit committee may occasionally spot an error or inconsistency in one of these Forms, or they may request clarification of certain statements made within the Forms. Nonetheless, only a few members of an audit committee usually have a strong financial background, so it is unlikely that the committee will spot significant issues. Consequently, the audit committee represents a relatively weak detective control over the financial statements.

The CEO is required to formally approve any financial statements filed with the SEC. It is possible that the CEO may spot problems in the financial statements, but only if he or she has significant financial knowledge of the company (which is not always the case). Thus, this should be considered a weak control.

In short, the participation of additional parties in the production of financial statements provides little additional control in the case of the audit committee and CEO; however the outside auditors may spot a number of issues that the controller can use as the basis for constructing additional controls.

Basic Financial Statement Controls

There are a number of financial statement controls worth considering. The accountant can select just one control to address a specific risk, or adopt a larger number of controls that provide multiple ways to mitigate the same risk. Here are some controls to consider:

Financial Statement Controls

Area	Description
General	*Closing checklist.* The most important control by far is a simple checklist of closing activities, which the controller monitors. This is a good way to verify that all steps required to close the books have been taken.
General	*Supporting documentation.* Anyone involved in the closing process should document the more complex journal entries, and have a second person review them for errors prior to entering them in the general ledger.
General	*Responsible person.* Assign responsibility for the entire closing process to one person, and assign responsibility for individual activities to those people assigned to the closing team.
General	*Limit journal entry authority.* It is more likely that an inexperienced person will incorrectly enter a journal entry in the general ledger, or not enter it at all, or enter it twice. Consequently, password-protect the journal entry screen in the accounting software and limit access to a trained general ledger accountant.
General	*Reconcile accounts.* There should be a mandatory reconciliation of all general ledger accounts that have ending balances larger than a predetermined amount, and which have had activity during the accounting period. This control may include a review of reconciled accounts by a supervisor. If some accounts persistently contain errors, consider requiring a preliminary review of them prior to the month-end close, when the accounting staff has more time for a thorough review.
General	*Analytical review.* Compare the preliminary financial statements to the results for the past few periods to see if there are any anomalies in the various line items, and investigate as necessary. This could be a simple search for blips in the trend line of results, or a more quantitatively-precise approach where changes over a specific dollar amount or percentage are investigated. A sample analytical review is shown after this list of controls.
General	*Retain spreadsheets.* If the information used to construct a journal entry was compiled in an electronic spreadsheet, lock down the spreadsheet to prevent it from being cleared out and used again in the next month. By doing so, one can retain a historical record of the justifications for journal entries.
General	*Review spreadsheets.* There may be calculation errors in the spreadsheets used to create journal entries, so periodically review the calculations to verify that they are correct.

Area	Description
Disclosures	*Independent review.* If disclosures are to be issued along with the financial statements, consider hiring a third party, such as a CPA firm, to review the disclosures for adequacy.
Disclosures	*Match disclosures to financial statements.* A huge problem area is that the information in the disclosures does not match the financial statements. Someone should match the information in every disclosure to the same information in the financial statements, and adjust the disclosures as necessary.
Report structure	*Match default to custom reports.* When a company creates a special version of the financial statements provided with the accounting software package, there is a good chance that some accounts will not be included in the custom reports, or that they will be repeated. These issues can be found by comparing the original default financial statements to the modified versions.
Cash	*Complete the bank reconciliation.* The main company checking account usually processes a large number of transactions, and so is almost certain to contain a transaction that the company either did not record, or recorded incorrectly. Consequently, it is very useful to either complete a full bank reconciliation before closing the books, or to complete a preliminary one a few days prior to closing the books.
Accounts receivable	*Reconcile trade receivables account.* There should be no journal entries impacting the trade accounts receivable account, so review the account for such entries.
Accounts receivable	*Reconcile other receivables account.* The other accounts receivable account is the home for many stray receivables, such as for employees and company officers, and is commonly subject to adjustment. If the balance in this account is large, review it every month.
Inventory	*Verify cutoff.* Verify that the recordation of received goods and shipped goods switched to the following accounting period as of midnight on the last day of the reporting period.
Inventory	*Verify inventory quantities.* Ensure that someone audits the inventory quantities in the warehouse on a regular basis, and follows up on errors found. This improves the likelihood that the ending inventory balance and the cost of goods sold are correct.
Inventory	*Audit bills of material.* In a standard costing system, the bills of material are used to compile the cost of ending inventory. Adopt an ongoing review system to verify that these bills are correct; otherwise, the ending inventory balance will be incorrect.

Area	Description
Inventory	*Verify inventory layers.* If an inventory layering system is in place, verify that the costs assigned to the cost of goods sold were properly taken from the correct inventory layers, and that the costs in those layers are correct.
Prepaid assets	*Monitor account.* Verify that all items listed as prepaid assets were not consumed during the month; if they were, charge them to expense.
Fixed assets	*Match detail to account balances.* Fixed assets are frequently recorded in the wrong accounts. Therefore, make sure that the asset classification totals in the fixed asset register match the fixed asset account balances in the general ledger.
Fixed assets	*Review sale transactions.* If fixed assets were sold during a period, verify that the transactions were correctly recorded. In particular, verify that the associated amounts of accumulated depreciation were removed from the inventory records, and that gains or losses were properly recorded.
Fixed assets	*Recalculate depreciation.* Verify that the correct useful lives have been assigned to all fixed assets, and that depreciation terminates at the end of the useful lives of fixed assets.
Accrued liabilities	*Review accrual calculations.* Review all accrual calculations for such items as wages, vacation pay, sick pay, commissions, and royalties, and verify that the general ledger accrual accounts have been properly adjusted for these calculations.
Revenue	*Match invoices to funding.* If a business has contracts with its customers, verify that there are sufficient funds available before issuing invoices. Otherwise, the invoices will be rejected by customers, and the company must subsequently reduce the amount of recorded revenue.
Revenue	*Review shipping log.* Compare the sales register to the shipping log to verify that all items shipped to customers have been billed.
Revenue	*Approve accrued revenue.* Have the controller review the proposed accrual of any revenue transactions.
Income taxes	*Verify percentage.* Verify that the income tax rate used to calculate the income tax liability is the estimated average amount that the company expects to incur during the calendar year.

Sample Analytical Review

Account	December	November	% Change	$ Change	Issue
Prepaid assets	$80,000	$60,000	33%	$20,000	Deposit on new machinery
Accounts receivable	720,000	480,000	50%	240,000	Christmas sales surge
Inventory	120,000	350,000	66%	-230,000	Draw down for Christmas sales
Debt	400,000	200,000	100%	200,000	Funding for receivables
Revenue	600,000	250,000	1405	350,000	Christmas sales surge
Cost of goods sold	390,000	175,000	123%	215,000	Christmas sales surge
Employee benefits	50,000	25,000	100%	25,000	Christmas bonuses

Controls for Form 8-K Reporting

The Form 8-K is used to report a wide range of material information to the SEC. The key control issue is to ensure that all such events are reported to corporate counsel, who can then include the appropriate information in a Form 8-K filing.

Most of the information that might be included in a Form 8-K originates in or passes through the accounting department, so this flow of information can be fairly easily monitored. However, it is also possible that other transactions or events might originate in other departments or in outlying subsidiaries; if there is no monitoring system in place, these latter items may not be reported to the SEC at all, or well beyond the required due date. The following controls can be used to reduce the risk of missing or late Form 8-K disclosures:

- Notifications regarding the 8-K process should be regularly sent to anyone who might be involved in a material event (usually department and subsidiary managers). The notification should include examples of what constitutes a material event, as well as a summary of the Form 8-K reporting requirements, and contact information for the reporting of such events.
- Corporate counsel is designated as the sole arbiter of which items are considered reportable. This centralization keeps disparate reporting from originating in different parts of the organization.
- Corporate counsel is to be copied on the minutes of all major company committee meetings, so that he or she can peruse them and see if any items constitute reportable events.

Controls for Forms 3, 4, and 5 Filings

A company may commit to file the Forms 3, 4, and 5 on behalf of its officers and directors. If so, it should first obtain a power of attorney from each of these individuals that authorizes the company to do so. Corporate counsel should retain these documents in a secure location, and update them whenever new officers or directors are added to the company. Otherwise, the company will be at risk of issuing these filings to the SEC without the permission of the officers and directors. See the Insider Securities Reporting chapter for information about the Forms 3, 4, and 5.

Controls for Non-GAAP Financial Measures

It is all too easy for a breakdown in processes to allow for the publication of an unauthorized non-GAAP financial measure. As noted in the Non-GAAP Reporting chapter, this tendency can be mitigated by using a standard approval form whenever someone wants to use such a measure. Once the form is in place, the following controls can be added:

- Require the person issuing SEC filings to periodically check the stored set of approved forms, to see if any non-GAAP financial measures have been added or discarded. This information is then used to update subsequent SEC filings.
- Have the internal audit staff compare the approval forms to the non-GAAP financial measures that were actually published, and note the consistency of presentation. Any variances are to be reported to management. Since internal audit reviews can be infrequent, a way to bolster this control is to also have an assistant controller conduct the same comparison on a more frequent basis.

It can be more difficult to control the presence of non-GAAP financial measures in oral presentations. As noted in the Non-GAAP reporting chapter, one way to do so is to require all presenters to submit the text of their presentations to the disclosure committee in advance. However, what if a presenter does not follow the text when making a presentation? There are two possible detective controls:

- Have a knowledgeable person, such as the investor relations officer or corporate counsel, attend the presentations. This person should know which non-GAAP financial measures are approved, and so may be able to spot any additional measures that a presenter mentions.
- Record all presentations, and have someone with knowledge of the approved non-GAAP financial measures review the recordings. This is a painfully slow process, but could be necessary, especially in cases where a person is a new presenter or has a history of departing from the prepared text.

If these controls note the presence of an unauthorized non-GAAP financial measure, corporate counsel and the controller will need to jointly prepare a Form 8-K for immediate distribution, in order to be in compliance with the SEC's Regulation G.

Controls for Regulation A Stock Sales

A key concern for a company contemplating a Regulation A stock sale is that such sales are limited to organizations whose directors, officers, principal shareholders, and others have not violated any securities laws. To ensure that this is not the case, a possible control is to have corporate counsel prepare a questionnaire that each of these individuals must complete, in which they note any infractions committed over the years, and which they must sign. Doing so gives the entity reasonable assurance that it is in compliance with the applicable SEC rules under Regulation A. Possible questions that could be included in the questionnaire (based on SEC Rule 262, Disqualification Provisions) are:

- Have you been convicted within 10 years prior to the filing of the offering statement of any felony or misdemeanor in connection with the purchase or sale of any security, involving the making of a false filing with the SEC, or arising out of the conduct of the business of an underwriter, broker, dealer, municipal securities dealer, or investment advisor?
- Are you subject to any order, judgment, or decree of any court temporarily or preliminarily enjoining or restraining, or subject to any order, judgment, or decree of any court, entered within five years prior to the filing of such offering statement, permanently enjoining or restraining you from engaging or continuing any conduct or practice in connection with the purchase or sale of any security, involving the making of a false filing with the SEC, or arising out of the conduct of the business of an underwriter, broker, dealer, municipal securities dealer, or investment advisor?
- Have you been suspended or expelled from membership in, or suspended or barred from association with a member of, a national securities exchange or a national securities association for any act or omission to act constituting conduct inconsistent with just and equitable principles of trade?
- Are you subject to a United States Postal Service false representation order within the five years prior to the filing of the offering statement, or are you subject to a restraining order or preliminary injunction?

Another control issue revolves around the SEC mandate to review all advertising solicitations. The company could be out of compliance with this rule if a solicitation were to be inadvertently issued without prior submission to the SEC. A reasonable control is to funnel all such solicitations through corporate counsel, who is responsible for reviewing these documents and submitting them to the SEC. Only after counsel has signed off on solicitations can they be issued to prospective investors.

Regulation A imposes a limitation of $5 million on the amount of money that can be raised under this exemption within a one year period. To ensure that no more than this amount is raised, impose a hard cap of $5 million on the amount of funding that will be accepted into the escrow fund. All other funds received by the escrow agent after this amount is reached will be returned to investors.

The offering circular sent to prospective investors must be accurate and up-to-date. If any material events occur during the offering period that are not described in the circular, the document must be updated. To ensure that the necessary updates take place, form a disclosure committee that meets regularly to examine the circular, and determine whether any updates should be made. This group should at least include the chief financial officer and corporate counsel, as well as anyone having access to information about material events.

A final control is to ensure that the Form 2-A is periodically issued to the SEC, as well as at the termination of the fund raising or funds expenditure periods. This can be accomplished by having corporate counsel set up action items in the legal department's calendar of activities, to warn the legal staff of when the report is due to be filed.

Controls for Regulation D Stock Sales

A Regulation D stock sale is a sale of restricted stock to accredited investors. The following controls can be used to ensure that the sale of securities under the Regulation D exemption does not breach the SEC's rules for such sales, and that the correct terms are offered to investors:

- *Match subscription agreements to master copy.* The subscription agreement contains the terms under which shares are to be sold to investors, including such information as the price, the number of warrants to be granted, and the exercise price of the warrants. There is a risk that the wrong terms will be issued to investors, especially if the sale continues for a number of months. To avoid a risk of making a sale under incorrect terms, manually compare each agreement to a master copy. In addition, conduct the same comparison for all signed agreements returned by investors, to guard against an investor altering the terms of the document.
- *Examine investor questionnaires.* The company must ensure to the best of its ability that investors buying shares under Regulation D are indeed accredited. To do so, the company relies upon the questionnaires filled out by investors. A reasonable control is to forward all completed questionnaires to corporate counsel for examination; no stock certificates can be issued without the signed approval of counsel.
- *Verify cash receipt.* Funds paid by investors for shares are routed through an escrow account that is maintained by a third party; this means that the company does not have direct access to payment information, and so could inadvertently issue stock certificates to investors even if the cash has not yet been received. To guard against this, only issue certificates after receiving verification from the third party that cash has indeed been received.
- *Verify authorization letter.* When shares are issued, this is done by the company's stock transfer agent, not directly by the company. Corporate counsel should match the information on the authorization letter sent to the stock transfer agent to the information received from each investor, to ensure that certificates are issued to the correct investor name, for the correct number of shares, and with the correct restrictive legend stated on the back of each certificate.

Controls for Rule 144

The SEC's Rule 144 sets the guidelines under which investors in a publicly-held company can have the restrictions removed from their stock, so that it can be sold. Most of the Rule 144 activity occurs between investors, the company's securities attorney, and its stock transfer agent. The company only needs to provide some structure to the information it gives to shareholders, which requires the following controls:

- Investors must be given the correct information regarding the rules under which they can sell their shares. To ensure that they receive the correct information, develop a standardized letter, stating the exact circumstances under which they can sell shares, which also notes the contact information for the company's securities attorney and stock transfer agent.
- Retain copies of all opinion letters received from the company's securities attorneys, stating which stock certificates are now unrestricted. This information can be used to estimate the additional number of unrestricted shares now in circulation.

Summary

A comprehensive system of controls should be considered an essential part of any publicly-held company. To ensure that controls are adequate, consider retaining a controls consultant who is tasked with continually examining existing processes and controls to see if they are sufficient. Better yet, task this person with a prior review of all new processes that are about to be installed, so that controls continue to be a central part of the planning for all new processes or system upgrades. The same concept can be applied acquisitions, where a controls specialist examines the control environment in any organizations being acquired by the company. Using an outside specialist is especially useful when the accounting staff is overburdened, and so has little time available with which to examine and test the existing system of controls.

Glossary

A

Accelerated filer. A company having an aggregate market value owned by investors who are not affiliated with the company of less than $700 million, but more than $75 million.

Accredited investor. A high net worth entity or individual; this investor is allowed to acquire shares under a Regulation D stock offering.

Affiliate. A person who can exercise control over an issuer, such as an executive officer, a director, or a large shareholder.

Amortization. The write-off of an intangible asset over its expected period of use.

Audit. The review and verification of an entity's accounting records, as well as the physical inspection of its assets.

Audit committee financial expert. A person who has an understanding of generally accepted accounting principles and financial statements, the ability to assess the application of these principles in connection with the accounting for estimates, accruals, and reserves, experience preparing and reviewing financial statements, an understanding of internal controls over financial reporting, and an understanding of audit committee functions.

B

Basic earnings per share. The earnings for an accounting period divided by the common stock outstanding during that period.

Blue sky laws. Laws enacted at the state level, requiring issuers of securities to register with the applicable state regulatory commission.

C

Change in accounting estimate. A change that adjusts the carrying amount of an asset or liability, or the subsequent accounting for it.

Change in accounting principle. A change from one generally accepted accounting principle to another, or a change in the method of applying it.

Chief operating decision maker. A person who is responsible for making decisions about resource allocations to the segments of a business, and for evaluating those segments.

Comfort letter. A letter issued by auditors concerning the validity of the financial statements and other information issued by an organization.

Common stock. An ownership share in a corporation that allows its holders voting rights at shareholder meetings and the opportunity to receive dividends.

Comprehensive income. The change in equity of a business during a period, not including investments by or distributions to owners.

Contingent stock. Shares that may be issued in the future under certain circumstances, such as the exercise of stock options.

Crowdfunding. The use of small individual investments from a large number of investors to fund a business.

D

Death spiral PIPE. A private investment in public equity where continuing declines in the stock price obligate the issuer to issue more shares to PIPE investors, possibly resulting in a change in control of the issuer.

Debt security. A security that involves a creditor relationship with a borrower, such as bonds, commercial paper, and Treasury securities.

Detective control. A control that detects an error after it has occurred.

Diluted earnings per share. The earnings for an accounting period divided by the common stock outstanding during that period and all potential common stock.

Discrete view. The assumption that the results reported for a specific interim period are not associated with the revenues and expenses arising during other reporting periods.

Dividend. A payment made to shareholders that is proportional to the number of shares owned.

E

EDGAR. An on-line report filing system operated by the Securities and Exchange Commission.

Emerging growth company. A company that has total annual gross revenues of less than $1 billion.

Employee share purchase plan. A plan under which employees can buy shares directly from their employer, usually at a discount and without paying a brokerage fee.

F

Fedwire. A payment system operated by the Federal Reserve Bank, using same-day gross settlements.

Form 10-K. The annual report filed by a public company with the SEC.

Form 10-Q. The quarterly report filed by a public company with the SEC.

Funding portal. Any person acting as an intermediary in a transaction involving the offer or sale of securities for the account of others, that does not offer investment advice, solicit purchases or sales to buy the securities listed on its website, or compensate its employees for soliciting the securities listed on its website, or handle investor funds or securities.

G

Generally Accepted Accounting Principles. A group of accounting standards used to standardize the recordation of business transactions and the reporting of financial statements.

Gross profit method. The use of the historical gross margin to estimate the amount of ending inventory.

I

Imputed interest. The interest assumed to be earned on a note that has a stated rate significantly different from the market interest rate.

Initial public offering. The registration of shares with the Securities and Exchange Commission by a business for the first time.

Intangible assets. Assets that have no physical substance.

Interim period. A financial reporting period that is shorter than a full fiscal year.

Integral view. The assumption that the results reported in interim financial statements are an integral part of the full-year results.

Intrinsic value. The difference between the conversion price and the fair value of the securities into which an instrument is convertible.

Issuer. An entity that registers and sells securities in order to finance its operations.

L

Large accelerated filer. A company having an aggregate market value owned by investors who are not affiliated with the company of a minimum of $700 million.

N

Net income. Revenues and gains, less expenses and losses, not including items of other comprehensive income.

Non-GAAP financial measure. A numerical measure of a company's historical or future financial performance that contains or excludes amounts that differ from a comparable measure as calculated under GAAP.

O

Operating segment. A component of a public entity.

Other comprehensive income. Revenue, expense, gain, and loss items that are excluded from net income but included in comprehensive income.

P

Phantom stock. A promise to pay cash on a future date to the recipient of an instrument that mimics changes in the market value of the issuing entity.

Potential common stock. Securities that can be converted to common stock, such as options, warrants, and convertible securities.

Preferred stock. A security that receives preferential treatment in comparison to common stock.

PIPE. A private investment in public equity, where investors purchase restricted stock that is intended to be registered with the SEC.

Preventive control. A control that keeps an error from occurring.

Public entity. A business that is required to file financial statements with the SEC.

Push down accounting. The convention of accounting for the purchase of an acquiree at the purchase cost, rather than its historical cost.

Q

Quiet period. The time period between the delivery of a registration statement to the SEC and its declaration that the statement is effective, when information releases to the public are restricted.

R

Registrant. An issuer of securities that files periodic reports with the SEC.

Reload feature. A stock option that grants additional options to an employee once that person exercises existing options that use company shares to pay the exercise price.

Restatement. The revision of prior financial statements to correct an error.

Restricted share. A share that cannot be sold for a certain period of time.

Reverse acquisition. A business combination in which the legal acquirer is the acquiree for accounting purposes.

Review. A service under which an auditor obtains limited assurance that there are no material modifications that need to be made to an entity's financial statements for them to be in conformity with the applicable financial reporting framework.

S

Segment. A distinct component of a business that produces revenue, and for which the business produces separate financial information that is regularly reviewed internally by a chief operating decision maker.

Shelf registration. The registration of securities that will be sold at a later date.

Shell company. An entity with no operations and minimal assets.

Short selling. The sale of company stock owned by a third party, with the intent of buying back shares on the open market at a later date and returning the shares to the third party.

Short-swing profit. A buy-and-sell or sell-and-buy transaction by a corporate insider of company securities within a six-month period that results in a profit.

Stock. Ownership shares in a business.

Stock dividend. A dividend paid in the form of additional shares, rather than cash.

Stock option. The right to purchase a certain number of shares at a later date and at a certain price.

Stock split. An issuance of shares to existing shareholders that exceeds a 20% to 25% increase in the number of shares outstanding prior to the issuance.

U

Unicorns. Startup companies with a valuation of at least $1 billion.

W

Warrant. An option to purchase a certain number of a company's shares at a pre-determined price, within a defined time period.

Well-known seasoned issuer. A public entity that has non-affiliate stock ownership of at least $700 million, or which has issued at least $1 billion of non-convertible securities in the past three years.

Index

CPSIA information can be obtained
at www.ICGtesting.com
Printed in the USA
FSHW021336220420
69471FS